BASIC
FRESHWATER
FISHING

BASIC FRESHWATER FISHING

*Step-by-step guide
to tackle and know-how
that catch the favorite fish
in your area*

Cliff Hauptman

*Fish and bait drawings by Ernest Lussier
Photos by author unless otherwise credited*

Stackpole Books

Published by
STACKPOLE BOOKS
5067 Ritter Road
Mechanicsburg, PA 17055

Printed in the United States of America

20 19 18 17 16 15 14 13 12 11

Library of Congress Cataloging-in-Publication Data

Hauptman, Cliff.
    Basic freshwater fishing.

    Includes index.
    1. Fishing. 2. Fishes, Fresh-water. I. Title.
SH441.H34   1988   799.1′1   87-18053
ISBN 0-8117-2226-0

This book is dedicated to my wife, Susie.
And so am I.

Contents

Section III
The Methods—How to Get the Fish and Tackle Together

Section IV
Extras and Fine Points

Acknowledgments

I would like to thank a few people who, through their variously sized gifts of time and effort, made this book better and easier to write. Thanks to Homer Circle of *Sports Afield* and Ken Schultz of *Field & Stream* for sharing some of their expertise about tackle. Thanks to Ray Nichols, owner of Nimrod Sporting Goods in Acton, Massachusetts, for many forms of help. Thanks to Mike Walker of the Walker Agency, Janel Patterson of the Juhl Agency, Patty Jo Clouse of the Michigan Travel Commission, Cindy Hendrickson of the Wyoming Travel Commission, and Carol Robinson of Bass Pro Shops for providing additional photos from their files. Thanks to Monte Kroner and Dean Thornblad of Creative Camera in Acton for their darkroom expertise. Thanks to Bill Cork of the Plano Molding Company for sending me tackle boxes to photograph and to Dick Healey of Lake Systems Division for providing me with a pH Guide and Color-C-Lector. Thanks to Chet Fish of Stackpole Books for his editorial guidance throughout this project and to Bill Rooney for improving my prose. Thanks to my father for acting as a photographic model and for teaching me to fish, lo, these many summers ago. Thanks to my wife, Susie, for her excellent judgment, patience, support, and all the things for which writers' wives deserve considerable thanks. And thanks to my daughter, Molly, for not pulling out the plug of my computer in the mid

Introduction

This book assumes you're an adult with no previous knowledge of freshwater fishing. You'll learn what freshwater fishing is all about, what equipment to use and why, what species to fish for, where to find them, what they eat, how to fool them into eating something that has a hook in it, what to do when that happens, and a lot of other things that will give you a comprehensive understanding of the sport without overwhelming you. You will come along on some imaginary fishing trips to get an idea of what it feels like to go fishing. More importantly, perhaps, you will find out what you do and do *not* need to buy.

The book is divided into four sections. Section I explains the functions of the most essential fishing equipment and describes the differences among the basic forms in which that equipment is available. You also learn the proper use and set-up of each of those types.

Section II is about fish. There you will learn the most popular types of fish that fishermen fish for in freshwater, where and how they live, what they eat, and what methods are most successful in catching them.

Section III explains the two major types of bait. The pros and cons of each are discussed, and the details and uses of each are further probed. This section also includes three fishing outings that are designed to acquaint the absolute beginner, as realistically as is possible in print, with the experience of going fishing.

In Section IV, you get additional information about equipment already introduced. Also, you learn about other equipment and techniques that will be useful, if not entirely necessary, for your well-rounded grasp of the basics. There is also a chapter on knots you should learn and some of my opinions on the value of many types of high-tech products that greet you and grab at your wallet.

The sequence of subjects in this book enables me to teach you about fishing as I feel it ought to be taught—as a natural process. You are, after all, seeking to catch a natural creature in its natural environment by luring it with baits that are either its natural food or a fair imitation of the things it naturally eats. It may seem contradictory to call the catching of a fish with a metal hook attached to other assorted hardware a natural process. Yet you will see that the most knowledgeable fishermen are those who best understand the natural workings of the fish, its environment, and the natural order of things.

One manifestation of that natural philosophy is my approach to artificial lures in Section III. Traditionally, writers have considered artificial lures according to the depth at which they are fished. And readers have read about surface, middepth, and bottom lures. But as a logical progression from your introduction to the fishes and their natural histories, habitats, and eating habits in Section II, and following a detailed discussion of live baits, I have chosen a different route. I discuss the artificials in terms of the natural foods they imitate. This approach underscores the natural aspect I believe essential to the full enjoyment of fishing.

Throughout, I aim to be as helpful as possible. While my ultimate goal is to give you a good enough grasp of the basics to enable you to make your own informed decisions, I fully appreciate the comfort a newcomer gains from knowing the opinions of an authority. That is why I have

given my opinion on manufacturers, brand names, and other product specifics when I have a strong one. At other times, I just give you the facts, realizing that your choice is likely to be as good as mine, no matter what you pick.

I have also chosen to use only the male forms of words like ''fisherman,'' ''sportsman,'' and ''outdoorsman'' and to use male pronouns almost exclusively. I find writing in which the terms ''his or her,'' ''he or she,'' and ''fisherman or fisherwoman''—or, worse yet, ''fisherperson''—are constantly repeated to be all but unreadable. It may be a more equitable form of communication, but I think that its fairness is at the expense of clear, painless writing. I assure you that I in no way discount the significant female constituency this book is designed to serve.

Finally, let me emphasize the ''beginner'' aspect of this guide. The book is not meant to be encyclopedic. It is meant to orient, to explain fundamentals, and to provide basic knowledge. To do that, certain concepts and data may be, by necessity, simplified or less than complete. Someone of advanced fishing experience, for example, might look through this book and say, ''Gee whiz, he never mentions salmon (or lake trout, or carp, or arctic char, or whatever).'' Well, there are *hundreds* of species of freshwater fishes in North America, so I have had to make some choices. I've undoubtedly omitted somebody's favorite. The same will be true of many topics in these chapters. One benefit of this selectivity, though, is that you can lift the results without needing a block and tackle.

I hope this book exceeds your expectations.

Section I

THE BASIC EQUIPMENT

What to Fish With

1

What Is Fishing?
What Is Tackle?

Fishing can be as basic as standing in a stream, grabbing a fish with your hands, and tossing it onto the bank before it has a chance to react. Commercial fishing usually involves netting huge numbers of fish. Still other types of fishing make use of spears, poisons, and even guns. But by far the most popular forms of fishing require the use of at least two pieces of equipment: a hook and some line.

The types of fishing explained in this book are those that are commonly called sportfishing or recreational fishing, and all are accomplished with a hook and line and, as you shall see, additional equipment designed to make the sport more fun, more efficient, and more successful.

As peculiar as it may sound, the kinds of fishing you will be learning have the basic goal of causing a creature of relatively little intelligence but well-developed instincts to attack a bait (real or artificial) out of hunger, anger, or mere curiosity, thereby becoming impaled on a hook attached to a line by which you may pull the fish toward you and capture it. Described that way, fishing sounds fairly ridiculous, but probably no sillier than the sport of counting how few hits it takes to knock a little white ball around a meadow and make it fall into holes in the ground.

Over a thousand years ago, fishing hooks were known as "angles" because the word "angle" was somehow related to the word "bend"—and, of course, a fishing hook has a bend in it. From that origin, the term "angling" evolved naturally enough to mean "fishing." And although we no longer use the word "angle" to mean "hook," we do still refer to the sport of fishing with a hook as *angling*,

Fishing can be as simple or as sophisticated as you choose to make it.

and to fishermen as *anglers*. That bit of etymology is given partly to avoid confusion when I start using the words "angler" and "fisherman" interchangeably, and partly to illustrate just how basic the hook is to fishing.

You can catch fish and have a lot of fun doing so with just a hook and a length of line. Many kids start out that way. They simply tie the line to a hook, place a piece of earthworm or cheese on the hook as bait, lower the baited hook into the water with the line, and catch fish. That basic system lends itself to a great deal of improvement. First, if you attach your line to a long stick, you gain several advantages.

THE ROD

By attaching your line to a fishing rod, you improve bait presentation in a number of ways, and you make it harder for a hooked fish to break your line.

One of the basic necessities of successful fishing is the ability to put your baited hook where there are fish to bite it. If you are standing on the shore of a pond, for example, you will likely notice that the water within a few feet of you is quite shallow, perhaps shallow enough for you to easily ascertain that it is devoid of fish. It is equally likely that farther out, in deeper water, there are some fish. Getting your baited hook out into that deeper area is made possible by a rod.

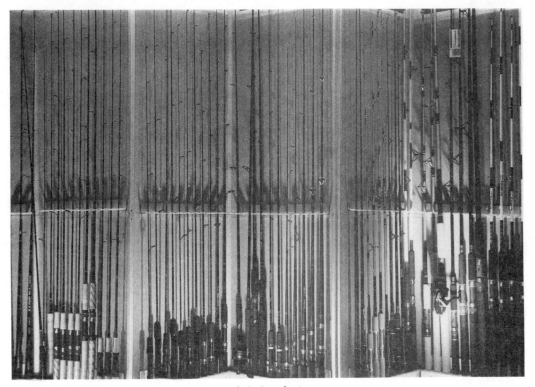

A display of rods.

A rod need not be anything more sophisticated than a 12-foot length of tapered bamboo (commonly called a cane pole). By tying your line directly to the thin end of such a rod and holding the thick end in your hand, you have added 12 feet to your reach. If your line is 12 feet long as well, as it normally is in this method of fishing, you have expanded your effective fishing area by quite a bit. By simply reaching out from your position on the bank and letting the hook hang straight down from the tip of the pole (a method of angling called *still-fishing*), you can dangle that bait in deeper water. And if you were to sort of flip the baited hook out so that it fell at a distance equal to the combined length of the line and rod, you would have increased your effective range even farther. That latter maneuver is called *casting*, and we will discuss it in greater detail a little later.

In addition to allowing you to present your bait to the fish more effectively, a rod helps to decrease the possibility of the fish's breaking your line, and it helps sap the fish's energy in the process. You may find it enlightening to try this experiment: take a three- or four-foot length of sewing thread, dental floss, or cake-box twine, and try to break it with your hands. You should have no trouble at all. Now take another length of the same string and tie one end to the tip of a slender, flexible branch on a bush or small tree. Hold the other end of the string so

Cane-pole fishing is a perfectly fine method that is ideal for the laid-back beginner.

that it forms an approximate right angle to the branch and, simply by yanking on it, try to break the string. You will wear yourself out before that string breaks. The whippiness of the branch dissipates most of your energy, allowing the string to remain intact.

That's how a rod works, too. Many fish you will be catching have the strength to break fishing line under certain conditions, but the chances of that happening are greatly reduced if the properties of a flexible rod are entered into the equation. It absorbs the fish's fighting power and saps its strength. Trying to force in a large, fighting fish, even with the help of a rod, can often result in a broken line if the fish is not ready to succumb. But fighting against the energy-robbing rod will soon weaken the fish sufficiently to let you bring it in safely.

So, the use of a rod can improve your fishing in two ways: by making it easier for you to present your baited hooks to

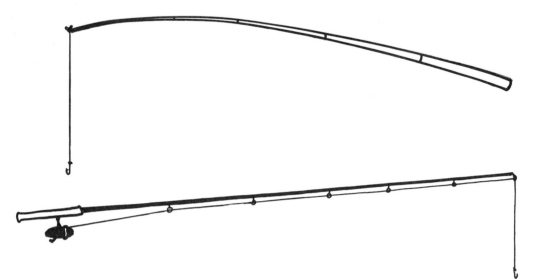

In cane-pole fishing, a fixed length of line is tied directly to the tip of the pole. A rod with line guides and a reel filled with line allow a variable amount of line to be let out and retrieved by the angler.

the fish you are trying to catch, and by raising the odds that you will successfully land the fish you do hook.

Without going into the relative qualities of the various rod-making materials, I can say with reasonable accuracy that the fish-fighting abilities of most rods are fairly equal. But any rod's ability to deliver your baited hooks to the fish can be improved enormously by the addition of one more piece of equipment: the reel. And in order to add a reel to a rod, certain modifications must be made to the basic cane-pole design.

A reel is mounted at the thick end of a rod, down near your hands. That necessitates a reel mount, which is simply a device for holding the reel onto the rod in a fixed place and position. The line, then, is no longer tied permanently to the tip of the rod, but is now spooled onto the reel. The line must be guided along the length of the rod from the reel to the rod tip and that requires the addition of line guides— five to eight rings along the length of the rod every few inches, which decrease in size as they approach the tip.

THE REEL

A reel performs four basic functions: storing line neatly, allowing line to be let out in an orderly fashion, allowing line to be retrieved in an orderly fashion, and providing an additional safety cushion, in addition to the rod, for keeping the fish from breaking the line.

You have no doubt flown a kite at some time in your life. Chances are you kept your string wound around a stick. When you wanted to let out more string, you simply let the stick turn in your hands as the kite pulled string from the windings around it. To bring the kite in, you wound

A pile of antique reels.

string back onto the stick. And if the wind got really strong, causing the kite to pull so hard that it seemed the string might break, you let some string pull off the stick, controlled carefully by your hands, to ease the strain. A fishing reel performs those exact functions, but it does so more easily and efficiently—and more expensive.

Depending upon the type of reel, which will be explored in the following four chapters, designs differ. Basically, however, all reels are comprised of a cylinder around which line may be wound and upon which it may be stored. That part corresponds to the kite-string stick. The important difference, however, is that the reel cylinder has ends that contain the string and allow it to be wound levelly and evenly. The kite string on the stick always took the shape of a football because most of the string had to be

Four types of reels. Clockwise from bottom-right: *baitcasting, spinning, spincasting, and flycasting.*

bunched in the center to keep it from falling off the ends of the stick.

Additionally, all reels have a crank that, by one means or another, causes the line to be wound around the cylinder. That takes the place of your arm and hands, which were your only means of winding the kite string onto the stick—an interminable chore if the kite was a few hundred feet up. Reels make that task nearly effortless, not only because of the mechanical advantage of the cranking mechanism but also because most reels are geared so that one turn of the crank results in four or five wraps of the line around the cylinder.

Most reels also provide a way to let line off the cylinder without having the crank turn. In other words, line can be pulled off the cylinder in such a way that the crank mechanism is entirely disengaged, thus eliminating any unnecessary interference to the free flow of the line—an essential factor in long and accurate casting.

In addition to allowing line to flow freely from the cylinder, most reels have a drag mechanism that lets line go out under tension. Thus, if a heavy, strong fish is on your line, and your rod cannot dissipate enough of the fish's pulling power, your reel will allow a pre-set amount of slippage of line off the cylinder to prevent breaking. That mechanism is called the "drag" and its setting can be varied from locked tight to very loose.

Now that you know the purpose of a reel and a rod, let's put the two together with some line and a baited hook and see how they can help you accomplish your goals.

Suppose you are sitting in a boat in the middle of a pond. You have with you a rod, a reel with sufficient line stored on its cylinder, a hook, and some bait (the kind is unimportant for now). The reel is secured near the butt end of the rod, and line has been threaded up through the guides and now dangles from the rod tip. You tie the hook to the line end (using a knot you will learn about in a subsequent chapter), place some bait on the hook, and you are ready to fish. Exactly what you are fishing for and how to go about it are not important right now. You are simply interested here in how a rod and reel work together and why you need them.

If you just want to still-fish, your newly acquired rod and reel give you no great advantage over the cane pole or the hook and line by themselves—except that the reel holds much more line. So you can more easily adjust the depth at which your bait dangles.

If you hook a large fish while still-fishing, your rod-and-reel combination, with its dual safeguards for protecting your line, will improve your chances of getting it into the boat over both the hook-and-line and the cane-pole approach.

A far more important advantage of the rod and reel becomes apparent when you want to cast. Suppose you are sitting in your boat with that same rod and reel and, instead of still-fishing with a worm or other live bait, you want to use an artificial lure that must be dragged through the water in order for it to perform the wiggling action that will cause a fish to mistake it for something to eat. Casting is the way to go about that. Basically, it involves throwing the lure out some dis-

tance and then pulling it back. Both the cast—of at least several yards, not just a few feet—and the retrieve are dependent upon the combined properties of a rod and reel. The rod provides the ability to catapult the lure great distances with relatively little effort, and the reel allows the line to be pulled out behind the lure with little hindrance. The reel also, of course, allows the line and lure to be retrieved smoothly and easily, and stores the line so it will be ready to perform properly on the next cast.

And again, as with still-fishing, both the rod and reel will insure a more successful outcome should a large fish be hooked.

LINE

Line is obviously some kind of filament that is attached at one end to a hook and

A reel allows an angler to cast.

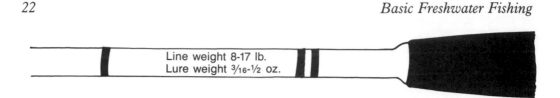

Line weight 8-17 lb.
Lure weight ³/₁₆-½ oz.

Most rods are stamped with the ranges of lure and line weights for which they are designed.

at the other end to a reel, a rod tip, or somebody's hand. But there are a couple of points about line that are necessary to your full understanding of these basic fishing tools.

For three of the four types of tackle you will be learning about in the following chapters—baitcasting, spinning, and spincasting—monofilament is the most widely used type of line. Mono is a clear or slightly tinted, single strand of synthetic material that provides a good combination of strength, flexibility, stretch, resistance to abrasion, knot-holding ability, invisibility, and minimum diameter-to-strength characteristics.

Mono comes in a selection of diameters that directly correspond to the amount of strain the line will bear. Ten-pound-test line, for example, is rated to sustain about 10 pounds of stress.

A 20-pound fish can be hooked and landed on a six-pound-test line, so it is not so much the weight of the fish you expect to catch that determines the weight (test) of the line you should use. Rather, it is the weight of the lures you will be casting and the characteristics of the rod that most influence your choice of line strength. An outfit—rod, reel, line, and lure—must be balanced, and that means that all of those parts must be allowed to work within the parameters for which they were designed. Most good rods are stamped on their shafts with in-

formation about the lure and line weights to be used.

The rod, reel, line, and hook—along with a multitude of additional fishing accessories that include everything from bobbers and sinkers to filleting knives, landing nets, lures, and boxes in which to carry all that stuff—are commonly known as *tackle*. In the next four chapters, you will learn about four common types of tackle, each characterized by specific types of reels and rods, which lend themselves to different techniques and situations. If you already have a rod and reel, the next four chapters will help you determine which type they are and for what type of fishing they are best suited. If you are starting from scratch, these chapters will help you understand what to look for when you are ready to buy or borrow tackle.

WHERE TO BUY TACKLE

There are, in my experience, three worthwhile sources of fishing tackle. By the time you have finished reading and absorbing the information in this book, you should be able to make use of all three. Their differences are based mainly on price and service.

The most expensive place is a local sporting-goods store that specializes in hunting and fishing equipment. In such a place you will usually pay close to list price for everything, but you will likely be dealing face to face with a knowledgeable person who uses the equipment and who can give you personal attention. You can also see, touch, and even (sometimes) use the tackle before you have to buy it.

A less expensive place to buy tackle is from a discount department store like K Mart. Such places sometimes offer substantial savings on national brands of rods, reels, line, lures, and accessories. Some discount stores are better than others in their selection of products, and some chains even vary from store to store. The K Mart chain, for example, has a particularly impressive fishing department in general, but the variety is highly changeable from one section of the country to another. In any case, you will be trading price for service by buying from a discount store rather than a sporting-goods store. Rarely do the chain stores have knowledgeable clerks to answer your fishing questions. The clerk manning the fishing-tackle department this week may have been stocking the housewares department last week and may be working at the local Burger King next week. It is hoped, though, that after reading this book you'll be able to take care of yourself in a discount store and take advantage of the lower prices.

Mail-order houses offer still greater savings, far more products, and yet less help. By ordering equipment from certain catalogs—by mail or phone—you can get top-quality tackle for the lowest possible cost. You will, of course, be at the distinct disadvantages of receiving little or no sales help and of seeing the equipment only in pictures. Still, after reading this book you should be able to handle that situation, especially if you can find and examine the tackle you want in a specialty or discount store, then go home and order it from a catalog.

Two catalog dealers with which I have had unblemished success in dependable service and value are Bass Pro Shops in Springfield, Missouri (800 227-7776), and Cabella's in Sidney, Nebraska (800 237-4444). The encyclopedic, full-color catalogs of both those outfits are, in themselves, invaluable educational tools for the beginner.

Now, before you run off and buy anything, read the rest of this book. There is much to be learned.

2

Baitcasting Tackle

If you were to stick a pencil through the hole in a spool of thread and then, holding the ends of the pencil with both hands, allow someone to pull thread from the spool so that the spool revolved around the pencil, you would have a basic approximation of the way a baitcasting reel works.

To wind the thread back on the spool, you would make the spool revolve in the opposite direction, much like the windings of a winch. In fact, a baitcasting reel basically *is* a winch. It consists of a cylinder upon which line is stored and which can be rotated by a crank. The crank mechanism may be disengaged from the cylinder when line is to be released during a cast (a condition called "free-spool") so that the cylinder can rotate with a minimum of mechanical interference and the line can leave the spool in

the most uninhibited manner. The crank mechanism automatically engages when the line is ready to be reeled in.

In addition, there is usually a guide on the front of the reel that moves back and forth along the width of the cylinder during line retrieval, placing the line on the spool in an orderly, level fashion. The vast majority of today's baitcasting reels employ such a guide and are called "level-wind" reels.

Baitcasting reels are used with baitcasting rods, which have a characteristic trigger-like projection on the underside of the butt between the grip and the reel seat. The trigger is not movable, however. It functions merely as a rest for your index finger. The reel is secured in the reel seat on top of the rod, and the line guides are aligned along the top of the rod as well. When the rod is held properly, your

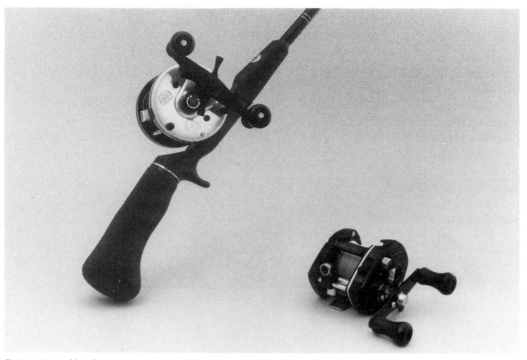

Baitcasting tackle, showing a conventional baitcasting reel on a baitcasting rod and a newer, magnetic baitcasting reel design.

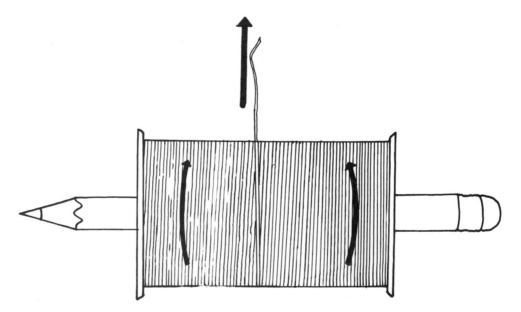

A spool of thread revolving on a pencil illustrates the principle of the baitcasting reel.

Three different makes and designs of baitcasting reels.

Casting or freespool button⎯⎯⎯⎯⎯

Drag⎯⎯

Spool tension knob⎯⎯⎯

Handle⎯⎯

Line

Line guide

Foot

The important parts of a baitcasting reel.

thumb will rest comfortably on the reel's cylinder. Baitcasting rods are most common in one-piece, 5½-foot or 6-foot lengths, but they can be found in two-piece models for easier transport.

Like all types of fishing rods, baitcasting models are a compromise among strength (for hauling in a fighting fish without breaking), lightness (so the fisherman does not drop from fatigue after making a few dozen casts), flexibility (to propel the lure when casting), and sensitivity (to transmit to the fisherman the sometimes subtle tugs that signal a strike). One of the very best rod materials is graphite. Although fairly expensive, graphite models combine an excellent mix of all the elements necessary for a top-grade fishing rod. Less expensive are rods made of fiberglass; they are heavier and less sensitive than graphite rods, but are still excellent and extremely popular because of their less aristocratic pricing.

Regardless of their raw materials, baitcasting rods are generally designed to function within certain parameters that are defined by the weight of the lures to be cast and the weight of the line to be used. That information is always printed by the better manufacturers right on the shaft of the rod, just ahead of the handle. Avoid buying rods that fail to provide that information.

But how are you, as a prospective buyer, to know whether you want a rod rated as "medium" and designed to handle lures weighing ¼ to ⅝ ounce on 8- to 15-pound line, or a "medium/heavy" rod designed for lures of ⅜ to ¾ ounce on 10- to 20-pound line—or something lighter or heavier? Well, that depends on the kinds of fish you plan to catch, the type of fishing you plan to do, and the circumstances under which you'll do

those things—none of which you have the foggiest notion of right now. But there are chapters in this book that will provide you with knowledge about all those aspects of fishing, so that you will soon be able to make your own judgments about not only what general types of tackle you want but also about the specific aspects of that tackle as well. Right now, however, suffice it to say that baitcasting rods are available in a whole assortment of materials, sizes, weights, and casting characteristics. Think of that diversity not as a potential source of confusion, but as a pleasant opportunity to choose exactly what you want.

Baitcasting is the preferred method of most experienced bass fishermen, for reasons we will get into later in the chapter. It is also one of the less-preferred methods for beginners because of the amount of practice required to master it. For in baitcasting, much more so than in spinning or spincasting, a lack of skill results not only in a lack of fish but also in a rat's nest of misery called "backlash."

Remember that spool of thread on the pencil? Imagine what would happen if the person pulling the thread off the spool gave it a sudden yank, causing the spool to revolve very fast around the pencil. Thread would begin spilling off the spool much faster than it was being taken up by your partner at the other end and would pile up on the floor in a tangled mess until the spool stopped revolving. If there were a housing around the spool, as there is on a reel, the thread would jam up in tangled coils inside the housing, resulting in the need to untangle, lost time, frustration, and perhaps the premature death of your budding interest in fishing.

Baitcasting reels have a tendency to backlash during a cast unless the revolving cylinder is controlled very precisely by the caster's thumb, and that takes a *lot* of practice. Makers of baitcasting reels, recognizing the problem, have devised a couple of clever mechanisms to reduce (*they* say "eliminate") the backlash problem. One mechanism involves magnets, meant to automatically slow the cylinder much the way your thumb is supposed to. Another solution makes use of a V-shaped spool rather than a parallel-sided one. The theory is that as the line leaves the spool, the spool's diameter decreases sharply because of its V-shape, thereby slowing the rate of revolution. Both ideas make more sense on paper than on the water. They may help the situation somewhat, but they do not replace the need for a highly educated thumb and plenty of serious practice.

SETTING UP YOUR BAITCASTING TACKLE

Baitcasting tackle is most often purchased as separate elements. The reel, rod, and line must then be put together properly before the tackle can be used.

If the rod is a two-piece model, join the two pieces by inserting the tip of the butt section into the opening in the tip section. While pushing the two sections together, twist them so that the guides are aligned exactly. Most baitcasting rods, however, are one-piece rods.

The baitcasting reel sits on top of the rod. If you hold the rod by its grip so that the trigger-like rest is downward and the guides are upward, you will notice that there is a place to secure the reel just forward of your hand. On the underside of the rod, at that point, there will likely be a knurled knob. Loosening that knob will loosen the bracket in the reel seat right above it. If there is no such knob, try turning the cone-shaped nose of the grip itself. That will loosen the bracket.

Hold the reel so that its flat feet are downward. The casting button should be toward the grip, or rear, of the rod, and the line guide that rides side to side when you crank the reel should be toward the

Seating the reel on the rod.

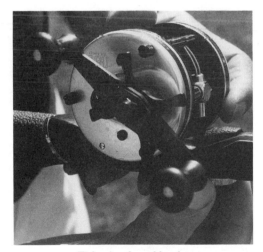

Tightening the reel bracket.

Threading the line down through the guides to the reel.

Be sure to thread the line through the reel's line guide before tying it to the reel spool.

Have your partner apply slight tension to the line spool.

rod's tip. Slide the front foot of the reel under the front bracket of the reel seat. Then seat the reel and slide it rearward as far as it will go. Hold it there and tighten the front bracket with the knurled screw or by turning the nose of the grip (whichever method your rod employs). The reel should be held securely with no play at all.

Now you must put line on the reel. (And by the way, do not skimp on the line. Buy a good brand like Trilene, Stren, Maxima, or Ande.) Most lines are available on spools that hold about 250 yards. Get the correct strength (test) for your rod and reel.

Find the end of the line, and thread it through all the guides on the rod, starting from the tip. After threading it through the largest guide near the grip, thread it through the line guide on the front of the reel and tie it around the reel spool, using the Reel Knot explained in Chapter 16. After pulling the knot tight and trimming the end, you can start loading the reel with line. You will need a partner.

Poke a pencil through the hole in the spool of line. Have your partner hold the pencil so that it is parallel to the ground, the spool is between his hands with its edge toward the tip of your rod, and the line is coming off the *top* of the spool. The line should be in a straight line between the spool and the reel. Have your partner apply slight pressure on the spool with both hands so that it does not turn entirely freely. Now, just crank your reel (you will notice that the line is also com-

Reeling the line from the spool onto the reel.

A properly filled reel.

HOW TO CAST WITH BAITCASTING TACKLE

Most baitcasting reels have their cranks on the right-hand side, so if you are right-handed, you will be casting with your right hand and then switching the rod over to your left hand so you can crank the reel handle with your right hand during the retrieve.

The following instructions are for right-handed casters. If you are left-handed, simply reverse all references to right and left.

In preparation for casting, your reel should be loaded with line of the proper weight, the reel should be mounted securely on the rod, and the line should be threaded up through all the guides. To the end of the line should be tied either an actual lure within the appropriate weight range for the rod—if you are practicing on water—or a hookless practice plug of appropriate weight if you are practicing on a lawn.

ing over the *top* of your reel's spool), and keep cranking until the line reaches the mark engraved near the edge of your reel's spool. In the absence of such a mark, fill the spool to within one-eighth inch of its limit.

Then cut the line near your partner's hands, and tie on a lure or practice plug (a plastic weight without hooks, made for casting practice), using the Improved Clinch Knot or the Jansik Special explained in Chapter 16.

1. *The Grip.* Hold the rod handle so that your right forefinger wraps comfortably around the trigger while your right thumb rests on the line on the reel's spool. Use a relaxed grip. Do not squeeze the rod handle; just hold it firmly.

The grip.

Setting the reel: press the freespool button.

Setting the reel: set the tension knob adjustment.

Hand position.

2. *Setting the Reel.* Press the freespool button on the reel (its location varies), and quickly move your thumb back to keep the spool from turning. If your reel has a spool-tension knob, tighten it all the way, let your thumb off the spool, slowly ease the tension with the knob, and watch for the point at which your lure begins to drop slowly from the rod tip. Then put your thumb back on the spool. Crank the lure back up to within two or three inches of the rod tip (that will turn off the freespool so that line can be retrieved). Then put the reel back in freespool and hold it stationary with your thumb again. The tension knob need not be reset unless the lure is changed.

3. *Hand Position.* Turn your hand so that your palm faces down and the reel handles are uppermost. This allows the greatest possible freedom of movement for your wrist.

4. *The Stance.* Face your target, then take a quarter-turn to the left so that your right shoulder points toward the target. Shift your left foot back to a comfortable position slightly to the rear of your right foot.

5. *Aim.* With your elbow held slightly away from your body and your forearm in

line with the rod, hold the rod so that the tip is just higher than your head while the handle is just higher than your hip. The rod itself should visually split the target in half.

6. *Cast.* By lifting your forearm with your elbow as the pivot, raise the rod so that your hand comes up to a point just below eye level. Keep the rod splitting the target, and stop its upward motion when it is just about vertical. The weight of the lure will put a backward bend in the rod. Do not allow the rod to drift back and absorb that bend. It is the potential energy in that bend that causes a good cast.

Without hesitation, start moving the rod back forward and down along the same path it took coming upward, but this time add a bit of wrist snap along with the elbow chop. At a point about halfway between the vertical rod position and your original starting position, lessen your thumb pressure on the spool so that the lure can pull line from the reel. NEVER TAKE YOUR THUMB EN-TIRELY OFF THE SPOOL. Always exert some slight pressure to keep the spool from overrunning the outgoing line, increasing the pressure as the lure nears the

The stance.

Aim.

Cast: back to about vertical.

Cast: without hesitation, back down, snap wrist, lessen thumb pressure.

target. The moment the lure lands, stop the spool dead with your thumb.

7. *The Retrive.* Switch the rod over to your left hand, and crank the reel handle with your right. The crank will re-engage with the spool and allow line to be retrieved.

The most critical aspect of learning to cast with baitcasting tackle is the control over the revolving spool by your thumb. Somewhere between total pressure and no pressure at all—and it varies throughout the progress of the cast—is the ideal amount of ''thumb'' that allows maximum freedom for the outgoing line without letting it overrun the spool and cause a backlash. Only practice will help you develop that educated thumb.

The very characteristics of baitcasting

The retrieve.

that make it somewhat difficult to master are those that give it its distinctive advantages over other forms of tackle. Because your thumb is in constant contact with the revolving spool and outgoing line throughout the entire length of the cast, you have more control over the accuracy of your casts. In playing a heavy fish, baitcasting tackle offers the advantage of a direct winching mechanism (you will see later how spinning and spincasting tackle differ). Baitcasting reels are also least likely to cause line-twist problems, have above-average drag mechanisms, and are generally the most durable.

Baitcasting's disadvantages are its tendency to backlash, the practice it requires of a beginner, the difficulty for the average person—especially a beginner—to achieve any great distance in casting, and the somewhat more limited range of lure weights that can be cast. Because lures must be heavy enough to cause the reel's spool to revolve, lures of about one-quarter ounce are the lightest that can be cast with baitcasting gear. In the next chapter, you will learn about another type of tackle that overcomes many of the disadvantages of baitcasting tackle, though it has shortcomings of its own.

3

Spinning Tackle

Let's take another look at that spool of sewing thread used to illustrate the workings of a baitcasting reel in Chapter 2. You know that you can pull thread off the spool by running a pencil through it and letting the thread come off at right angles to the pencil, thus causing the spool to revolve. A baitcasting reel works on that principle.

But there is another way to get thread off the spool. Suppose you hold the spool by one end, with just your fingertips around the lip on that side, and pull thread off the other side. The spool does not move at all—the thread simply spills off over the lip.

That is how a spinning reel works. It is known as a "fixed-spool reel" (whereas a baitcasting reel is a "revolving-spool reel"). On a spinning reel, the spool is aligned parallel with the rod so that the line is pulled off the forward end of the spool during a cast.

When the line is retrieved, the spool still does not revolve. A cup in which the spool sits, however, revolves around the spool when the reel handle is turned. A wire hoop, called the *bail*, gathers the line and wraps it neatly back on the spool. The bail is moved out of the way during a cast and automatically pops back into line-gathering position when the crank handle is turned for the retrieve.

Spinning reels come equipped with a drag mechanism that can be tightened and loosened by a knob or similar device located at the front or rear of the reel or atop the spool. The drag, as on all types of reels, allows a preset amount of line slippage to prevent the line's breaking when you are playing a strong fish.

Unlike baitcasting reels, spinning reels

Spinning tackle, showing a rod-and-reel setup and a separate spinning reel.

hang under the rod. Rather than the thumb, the index finger is used for casting with spinning tackle, so the reel must be positioned below the rod where the index finger is naturally positioned when the rod is gripped correctly.

Because the reel hangs below the rod, spinning rods have their line guides arranged along the lower side of the rod. In

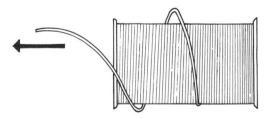

A stationary spool with thread looping off its end illustrates the principle of the spinning reel.

addition, because the line uncoils off the end of the spool in a looping motion (rather than pulling straight out as from a baitcasting reel), the first guide—the one closest to the reel—is quite large in diameter so as to interfere as little as possible with the outgoing line. From that first guide to the *tip top* (the last guide at the tip of the rod), a spinning rod's guides taper more obviously than those on a baitcasting rod.

Because there is no inertia to overcome when casting with a stationary-spool spinning reel, there can be no backlash. The spool cannot outrun the outgoing line because the spool is not turning. The line is simply spilling off the end. This also means that lighter lures can be cast with spinning tackle.

Like baitcasting rods, spinning rods come in a variety of lengths, weights, materials, and quality. Most spinning rods are six to eight feet long and are stamped with the recommended line and lure weights that will provide a balanced setup. The most popular rod materials are graphite and fiberglass. Graphite provides greater sensitivity and lighter weight, while fiberglass is more afford-able.

Spinning tackle can be designed for a much broader range of lure and line weights than baitcasting tackle can. Both types handle lines in the eight- to 20-pound-test range, with corresponding lure weights of one-quarter to three-quar-ters of an ounce, but only spinning tackle comes in *ultralight* designs to handle line down to two-pound test and lures as light as 1/32 of an ounce.

Although there is no disputing the fact

Three different makes of spinning reels.

that spinning tackle has licked the back-lash problem, it does have a problem of its own. Because the line comes looping off the end of a spinning reel spool, there is a strong tendency for the line to be-come twisted in the course of normal use,

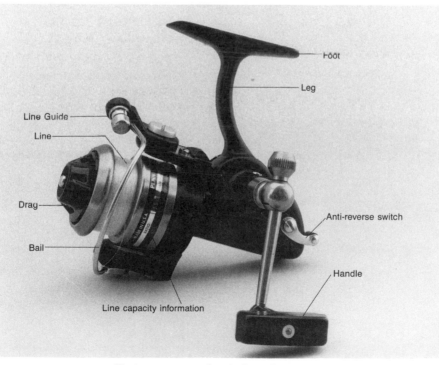

The important parts of a spinning reel.

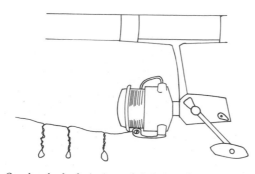

One drawback of spinning reels is their tendency to cause line twist.

Joining rod sections.

and even more so with normal *mis*use. The misuse usually comes when the user continues to crank the reel even as line is being pulled out against the drag while a fish is being played. At such times, the line does not get wound onto the spool—it just gets several twists put in it each time the crank is turned. While the line is under tension, twists are invisible. But when twisted line is allowed to go slack, it tends to form loops, loops tend to form bunches, and bunches tend to form snarls that fluff off the end of the spool in great clumps of tangled line and jam up in the rod guides, necessitating immediate and lengthy attention.

Nonetheless, spinning tackle is easier to learn to cast than baitcasting tackle, and the beginner can achieve greater distance with it.

SETTING UP YOUR SPINNING TACKLE

Spinning tackle is most often purchased as separate elements—reel, rod, and line—which must then be put together properly before use. The rod will

Seating the reel on the rod.

Tightening the reel ring.

Threading the line down through the guides to the reel.

most likely be a two-piece model. Join the two by inserting the tip of the butt section into the opening in the tip section. While pushing the two sections together, twist them so that the guides are aligned exactly.

If you hold the rod by its butt so that the guides are downward, you will notice that there is a place to secure the reel just forward of your hand. It will likely consist of one or two movable rings on a threaded part of the rod shaft, and two cup-like brackets separated by a space of about three inches. One bracket is stationary; the other is movable.

Hold the reel so that the flat feet form the top of a T with the stem. The body of the reel should be hanging below, with the spool and bail toward the rod's tip.

Remember to open the bail.

Slide the rear foot of the reel into the rear bracket of the reel seat. Then seat the reel against the rod and slide the reel and bracket up as far as they will go, making sure the foot aligns with the front cup. Hold it there and tighten the frontmost ring (if there are two) or the single ring (if there is only one) so that the reel is held securely. If there is a second ring, screw it up tightly to the first. There should be no play at all whether there is one ring or two.

Now you must put line on the reel. (And by the way, don't skimp on the line. Buy a good brand like Trilene, Stren, Maxima, Ande, or one of the other premium lines). Most lines come on spools that hold about 250 yards. Get the correct strength (test) for your rod and reel.

Thread the end of the line through all the guides on the rod, starting from the tip. Open the reel's bail until it stays open by itself, and tie the end of the line around the spool, using the Reel Knot explained in Chapter 16. After pulling the knot tight and trimming the end, you can start loading the reel with line. You will need a partner.

Poke a pencil through the hole in the spool of line. Have your partner hold the pencil so that it is parallel to the ground, the spool is between his hands with its edge toward the tip of your rod, and the line is coming off the *top* of the spool. The reel should be "aimed" at the spool. Have your partner apply slight pressure on the spool with both hands so that it does not turn entirely freely. Now, just crank your reel (that will close the bail), and keep cranking for about 20 turns of the handle. Then stop. Move a couple of steps closer to your partner so that a belly of slack line forms. If that belly is free of twists, you may step back and continue reeling line onto the reel, but if the slack line shows any tight, twisted loops, have your partner turn the spool so that the line comes off the *bottom* instead of the top. That will eliminate the twisting when you continue. Crank line onto the reel until the spool is filled to within the thickness of a new penny of its lip. Cut the line near your partner's hands, and tie on a lure or practice plug, using the Improved Clinch Knot or the Jansik Special explained in Chapter 16.

Tie the line to the reel's spool while the bail is open.

Your partner can apply slight pressure to the line spool.

Reeling line onto the reel from the line spool.

HOW TO CAST WITH SPINNING TACKLE

Most spinning reels have the crank handle on the left side, so you will be casting with your right hand and, keeping the rod in that hand, cranking the reel handle with your left hand for the retrieve.

1. *The Grip.* Hold the rod so that the reel hangs down. The leg of the reel (the stem that extends between the rod handle and the reel) should be between your second and third fingers so that two fingers are ahead of it and two are behind it. Your thumb should be on top of the rod grip.

2. *Setting the Reel.* Most spinning reels have an anti-reverse switch that keeps the handle from turning backward and letting out line when you do not want it to.

Properly filled reel.

The grip.

Setting the reel: releasing the anti-reverse switch.

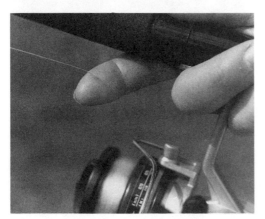

Catch the line on your index finger.

The switch is usually located on the same side of the reel as the crank handle. Make sure the switch is off so that the reel can be cranked both forward and backward. Then, by cranking either backward or forward, let out or reel in enough line so that the lure hangs about six inches from the rod tip.

Next, extend your right index finger and take the line onto its tip. Do not let the line fall into your finger joint, and don't press the line against the rod handle with your finger. Simply allow the line to rest on the ball of your fingertip. With your left hand, open the bail of the reel until it clicks into place and is held open.

3. *The Stance.* Face your target with slightly more weight on your right foot.

4. *Aim.* With your arm bent at the elbow, point the tip of your rod directly at your target. Your forearm should be in line with the rod, so your wrist should not be bent.

5. *Cast.* Quickly lift your forearm with your elbow as the pivot so that your hand comes up to a point just below eye level.

Open the bail.

The stance.

Aim.

Cast: stopping at vertical.

Keep the rod splitting the target, and stop its upward motion when it is just about vertical. The weight of the lure will put a backward bend in the rod. Do not allow the rod to drift back and absorb that bend—it is the potential energy in that bend that causes a good cast.

Without pausing, move your arm back down the same path it took coming up. Apply a slight amount of wrist snap at the same time. When the tip of the rod is again pointing at the target, release the line from your index finger and freeze the motion of the rod. The lure will fly straight toward the target, pulling line off the reel as it goes. By keeping your index finger extended, you can allow the outgoing line to brush against it, thereby "feathering" the line and controlling its flight to some extent. When the lure hits the water (or sooner, if you fear over-shooting the target), touch your index finger solidly to the lip of the reel spool. That will snub the outgoing line completely.

6. *The Retrieve.* With your left hand, crank the reel handle counterclockwise (as looked at from the handle side of the reel) so that the bail-pickup mechanism is re-engaged. Some slight force is usually needed to trip the mechanism, and you will hear the bail click back into place. Line will then be wrapped onto the spool and your lure will return to you as you crank.

The trickiest part of the whole operation is the timing of the line release. If your casts are firing down into the water short of your target, you are releasing the line too late. If they are sailing up into the

Cast: without pausing, back down, snap wrist, release line from finger.

Feathering the line.

The retrieve.

air like space shots, you are releasing too early. The casts should have a certain amount of arc to them, but not so much that accuracy becomes a matter of luck, or so little that all your casts are fish-scaring line drives.

The fixed-spool design of spinning reels eliminates the backlash problems of baitcasting reels, and so spinning tackle allows the beginner to quickly achieve a level of proficiency that gets him fishing in a relatively short time. He can also cast a wide variety of lure weights and make casts of very good distances with most of them. Additionally, spinning tackle, because of the reel's hanging arrangement, offers a comfortably balanced setup that

can be cast for hours with little fatigue. Spinning rods also offer room behind the reel so anglers can cast two-handed to attain greater distance or to divide the work of casting between both arms.

The shortcomings of spinning tackle are its tendency to cause line twist, less casting accuracy than is possible with baitcasting tackle, and a slight mechanical disadvantage (caused by the parallel rather than perpendicular position of the reel spool) when playing a heavy fish.

In the next chapter, you will learn of a third type of tackle that makes use of both spinning and baitcasting techniques and, despite its drawbacks, may be the best type for the absolute beginner.

4

Spincasting Tackle

Spincasting tackle borrows some design aspects from both spinning and baitcasting gear and, in doing so, compromises the best characteristics of each. The result is a second-rate system that has one very important advantage—it is extremely easy to master.

Many experts downplay spincasting, believing that beginners may as well learn on a good system that will stand them in good stead even after they become proficient and serious anglers. Others, including myself, feel that though spincasting does have its drawbacks, and the equipment will inevitably be replaced, it is a method so free of hassles that it allows the absolute beginner to quickly experience the joys of fishing without burdening him with equipment-caused frustrations.

Like the spinning reel, the spincasting reel is a "fixed-spool" device. The spool

lies parallel to the rod, and line peels off the end. Unlike the spinning reel, however, the face of the spincasting reel is enclosed in a cone-shaped housing. A hole at the front of the cone allows the line to escape, so the workings of the reel are entirely hidden from view and need not concern the angler. Such a reel is called "closed-face," as opposed to the "open-face" design of the spinning reel.

With the spool of the spincasting reel hidden from eyes and fingers, there is no bail to deal with as there is on a spinning reel. Release of the line is controlled by a reel-top button that is triggered by the thumb, much like the free-spool button on baitcasting reels. Because of this arrangement, the spincasting reel sits on the top of the rod, as does a baitcasting reel. In fact, spincasting reels usually make use of baitcasting rods.

Spincasting tackle, showing a spincasting reel mounted on a spincasting rod.

With no bail to open, no revolving spool to thumb, and no exposed innards, you simply press the button, cast your lure, and crank the handle to retrieve. Casting is done entirely with one hand, and then the rod is switched to the other hand for retrieving.

To make matters even simpler, spincasting tackle—to a far greater extent than any of the other types—is marketed in such a way that the absolute beginner can buy it and use it without having to make any anxiety-provoking decisions or perform any unfamiliar tasks. Nine times out of 10, spincasting outfits will be packaged as a matched rod and reel, and the reel will already contain the proper

The important parts of a spincasting reel.

amount of the proper weight line. It is virtually ready-to-use right off the shelf.

Spincasting gear is also relatively inexpensive. The very best spincasting reels are less than half the price of the best baitcasting reels, and an average-quality spincasting reel can be less than the price of a hardcover novel.

So, what is the bad news? Well, first of all, spincasting tackle has the same disadvantages as spinning tackle—reduced casting accuracy, a tendency toward line twist, and a mechanical disadvantage when playing a fish—and then some. Because outgoing line loops off a stationary spool in spincasting, as in spinning, the line swings in wide arcs near the spool during a cast. Spinning tackle is designed to minimize that problem. But in a spincasting reel, the looping line is severely inhibited by the small hole in the end of the housing, causing a great deal of friction and loss of casting distance. In addition, spincasting reels are usually less well crafted than other types, and their drag systems leave much to be desired.

The biggest problems, however, are caused by the very design that makes these reels so appealing—the invisibility of the innards. Small problems with line tangles are not noticed until they have become severe. Worse yet, in the normal course of fishing—as lures and hooks are tied to the line and removed, line ends are clipped off, line is broken by fish and snags—the housing keeps the angler in the dark about how much line is left on the reel. It is entirely possible for the fisherman to use up nearly all his line before realizing it must be replaced.

Spincasting tackle is also more limited than spinning tackle in the range of lure weights it can cast effectively. Mainly because of the friction problem, spincasting tackle is not good for lures much lighter than a quarter ounce or so. The very light lines required to cast tiny lures also have a tendency to pile up inside the housing.

SETTING UP YOUR SPINCASTING TACKLE

Because the greatest advantages of this type of tackle are its hassle-free elements for the absolute beginner, I strongly advise that you take advantage of them by

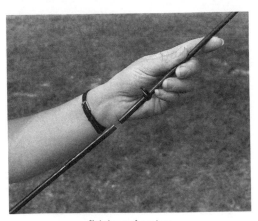

Joining rod sections.

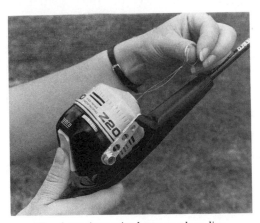

Thumb pressing casting button to release line.

Threading line up through guides from reel.

inserting the tip of the butt section into the opening in the tip section and aligning the guides.

Now you can thread the line up through the guides by first pressing and releasing the casting button. That step will allow line to be pulled from the reel. Usually there is a small ring tied to the end of the line to keep it from disappearing into the housing. Pull on the ring until a couple of feet of line extends from the reel, then snip the line near the ring. Thread the line through each guide from the reel to the rod tip. Then tie on a lure or practice plug (a plastic weight without hooks, made for casting practice), using the Improved Clinch Knot or the Jansik Special explained in Chapter 16.

HOW TO CAST WITH SPINCASTING TACKLE

Most spincasting reels have the crank handle on the right side, so you will be casting with your right hand and, switching the rod to your left hand, cranking the reel handle with your right hand for the retrieve.

Now, to get an idea of the working of the reel before making an actual cast,

buying an outfit that is already set up. The reel should already be attached to the rod and come pre-spooled with line. The only thing you should have to do is put the two sections of the rod together by

The grip.

Hand position.

The stance.

hold the rod as in Step 1 below. Point the rod straight out in front of you, parallel to the ground. The lure should be hanging a couple of inches below the rod tip. Press the reel button with your thumb and *hold it down*. Nothing will happen. Now release the button—the lure drops to the ground and the button stays down. Crank the handle—the button pops up and the lure comes back up to the rod tip. Until the crank is turned, however, the line is still free to leave the spool. Bring the lure up to within about six inches of the tip. Now try a cast, following the directions below.

1. *The Grip.* Hold the rod handle so that your right forefinger wraps comfortably around the trigger while your right thumb rests on the line-release button. Do not squeeze the rod handle; just hold it firmly.

2. *Hand Position.* Turn your hand so that your palm faces down and the reel handles are uppermost. This allows the greatest possible freedom of movement for your wrist.

Setting the reel: thumb pressing and holding the casting button.

Aim.

Cast: back to vertical.

Cast: without hesitation, back down, snap wrist, release button.

3. *The Stance.* Face your target, and then take a quarter-turn to the left so that your right shoulder points toward the target. Shift your left foot back to a comfortable position slightly to the rear of your right foot.

4. *Setting the Reel.* Press the line-release button with your thumb, and hold it down. As long as you maintain pressure on the button, the line will not be released.

5. *Aim.* Line up your eye, your rod, and your target.

6. *Cast.* Quickly lift your forearm with your elbow as the pivot so that your hand comes up to a point just below eye level. Keep the rod splitting the target, and stop its upward motion when it is just about vertical. The weight of the lure will put a backward bend in the rod. Do not allow the rod to drift back and absorb that bend—it is the potential energy in that bend that causes a good cast.

Without hesitation, start moving the rod back downward along the same path it took coming upward, but add a bit of wrist snap along with the elbow chop. At a point about halfway between the vertical rod position and your original starting position, release the button you have been holding with your thumb all this time. The lure will be cast toward the target, pulling line behind it from the reel. As the lure reaches the target, you can do one of three things: press the thumb button again, which will stop the lure dead; do nothing; or slow the lure gradually by using your left index finger to create increasing interference with the line as it exits the hole in the front of the reel. The last of the three options is preferred for a soft, controlled lure landing.

7. *The Retrieve.* Switch the rod to your left hand, and crank the handle with your right hand. The thumb button will pop up, re-engaging the line-retrieve mechanism. Unseen by you, line will wrap onto the reel's spool inside the cone housing, and the lure will return to you.

The timing of the release is the most difficult part of the cast. Release the line too soon, and your lure will sail high into the air, usually falling far short of the target. Release the line too late, and the lure will fire down into the water, also far short of the target. But because of the relative simplicity of this type of tackle, your concentration on timing can be com-

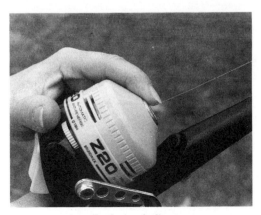

Feathering the line.

The retrieve.

plete, and you should get the hang of it very quickly.

That simplicity is the overwhelming advantage of spincasting tackle. There is so little to think about in terms of physical actions and tackle mechanics that spincasting comes close to being an immediate success. Add in the fact that spincasting tackle comes in ready-to-use, right-off-the-shelf packaging, and you have the closest thing to instant gratification that fishing has to offer. The most difficult task involving spincasting tackle

may well be removing it from the shrink-wrap package.

The disadvantages of spincasting have already been discussed. Nonetheless, I highly recommend spincasting tackle as the initial equipment for the absolute beginner who is looking for a versatile, simple, hassle-free, and inexpensive way to find out if fishing has any attraction for him.

In the next chapter we will take a look at a method of fishing that, in many respects, is quite the opposite.

5

Flycasting Tackle

Flycasting is fundamentally different from any of the other types of casting discussed in previous chapters. Baitcasting, spinning, and spincasting all share one basic principle: the weight of the lure is propelled through the air, pulling the line behind it. In flycasting, the opposite is the case—the weight of the line is propelled through the air, pulling the lure behind it.

In baitcasting, spinning, and spincasting, the lures used are generally imitations of baitfish, frogs, crayfish, eels, and other more or less substantial critters. The lures are most often made of plastic, rubber, wood, or metal, and generally weigh one-eighth to three-quarters of an ounce. The very lightest of those lures, which can be cast only with ultralight spinning tackle, may be as light as 1/32 of an ounce. But the lures used with flycast-

ing tackle are usually imitations of insects. They are made of tiny bits of feathers and furs tied with thread to very small hooks, and they weigh—for all practical purposes—nothing. The line is heavier than the lure. And so in flycasting you cast the line, and the fly is carried along with it.

Fly line, as you may already suspect, is quite different from the filmy monofilament used with baitcasting, spinning, and spincasting tackle. Fly line is substantial stuff, usually a core of braided nylon surrounded by a plastic coating of variable thickness. Depending upon the configuration of the coating, the line may be a weight-forward (WF) type that is fattest—and therefore heaviest—at one end, tapering down to a much narrower diameter for the rest of its length; or a double-taper (DT), in which the midsection is

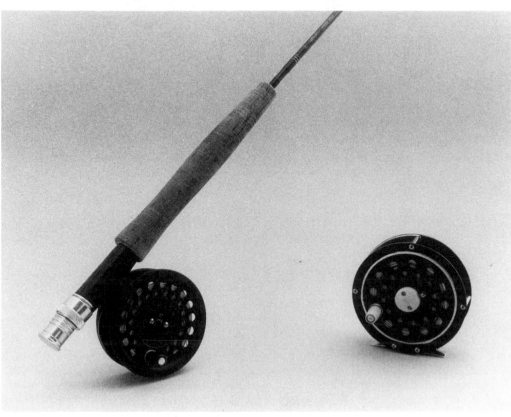

Flycasting tackle, showing a fly reel on a fly rod and a separate reel.

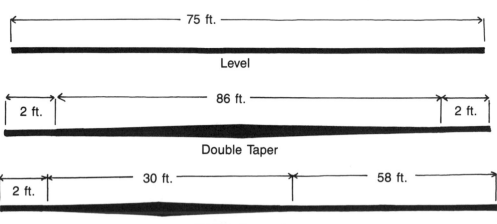

The three most common forms of fly line, with thickness greatly exaggerated in proportion to length.

thickest and heaviest, tapering in both directions toward the ends; or a level (L) type with a uniform thickness throughout.

Because the fly line is relatively thick and the fly's hook is relatively delicate, a leader of tapered monofilament intervenes. The end of the leader to which the fly line is tied is nearly as thick as the fly line, and the end to which the fly is tied is much finer, its thickness depending upon the size of the fly being cast. The leader usually ranges from the length of the rod to twice that long.

The fly line—and thereby the leader and the fly itself—is cast by waving a length of it in the air with the rod until sufficient velocity is attained to shoot the line out toward the target. At the end of the cast, the line straightens out in such a way that the fly flips out ahead of the leader and line.

Fly lines come not only in different thickness configurations (tapers) but in different weights as well. The weight rating of a line is determined by the weight of the first 30 feet of the line in grains, which is then assigned a number from 1 to 12. In addition, fly lines may float, sink, or have a 10-foot tip section that sinks while the rest of the line floats. All those variables are identified by a series of letters and numbers that are used as the standard method of labelling fly lines. A DT-6-F fly line is a double-tapered line with a weight of 160 grains that floats. A WF-8-S line has a weight-forward taper, weighs 210 grains, and sinks.

Although there is no easy way to remember the actual weight equivalents (in grains) of the numbers 1 through 12 in the ratings, it is not particularly important to do so. The important factor is to correctly match that weight of line with a rod that is designed to handle it. Fly rods are also assigned the 1 through 12 rating. A No. 7 rod works best when casting a 7-weight line; its resistance to bending is perfectly matched by the 185 grains in the first 30 feet of a 7-weight line in order to achieve the best casting characteristics. So matching line of the proper weight with the proper rod is simply a matter of matching the numbers. Everything else is more complicated.

There are reasons for choosing one weight of line over another; for using one type of taper over another; for using floating, sinking, or sinking-tip lines, and for using 7½- , 9- , 12- , or 15-foot leaders. There are a million variables in almost every possible aspect of fly fishing, and it is one of the most written about and nit-picked sports in history. Yet for the beginner, it need not be particularly complicated. As you gain experience and knowledge, you may add complexities— and that is unquestionably a large part of the fun of fly fishing. For now, however, let it suffice to say that the absolute beginner will do very well for a long time with a flycasting outfit that includes a double-taper, 6-weight, floating line (DT-6-F); the best eight-foot, No. 6 fly rod you can afford; and a reliable single-action reel about 3½ inches in diameter. In addition, you will need a 7½-foot tapered leader, either knotted or knotless, with a 4X tippet; a spool of 15-pound-test Dacron backing; and a selection of both wet and dry flies in the No. 12 to No. 16 size range.

That selection of tackle is suitable for trout in small to medium-size rivers and streams and for panfish and small bass in lakes and ponds. For larger bass in lakes and ponds, a weight-forward, 8-weight, floating line (WF-8-F) is more appropriate. It should be matched with an 8½- or nine-foot, No. 8 rod; a single-action reel about four inches in diameter; a six-foot, tapered leader with a 1X or 0X tippet; and an assortment of bass bugs in the No. 2 to No. 4 size range.

Now I will try to explain some details about those two outfits I just suggested.

The Line. For trout and panfish, I have recommended a DT-6-F line. The *double taper* makes the line economical because it is reversible. Both ends of the line are relatively thin, and the center portion of the line is thickened to provide the weight necessary for easy casting. Because both ends of the line are identical, the line can be reversed on the reel when one of the ends wears out. Because the ends are more delicate than the middle, a delicate cast can be made to wary fish; the heavy part of the line is far from the fly.

Six-weight line is suggested because it is not so fine as to be difficult for the beginner to cast, yet not so heavy as to cause much commotion on the type of water you'll be fishing. Heavier lines are useful for attaining long casts (40 feet or more) and for fighting wind. On woodland streams and smaller lakes, your casts will average about 20 feet and wind will not be too great a factor.

Floating line is recommended because it is easier to cast and because, for the most part, you will not need to sink your flies deeper than the length of your leader.

For serious bass fishing, I have suggested a WF-8-F line. The *weight-forward* taper is used in bass bugging (flycasting for bass) because it makes casting the bushy, wind-resistant bass bugs much easier. Weight-forward lines increase casting distance but make a much less delicate delivery of the fly because their

forward portion is relatively thick and heavy, tapering down fairly rapidly to thinner line for the remainder of their length. Weight-forward lines look like double-taper lines that have had their bellies squeezed up toward one end. They are, of course, not reversible. Bass are generally not as easily frightened as trout and can therefore be fished for with weight-forward lines, which make a bit more commotion closer to the fly or bug than do double-taper lines.

An *8-weight* line is suggested for bass because the extra weight helps punch out the big bass bugs and is easier to cast in the inevitable breezes that haunt larger lakes.

Floating line is recommended because it is easier to handle and because most of the bugs you will cast for bass are floating flies.

The Rod. Within limits, it can be said that using a longer rod makes flycasting easier. However, on a typical trout stream, with overhanging trees and assorted other streamside shrubbery, a long rod (over 8½ feet) can make life terribly difficult in a hurry. Rods shorter than 7½ feet, however, require line-handling precision that you do not yet have (and may not have for some time). Therefore, an eight-foot rod is about perfect. You will need a No. 6 rod for trout and panfish because you will be using a 6-weight line, and the rod must match the line. For bass, you will want an 8½-foot No. 8 rod because the longer rod is no hindrance out on an open lake (you might even consider a nine-foot rod) and because the No. 8 rod will best handle the 8-weight line you will be using.

Fly rods are available in a startling range of prices, and, as with other types of fishing rods, you should get the best you can afford. The least-expensive fly rods are made of fiberglass. The best glass rods are pretty good; the least expensive are pretty awful and may make your learning experience more difficult than necessary. More expensive fly rods are made of graphite, and good ones can be bought for a reasonable price. Some graphite rods are very costly without being all that much better in quality than some less expensive graphite models. In those cases, you are paying extra money for a brand name and/or cosmetics. I recommend that the beginner buy the best graphite rod he can afford for under $100. Some very expensive fly rods are made of bamboo and start at an arm-and-a-leg, increasing in price from there.

Fly rods usually come in two or three pieces for ease of transport. They have several line guides along their underside, the first of which (the one closest to the butt) is the largest and is ring-shaped. The rest of them are called snake guides and are of a special shape to allow easy back-and-forth movement of the line. The rod handle is most often made of cork and may have any of a variety of shapes. Endmost on the rod is the reel seat, meaning that the rod is actually held ahead of the reel, unlike all the other tackle you have learned about. The fly reel hangs down below the rod.

The Reel. Unlike other types of reels, the fly reel will do little more for the absolute beginner than store line. Casting has nothing to do with the reel. Playing a fish can be done from the reel but is more often accomplished by stripping (or pulling) in line with the hand not holding the

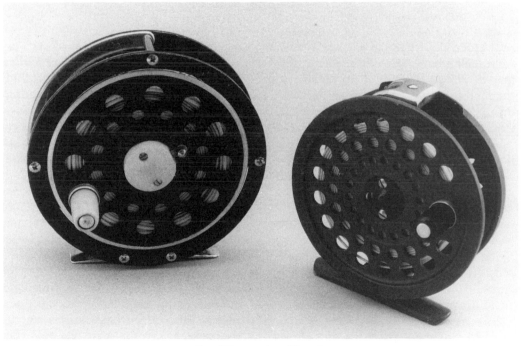

Two different makes of fly reels.

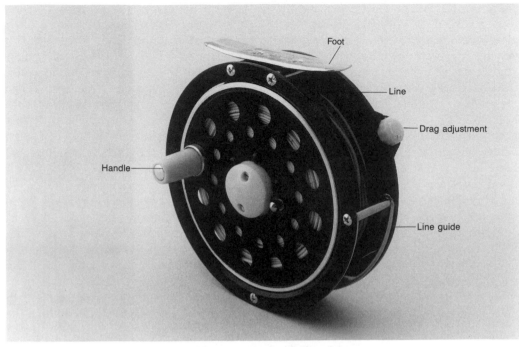

Foot

Line

Drag adjustment

Handle

Line guide

The important parts of a fly reel.

rod, especially when the catch is a small trout, small bass, or panfish. Larger fish may be played off the reel, in which case the reel's drag may help control the fish.

Generally speaking, though, the fly reel simply holds the line, and the free hand (the one not holding the rod) grabs the line itself and yanks lengths of it off the reel when more is needed for the cast. A crank on the reel allows the line to be wound back on for storage or to temporarily get various amounts of it out of the way. Fish played off the reel may be brought in by cranking in line as well. Most fly reels can be arranged so that the crank handle is on either the left or the right. Traditionally, it is on the right.

A *single-action* reel, as I have recommended, is simply a reel that has a one-to-one line-take-up ratio. The handle is connected directly to the spool itself, exactly like those reels used to store garden hose. There are other types of reels, including automatic reels that are spring-loaded for automatic retrieval of line, and reels that are geared for faster line retrieval than the single-action models, but they are not necessary for the absolute beginner.

Usually, the 30 yards of fly line is not enough to fill up a reel. It is therefore advisable to first load the reel with your fly line, then tie to it some 15-pound-test, braided Dacron backing. Continue loading the reel until it is filled, then cut the backing. Next, wind the backing back onto an empty reel, untie the two lines, remove the fly line from your reel, and tie the backing from the spare reel onto your fly reel, using the Reel Knot explained in

Chapter 16. Then tie the fly line to the backing and wind it on the reel. With a DT fly line, it doesn't matter which end is tied to the backing—the ends are identical. But with a WF taper, make absolutely sure that the weighted end is outermost and is not tied to the backing. When playing strong fish like salmon and steelhead that fight hard and take line off your reel, the backing ensures that you will not run out of line. But even with fish that are unlikely to do that, the backing provides a means of filling your reel so that your line is wound in larger coils, thereby diminishing the likelihood of kinking. (See *Setting Up Your Flycasting Tackle* below.)

The Leader. The whole object of flycasting—for *all* fishing, actually—is to present a lure without letting the fish become aware that the lure is a fake. Therefore it is necessary to connect the fly to the fly line in the least conspicuous manner. Partly to make the fly seem unconnected to anything, and partly because most flies cannot physically be tied directly to the fat fly line anyway, a monofilament leader is tied between the fly line and the fly. (See *Setting Up Your Flycasting Tackle.*) The leader should be tapered in such a way that its butt end is about two-thirds the diameter of the fly line, and its tippet end is just right for attachment to the fly (explained below). The correct rate of taper is important to making a good cast. Leader length, which can be anywhere from six to 15 feet, is usually determined by water and wind conditions.

Many fly fishermen build their own leaders by tying together several specific lengths of different-diameter mono. You should simply buy a ready-made leader, either knotted or knotless, that is 7½ feet long and tapers to a 4X tippet. That will serve you well with your trout and panfish outfit. For your bass outfit, I recommend a six-foot leader with a 0X or 1X tippet. When you become more knowledgeable about fly fishing (beyond the scope of this book), you can make your own choices regarding leaders. Tippet sizes run from 0X to 7X. 0X is relatively coarse and 7X is ridiculously fine. The X-ratings correspond to the thickness of the monofilament in thousandths of an inch.

Rating	Diam. (inches)	Approx. test (pounds)
0X	.011	10
1X	.010	9
2X	.009	7
3X	.008	6
4X	.007	5
5X	.006	4
6X	.005	3
7X	.004	2

The choice of tippet size is determined mainly by the size of the fly you will be casting. A tippet incorrectly matched to the fly will not do a good job of transferring the energy of the cast through the line, leader, and tippet. The fly will then not fall where and how it is supposed to, and you may as well not bother flycasting at all.

The Flies. There are two broad categories of flies: those that float on the surface of the water and those that sink below it. Flies that float are called dry flies; flies that sink are called wet flies.

All flies are classified in terms of their size, using a numbering system that assigns to the tiniest flies the highest numbers. Thus a No. 28 fly is a barely visible, midge-size thing, while a No. 2 fly is a fairly substantial lure. Flies larger than

No. 0 bear numbers such as 1/0, 2/0, 3/0 (pronounced one-ought, two-ought, three-ought where I come from) in increasing size.

For general-purpose fishing for trout and panfish, I suggest a selection of wet and dry flies in the No. 12 to No. 16 size range. Those sizes are best handled by a tippet of about 4X, which is why I told you to buy that size of leader. Bass flies—usually called bass bugs because of their bulky designs (which, by the way, often are meant to imitate frogs and mice, although they are still referred to as bugs)—should be larger. A selection of bugs in the No. 2 to No. 4 range is a good bet, and with them you should use a leader that tapers to a 0X or 1X tippet.

SETTING UP YOUR FLYCASTING TACKLE

Flycasting tackle is most often purchased as separate elements. The reel, rod, backing, line, and leader must then be put together properly before the tackle can be used.

The rod will most likely be a two-piece model. Join the two pieces by inserting the tip of the butt section into the opening in the tip section. While pushing the two sections together, twist them so that the guides are aligned exactly.

I suggest you have a reputable tackle shop perform the job of connecting the backing to your fly line and tying on your leader. Special knots and techniques are involved here that need not be the concern of the beginner. If the store where you bought your tackle cannot do this for you, take your backing, line, leader, and reel to a better store. They may charge you a minimal fee to do the job, but they are unlikely to refuse. You will end up with your backing, line, and leader joined together and wound onto your reel.

The flycasting reel hangs below the rod. If you hold the rod by its grip so that the guides are downward, you will notice that there is a place to secure the reel just behind your hand. It will usually consist of one or two movable rings on a threaded part of the rod shaft, and two cup-like brackets separated by a space of about three inches. One bracket is stationary; the other is movable.

Joining rod sections.

Seating the reel on the rod.

Hold the reel so that its flat feet are uppermost. The body of the reel should be hanging below, and the round or U-shaped line-opening of the reel should be toward the rod's tip. The crank will most likely be toward the right. First, slide one foot of the reel under the stationary bracket of the reel seat. Then seat the reel against the rod and slide the movable bracket forward or back as far as it will go, making sure the cup is aligned to hold the foot of the reel. Hold it there and tighten first the ring closest to the reel (if there are two) and then the other, or the single ring (if there is only one), so that the reel is held securely. There should be no play at all.

Find the end of the leader, and thread it out the line-opening of the reel and up through all the rod guides, starting with

Tightening the reel ring.

the large ring-guide closest to the reel and ending with the little ring-guide that is the tip top. Tie on a fly of the recommended size for your outfit, using the Improved Clinch Knot explained in Chapter 16.

The line threaded up through the guides from the reel.

Holding the rod after laying line out on the grass.

HOW TO CAST WITH FLYCASTING TACKLE

First of all, it is important to know that when flycasting you need as much clear space behind you as in front of you, so position yourself in the middle of a lawn

The grip.

or other uncluttered space, and make sure that you have at least 20 feet of room behind and in front.

With either the trout/panfish or the bass outfit I have recommended, rig up your tackle so that it is complete and ready to use, including a fly tied onto your tippet. It is important always to practice casting with a fly tied on, in order to sense the proper action of the line, but cut the point and barb off the hook with a wire snip so that it does not catch in the lawn or the back of your head (sooner or later you will see what I mean).

To start, lay your rod down on the grass and pull about 20 feet of line (including the leader) off the reel and through the guides so that it extends straight out from the rod tip and rests on the grass. Then go back and pick up your rod in your right hand if you are righthanded.

1. *The Grip.* Hold your rod handle as you would grip the handle of a suitcase,

but with your thumb resting on top, in line with the rod. The reel should be hanging straight down. There is no need to strangle the rod; just hold it with a firm but relaxed grip. Your forefinger should press the line against the handle.

2. *The Stance.* Squarely face the direction in which you are going to cast, placing a bit more weight on your right foot. Point your rod out toward the extended line lying on the grass, the rod tip at about eye level.

3. *The Backcast.* Keeping your wrist stiff so that the rod becomes an extension of your forearm, raise the rod with a smooth, accelerating lift by pivoting on your elbow. The line will come up off the grass and be thrown into the air behind you. *Stop* all rod and arm movement as the rod approaches the vertical position. If you were holding an ice cream cone in

place of a rod, it would be just about in position for you to lick at this point. Keep your wrist absolutely stiff; do not let it bend and allow the rod to sag backward.

4. *The Pause.* The temptation is to begin the forward cast immediately. Resist it. You must get used to the idea that the fly line at this point is actually moving upward and backward and will take a surprisingly long time to start falling downward behind you. Wait until you feel the line pulling against the rod, which it will do once it straightens out behind you. You may even find it helpful to glance over your shoulder to see what the line is doing. Starting the forward cast too soon will result in a mess.

5. *The Forward Cast.* When the line has straightened out behind and you feel its pull, swing your arm downward sharply but smoothly, emphasizing the forward

The stance.

The backcast: starting the line in motion toward the rear.

stroke with a slight forward bend of your wrist. *Stop* the forward cast when the rod is still quite high, allowing your arm and the rod to drift down as the cast straightens out and the fly falls to the ground.

The rod positions in flycasting are traditionally described in terms of the numbers on a clock face. Think of three o'clock as being straight out in front of you and of nine o'clock as being straight behind you. Twelve o'clock is straight up over your head. In those terms, your rod should stop at eleven o'clock on the backcast described in Step 3, and your forward cast should stop at one o'clock on the forward cast described in Step 5. That is not much rod movement, and it is tempting to let your wrist do the work. But you must keep that wrist stiff during those movements and let your whole arm do the work. Otherwise, your cast will be

The pause: waiting for the line to straighten behind you.

The forward cast: stopping as the line straightens in front.

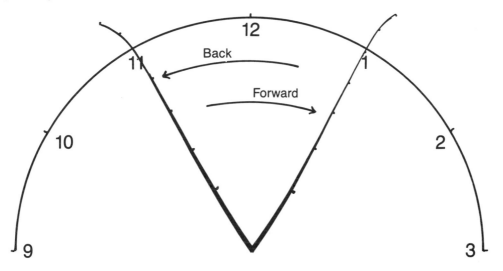

Rod position during flycasting can be thought of in terms of a clock face. The important action takes place between 11 and 1 o'clock.

sloppy, and you will become frustrated and disenchanted with flycasting. And that would be a shame.

Fly fishing, perhaps more than any other type of fishing, can become an all-encompassing hobby in itself. There is more esoterica accompanying fly fishing (particularly for trout) than you can imagine. Yet you can ignore or embrace as much of it as suits your personality. You can even get involved in tying your own flies.

The disadvantages of flycasting are that you need room for your backcast; it requires more practice than does other tackle; flycasting is more affected by wind than are other forms of casting; and, although most types of fish can be caught on flies, most fly rods effectively handle only a very narrow range of lines and flies, thereby requiring different rods for different types of quarries.

One of the advantages of fly fishing involves the flies themselves. Because of the materials from which they can be made, flies represent realistic imitations of the creatures fish eat. In addition, because of their lack of weight, flies can be presented to the fish in the most natural and least frightening manner. Another advantage is the caster's ability to hit a target with repeatable precision, for the line need not be reeled in after each cast; it is simply backcast and cast again to the same spot. Related to that factor is flycasting's advantage of being able to work the lures *over* troublesome areas that would snag baitcasting, spinning, or spincasting lures, most of which have to be retrieved *through* the area before you can cast them again. And casting with a fly rod can be extremely precise. If you see that your fly is not going to hit the target perfectly, you do not have to let it land, as you must with other types of tackle. You can simply throw the line back into a backcast and try again without disturbing the water.

Flycasting may be the most difficult form of casting in which to gain proficiency, but it is arguably the one that offers the devotee the most depth of interest. Many anglers will fish with nothing but a fly rod, and others will not take the time to learn to use one at all. I think that if you find fishing interesting, you should try your hand with *all* the tackle I have discussed in these chapters.

Section II

THE FISHES

What to Fish For

6

Panfish

Panfish are not a scientifically recognized taxonomic group. They are rather an indefinite collection of common fish that most anglers, for one reason or another, refuse to recognize as gamefish. One reason may be the fish's failure to attain any great size, even in adulthood—in fact, the term "panfish" may derive from those fishes' ability to be placed in a frying pan whole. Another reason may be that all panfish are perceived as sharing a low level of challenge in both the ease and numbers in which they are often caught. So they are more often caught for food than for sport—for the pan rather than for the thrill or the trophy.

Not all fishermen agree on which fish should be designated as panfish. Some panfish are so scrappy when hooked that they are regarded by some as gamefish. Some anglers consider as panfish many more species than are usually included in the group. But a consensus undoubtedly regards as the most common panfish the various species of sunfish, bluegills, crappies, yellow perch, and bullheads—most of which are known by a remarkable assortment of local monikers, and most of which are close relatives of popular gamefish.

SUNFISH AND BLUEGILLS

These are arguably the most commonly caught fish, especially by beginners. Some reasons are that sunfish and bluegills, which are closely related and similar in appearance, can usually be found near shore; they are abundant; they readily take several types of live baits as well as some types of artificial lures; they usually are not subject to size, number, or sea-

Bluegills (foreground) *and sunfish*. Drawing by Ernest Lussier.

sonal limits by state fishing laws; they can be caught with any kind of tackle; they are fun to catch; and they make good eating. What more could you ask?

Well, for one thing, you could ask for more size, and as your skill and experience increase, you will discover why most good fishermen seek encounters with the larger gamefish while still occasionally taking a dose of simple fun from the bluegills, sunfish, and other panfish.

Bluegills, also called bream, and the sunfish, of which there are several species called by a variety of names, are actually different fish, though all belong to the sunfish family. I am discussing them together here because having to know the exact differences between bluegills and the various sunfish seems an unnecessary complication for the beginner. At this stage, it is enough that you be able simply to tell the bluegills and sunfish from all other fish.

Bluegills and sunnies have a distinctive shape, for one thing. Technically they are described as having an ovoid and laterally flattened body—meaning that if you took a slightly oval saucer and stood it on edge, you would have a fair approximation of a bluegill or sunnie. The mouths of bluegills and many sunfish are noticeably small for their size, and many of the various fish have beautifully colored cheeks streaked with electric blue, and chins and bellies aflame with brilliant yellows, oranges, and reds, while the remainder of the body varies through olive, brown, bronzy brown-green, and dark green.

Generally speaking, bluegills and sunnies share similar weedy habitats, which include ponds, the coves and shallows of larger lakes, and the slow-moving backwaters of rivers and streams. Notice the key word here: weedy. Weedy areas pro-

vide bluegills and sunnies with food and protective cover. The fish usually do not eat the weeds, but they do eat many of the insects, crustaceans, tadpoles, and minnows that are also attracted to the weeds for food and shelter. Other common areas where sunnies and bluegills can be found include brushpiles, areas under docks and boathouses, and among the pilings of bridges and piers. Sunnies and bluegills normally take their food at mid-depths, shallow depths, and right off the surface.

In late spring, when the water warms to over 50° F, the bluegills and sunnies begin to spawn, an activity that can continue throughout most of the summer. Generally, these fish clear round, dishlike clearings on the bottom of shallow waters. The males guard these nests, which may be so dense in an area that their edges may actually touch. And it is the males that watch over the fry once they hatch from the several thousand eggs laid by the females.

In size, the bluegills tend to get larger than the sunnies, the largest bluegills reaching a length of about 15 inches while the largest sunnies rarely exceed nine inches. Far more common, however, are bluegills in the nine-inch size and sunnies of about six inches. Small ponds without large, predacious fish, however, can hold enormous numbers of stunted bluegills and sunnies that never grow much beyond a couple of inches.

In subsequent chapters, you will learn about the methods of catching bluegills and sunnies, but it is safe to say that if you were to go to any local pond and drop a hook baited with a piece of earthworm into a hole in the weeds, the fish you would most likely catch would be a sunnie or bluegill. Other good baits and lures include small, live crickets, grasshoppers, grubs, and nymphs (all tackle); small artificial lures (spinning and spincasting tackle); and wet and dry flies (fly fishing tackle).

CRAPPIES

Crappies, too, are members of the sunfish family. But they're different enough in habits, in appearance, and in the techniques used to fish for them to warrant their own listing. There are two types of crappies, white and black; each is slightly different from the other in habitat preferences and in appearance. Again, it is more important that the beginner be able simply to tell crappies from other fish than to be able to tell black crappies from white.

Crappies have a lot of common names, including speckled bass, specks, calico bass, strawberry bass, silver bass, and papermouths. Some of these names give clues to the crappies' appearance, physical characteristics, and family ties. For one thing, the black crappie is generally a brassy color with many black spots. It is therefore the black crappie that is usually referred to as a speck or calico. The white crappie is more silvery and is marked with six or seven pale vertical stripes. Both are much less round in profile than their cousins the sunfish, but they are still fairly flat. Their mouths are much larger than those of the bluegills and sunnies, and when fully open reveal a papery membrane behind the lips. It is from that characteristic that both species of crappies get the name papermouth, which also hints at the ease with which a hook pulls out of that membrane.

Crappies live in areas very similar to those preferred by sunnies and bluegills and, like their cousins, have a tendency

Catching bluegills and sunnies. Michigan Travel Commission photo.

to form schools. Crappies, however, are much more closely associated with brushpiles than are other members of their family, and if you can locate a submerged treetop, flooded bushes, or an area in a slow river where brush and branches collect, you will likely have found a place where crappies congregate. In lieu of brushpiles, crappies will seek out weedy areas much like those preferred by sunnies and bluegills.

Young crappies eat insect nymphs and larvae and crustaceans, but after a couple of years their diet shifts mainly to minnows and other small fish. They may feed on young sunnies and bluegills if those are in abundance.

Like sunnies and bluegills, male crappies clear nests on the bottom in shallow water and guard them from intruders. Spawning takes place in late spring and

Black crappies. Drawing by Ernest Lussier.

Yellow perch. Drawing by Ernest Lussier.

early summer, and the males continue to guard the young for a short time after they hatch.

Crappies can get a good deal larger than sunnies or bluegills, some reaching a weight of five pounds. But crappies most commonly weigh a pound or less and reach about 10 inches to a foot in length. Crappies can put up a good fight when hooked, and the papery mouth makes it uncertain that the angler will actually land one. They make delicious eating and are not so easily found as their cousins the bluegills and sunnies—all of which makes them a panfish with many of the characteristics of gamefish. While randomly fishing, you are much less likely to catch a crappie than a bluegill or sunnie, but if you actively seek out and find a place where they have congregated, your success is nearly assured. Crappies are fished for with live minnows 1½ to 2½ inches long (baitcasting, spinning, or spincasting tackle), artificial lures resembling minnows of that same size range (spinning or spincasting tackle), or streamers of the same size (fly fishing tackle).

YELLOW PERCH

Yellow perch are not related to any of the fish you have read about so far and are not likely to be confused with any of them. Yellow perch, though somewhat flattened laterally, are much more elongated than the panfish in the sunfish family, and their coloration makes them easily identifiable. Yellow perch are almost tropical in appearance. They have bright yellow sides blending to a snow-white belly, overlaid with six to eight bands of olive green that seem to drip down from the top of the back. In addition to those beautiful markings, the lower fins are all bright orange.

Although yellow perch will often be found in the same lakes and ponds as bluegills and sunnies, they actually prefer cool, clear lakes with sandy or rocky bottoms. Nonetheless, they have the same needs of food and cover as do other types of fish and so will be found around weedy areas. There they feed on aquatic insects, crustaceans, and small fish, the adults feeding almost entirely on other fish and crayfish.

Generally speaking, yellow perch like to stay in the deepest water that suits their needs. That usually puts them deeper in a lake than bluegills and sunnies. Unlike those panfish, yellow perch very rarely feed at the surface.

During spawning, though—which takes place early in the spring when the water temperature is still between 45° and 52° F—yellow perch can be found in shallow water. There each female lays as many as 50,000 eggs that are enveloped in strings of a gelatinous substance, much like the eggs of frogs. The males fertilize the eggs, and thus ends all parental responsibility. The result is that large numbers of yellow perch never get much beyond the hatchling stage. Though each yellow perch may lay more than twice the number of eggs laid by each bluegill, our lakes and ponds do not necessarily hold more yellow perch than bluegills. Even minimal parental care, as provided by fish in the sunfish family, seems to make a tremendous difference in the survival of the young.

Yellow perch are schooling fish, and the schools tend to consist of fish of similar size. Thus, if you catch a yellow perch, you are likely to catch more from that spot and find that all of them are nearly identical in size. Yellow perch of a different size will be in a separate school elsewhere in the lake.

Most yellow perch that you will catch will weigh around half a pound and measure about 10 inches in length. Occasionally, you may be lucky enough to chance upon a school of one- to two-pounders, fish 12 to 15 inches long. The very largest yellow perch attain a weight of about four pounds.

In terms of delicious eating, yellow perch are hard to beat if they are caught in relatively cold water in the early part of the season or through the ice during the winter. Once the water warms to midsummer temperatures, the meat of yellow perch tends to become less firm and may pick up a muddy flavor.

Yellow perch are fished for with a variety of small, live baits (all tackle); small artificial lures such as minnow-imitating crankbaits, spinners, and spoons (spinning and spincasting tackle); and wet flies and streamers (fly fishing tackle).

A fine catch of hefty yellow perch. Michigan Travel Commission photo.

BULLHEADS

Bullheads are small (10 to 12 inches; about a pound in weight) catfish that inhabit the same lakes, ponds, and rivers as the other panfish you have just learned about. When hooked, they put up a terrific fight and feel as though they are much larger than they turn out to be. For sheer sport, no panfish is scrappier than a bullhead. Despite that fact, I find bullheads not entirely pleasant to catch.

For one thing, bullheads are ugly. Like most members of their family, they are broad, solid fish with wide, somewhat flattened heads, relatively small eyes, and extremely wide mouths surrounded by several fleshy whiskers (barbels). In addition, bullheads have a sharp spine on each pectoral fin that can inflict a nasty injury to your hand while you are trying to get the fish off your hook—a task made more difficult by the bullhead's fleshy lips and exceedingly slimy, scaleless body. Worse yet, the fish has the ability to utter sounds while you are handling it. Bullheads are generally muddy olive brown over most of their bodies, grading gradually into a white, cream, or yellow belly.

It is not my intention to turn you off to bullheads. I really do not mind catching them, and bullheads are a particular favorite of many fishermen (some of whom, I am certain, will write me nasty letters for calling their favorite fish ugly). There

Bullhead. Drawing by Ernest Lussier.

is no denying that they are truly delicious when prepared properly, and a thrill to have on the line. So please make your own decisions about bullheads, but know that they are very different in appearance from the other panfish discussed in this chapter.

There are actually several species of bullhead, but—again for the sake of sanity and simplicity—suffice it to say that at your stage of angling, it is enough to know the generic bullhead from the rest of the panfish.

Bullheads, also called horned pout, are designed for feeding on the bottom. They have poor eyesight, but their senses of touch, taste, and smell (all of which are located in their skin and barbels) make them highly efficient feeders. And their diet—which consists of just about anything they can fit in their mouths, alive or dead—makes them fairly easy to catch if you are in the right place.

Bullheads are most often found in slow rivers but can also be found in lakes and ponds. They manage to survive under extreme conditions of high water temperatures and low oxygen levels. Bullheads spawn in nests in shallow water during the early summer, laying very few eggs, usually less than 1,000. Due to the care of both parents, however, the survival rate of the hatchlings is very high.

Bullheads are most often fished for with earthworms (all tackle), but are occasionally caught on artificial lures (all tackle), usually by accident.

Those are the panfish you are most likely to catch as you pursue your interest in fishing. There are others that are less commonly encountered but may be abundant where you live. If so, please forgive me for not mentioning them. What I am trying to do is introduce anglers to those species that are most common in most places.

The next chapter, similarly, will introduce you to the most common gamefish, the ones that provide the best sport, if not necessarily the best eating.

7

Gamefish

Gamefish are, in a way, the big brothers of panfish. Though each of the panfish may be fun to catch, it is not only fun but *exciting* to catch a gamefish. Gamefish grow substantially larger than panfish, are harder to catch, fight harder and longer when hooked, and are generally more challenging and rewarding. Gamefish are commonly kept for food, as are panfish, but unlike panfish, they are also commonly released, their hooking and landing often being the ends in themselves.

For those reasons, gamefish are considered an important natural resource in all states and provinces in North America. With gamefish, unlike panfish, there usually are legal limits to the numbers you can keep in one day, size limits, and seasonal restrictions as well.

Many of our most popular gamefish have close relatives among the panfish you have learned about in the previous chapter, and so share similar habits and habitats. Others are unique. But, again, as with the panfish, I am introducing only those gamefish that you are most likely to encounter as a beginning angler. If other species are abundant in your area, my apologies.

LARGEMOUTH BASS

The largemouth bass is arguably the most popular freshwater gamefish in the United States. That popularity is due largely to the relatively recent outbreak of bass-fishing tournaments, professional bass fishermen, organizations and publications dedicated to the catching of bass—mainly competitively—and all the attendant macho and celebrity connota-

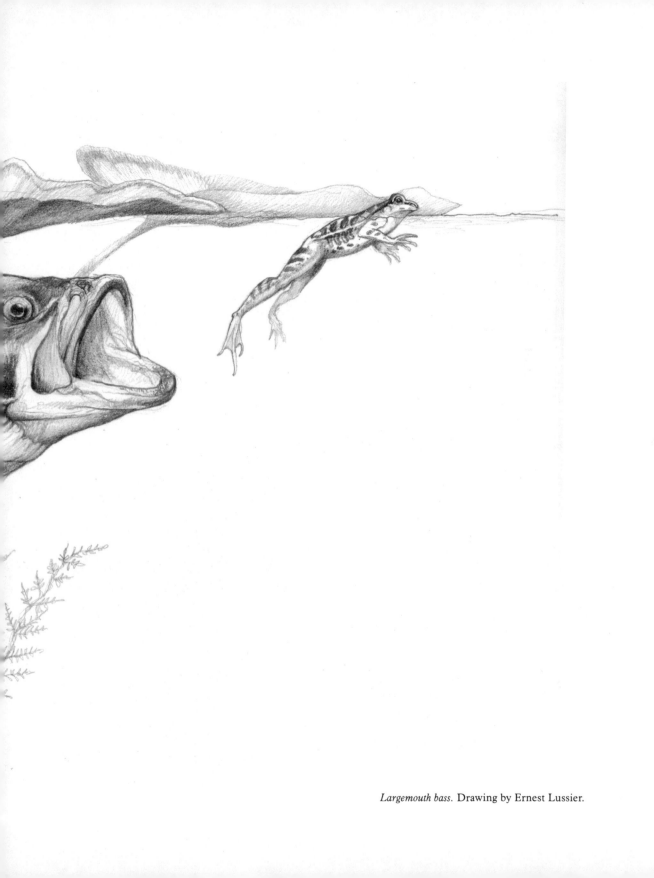

Largemouth bass. Drawing by Ernest Lussier.

tions that can accompany the pursuit of the species.

On the other hand, largemouth bass were sought by anglers even back in the days before the ''mystique'' developed and so they are a well-established part of American fishing heritage. Now, however, bass fishing is being touted as a booming, commercial endeavor rather than a simple, pleasant pastime. Of course, it does not have to be. You can still go out and have wonderful, peaceful, noncompetitive days of bass fishing. But it is difficult nowadays to pick up a fishing magazine or tackle catalog without feeling as though your worth as a human

being is determined by the size and number of bass you can catch.

Despite my obvious annoyance with the competitive direction bass fishing (and, by indirect association, *all* fishing) has taken, let me assure you that there is ample reason to pursue the largemouth bass. First of all, the small ones are scrappy, the big ones are strong, and the mid-size ones are both. After you catch your first good panfish, you may become hooked on the sport of angling; but after you land your first good-size bass, you will have taken a quantum leap in your dedication and enthusiasm.

Largemouth bass are in the sunfish

Typical largemouth habitat.

family. But saying that a bass is just a large sunnie is like saying that a Porsche is just a sporty Volkswagen. Largemouth bass do get large. The world-record fish weighed a bit over 22 pounds. Fifteen-pounders are caught on occasion in the South and far West, where they attain their greatest size due to the year-long growing season. Yet even in the North it is not uncommon to catch five- to seven-pound largemouths, though in most of the country the fish is usually encountered in its one- to three-pound size.

The largemouth bass varies in coloration with location and habitat but is generally blackish on top, shading down the sides to green, with a dark band extending from head to tail, and blending into a belly of white, cream, or yellow. It does have a large mouth, and comparatively large eyes.

Shallow, weedy lakes and slow rivers are the natural homes of the largemouth. These gamefish have also been able to thrive in the large impoundments created by dammed rivers throughout the South and West. But their classic environment is natural lakes containing plenty of subsurface weedbeds and large expanses of lily pads.

Largemouths are voracious predators with an extensive diet that includes fish, crayfish, frogs, insects, and anything else they can catch and swallow, including snakes, mice, and baby ducks. They feed through the full range of water depths from the bottom to the surface, and there is no greater thrill than suddenly to have a bass come up and smash your surface lure on an otherwise calm lake.

Largemouths spawn much like their cousins the sunnies. They clear shallow depressions in the bottom in about two feet of water when the temperature

A better-than-average largemouth bass. The Walker Agency photo.

reaches about 63° F. The eggs and hatchlings are guarded by the males until the tiny fry form large schools that remain in the weedy shallows until the fry reach an inch or so in length.

The adult largemouths—the ones you will be trying to catch—seek those areas that offer as many of their requirements for comfort and survival as possible. Like most other fish, they need food and cover, water of the proper temperature and oxygen content, and other environmental factors about which we have varying degrees of reliable information and insight. Generally, though, largemouth bass can be found in weeds; along steep, rocky dropoffs; over submerged islands and rockpiles; and in submerged brush and timber.

Largemouths make excellent eating, and most keepers (those you are allowed

Smallmouth bass. Drawing by Ernest Lussier.

by law to keep) are large enough for filleting.

Largemouths are fished for with live bait including worms, frogs, crayfish, and minnows (baitcasting, spinning, and spincasting tackle); many types of artificial lures including crankbaits, spinnerbaits, surface lures, spoons, spinners, and plastic worms (baitcasting, spinning, and spincasting tackle); and with deerhair, cork, feather, and wooden bass bugs (fly fishing tackle).

SMALLMOUTH BASS

If you have deduced from the slight difference in names that the smallmouth bass is a smaller-mouthed version of the largemouth, you are partly correct. There is more to it than that, though.

In shape the two fish are very similar. In color, however, the smallmouth is much more bronzy—hence the nickname ''bronzeback''—and has dark, vertical bars along its sides in place of the largemouth's horizontal band. Smallmouths do not achieve the size of largemouths, the world-record size being around 14 pounds.

The smallmouth generally prefers a different habitat from that of the largemouth as well. Rockpiles in clear, cool lakes and in clear, flowing rivers are where the smallmouth is found. Its comfort range is between 60° and 80° F in the summer, whereas the largemouth will tolerate warmer waters.

Like largemouths, smallmouths spawn in late spring and early summer, clearing nests in the bottom in which the eggs are laid. The fry may be guarded by the males even after they have left the nest.

Smallmouths seem more selective than largemouths in their food preferences, feeding mainly on minnows, crayfish, and the largest insect larvae, particularly the large dobsonfly larvae known as hellgrammites.

Smallmouth are a gamefish *par excellence*. There is no comparison between the fight of a three-pound largemouth and that of a smallmouth of the same size. A hooked smallmouth is like a runaway locomotive—or more aptly a runaway jet, for it seems airborne much of the time. It strikes hard and fights hard and is an unmitigated thrill to catch. But it is not easily caught, for it is wary and difficult to land as a result of its fighting skills.

Smallmouths are fished for with live bait in the form of worms, minnows, crayfish, and hellgrammites (all tackle); artificial baits such as crankbaits that imitate minnows and crayfish, small spoons, spinners, and jigs (baitcasting, spinning, and spincasting tackle); and deerhair, cork, plastic, or wooden poppers and hair or feather crayfish imitations (fly fishing tackle).

NORTHERN PIKE

The northern pike is not related to any fish we have yet discussed in this book. It is in the pike family, which consists of five species, all characterized by their greatly elongated shape, duck-like snout, and fearsome numbers of long, sharp teeth.

Northerns are widely distributed in North America north of Missouri. They tend to be large fish, reaching weights of 20 pounds and more. Coloration is generally greenish with many rows of creamy, bean-shaped spots along the sides that blend into the whitish belly. The fins are orangy with irregular dark markings. Pike often appear to be flecked with gold.

Northern pike are loners that lurk in relatively shallow weedbeds near the shores of lakes and in the backwaters of rivers. Their main foods consist of other fish, particularly young perch, shiners, and other panfish. But they will go after frogs and other aquatic life as well. They feed entirely during daylight hours.

Pike spawn early in the spring when the water is between 40° and 52° F. They make no nests; the females simply drop their eggs randomly, and one or two smaller, accompanying males fertilize them as they fall. The eggs hatch in about two weeks, and the young are inactive for about 10 days, living off stored nutriments. Then they begin their voracious feeding, often eating each other where populations of fry are dense. Northern pike are among the fastest-growing freshwater fish.

Although pike are excellent fish for eating, many anglers are interested only in their sporting qualities, which are considerable, thanks to their size and fighting ability. Their use as food is somewhat reduced by the Y-shaped bones that make them difficult to fillet effectively.

Except in the most northern parts of their range, where the lakes stay relatively cold throughout the summer, the best fishing for pike is in the spring and fall. Because of the pike's sharp teeth and large size, some anglers tie in a wire leader between their monofilament line and their bait or lure to keep the fish from shearing the line. Others believe that the wire cuts down on the number of strikes—they prefer losing an occasional fish over getting fewer hits. Northern pike are fished for with live minnows (baitcasting and spinning tackle) or with large, shiny, fast-moving artificial lures like spoons and spinners that resemble baitfish (baitcasting and spinning tackle).

CHAIN PICKEREL

The chain pickerel is a widely distributed, smaller cousin of the northern pike, generally occurring where the northern pike does not. It shares the pike's elongated body, duckbill snout, and tooth-filled mouth. The pickerel, however, is a relatively small fish, often appearing almost snakelike. Most commonly, pickerel are caught in lengths of around 16 inches and are only about as big around as your wrist. Older specimens can attain a length of three feet and weigh about nine pounds.

Chain pickerel are named as a result of the black chain pattern along their greenish, golden sides. They are usually quite beautiful fish and can fight like the Furies. Their habits and preferred habitat are much like those of their larger cousins. They are found in both lakes and slow rivers, in the heavily weeded, shallow areas near shore. They eat other fish, and are particularly fond of small yellow perch. They will also go after frogs. Pickerel are loners, feeding entirely during the day.

Their spawning habits, too, are similar to those of the pike. Without making nests, they lay eggs soon after the water temperature reaches 45° F. The eggs hatch after one to two weeks, and the young eat small aquatic organisms of many kinds, switching mainly to fish when they reach a length of four to six inches.

Pickerel put up a wonderful fight and

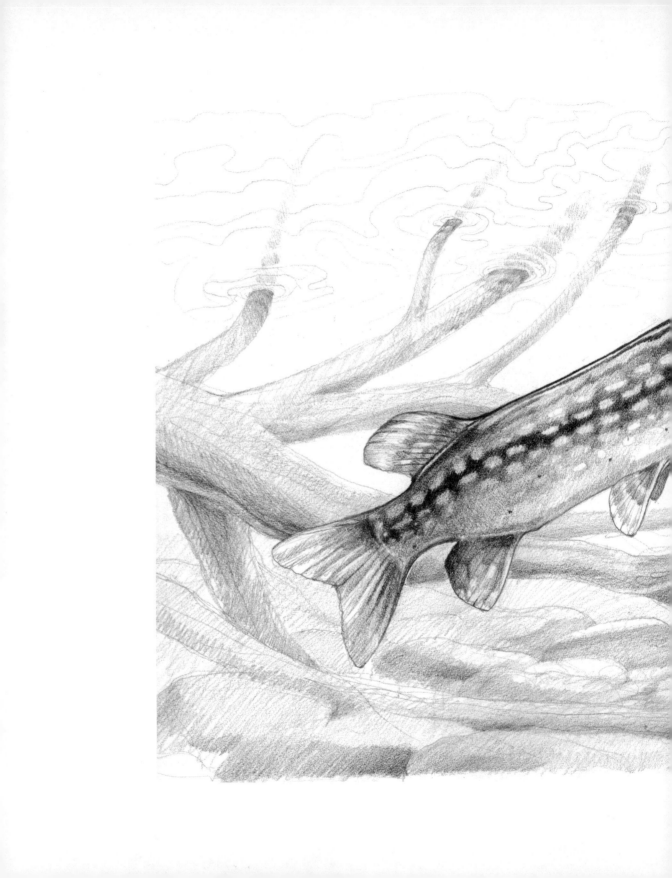

Northern pike. Drawing by Ernest Lussier.

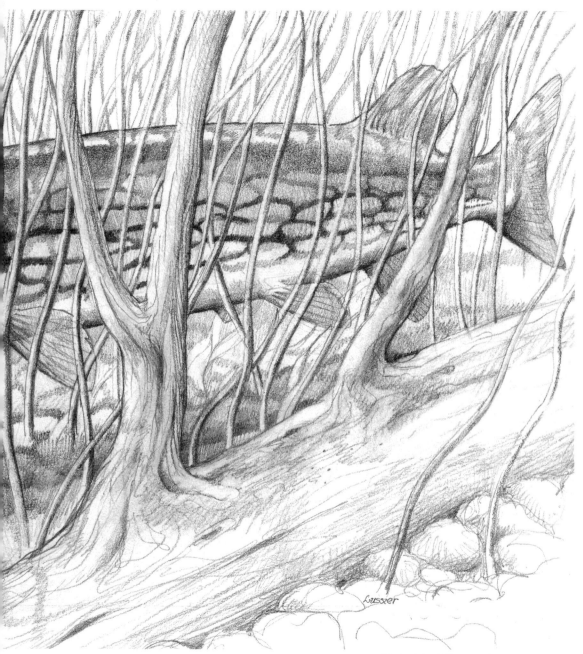

Chain pickerel. Drawing by Ernest Lussier.

Typical pickerel habitat.

can be voracious feeders, taking a lure with heart-pounding violence. It is common to see a pickerel coming after your lure from 15 feet away, raising a wake like a torpedo. Sometimes, though, in water where you have caught dozens of pickerel on previous occasions, you will not see one all day. No one fully understands the reasons for that behavior.

Few anglers actually go after pickerel on purpose. Most pickerel are caught by fishermen who are trying to catch bass.

The baits and techniques that work for bass also work well for pickerel, which share much of the bass's weedy habitat. Like pike, pickerel make good eating, but the Y-bones make them hard to fillet.

Pickerel are best fished for with light tackle. Live minnows or frogs (spinning tackle), artificial lures such as crankbaits, spoons, and spinners that imitate yellow perch and other baitfish as well as frogs (spinning tackle), and streamers (fly fishing tackle) may be used.

WALLEYES

The walleye is the gamefish relative of the yellow perch. It makes for delicious eating, puts up a great fight when hooked, and can attain weights of over 20 pounds. In contrast to its beautiful, smaller cousin, however, the walleye is a homely fish.

The walleye gets its name from its large, milky eyes. Its coloration is more or less olive green on the back, lightening to cream on the belly. There is some darker banding along the sides.

The walleye used to be found only in Canada and the northernmost states, but, as with most of the fish mentioned in this book, its range has been extended through stocking so that it now occurs throughout most of North America. It is, however, normally found only in lakes of at least 100 acres with an average depth greater than 10 feet. In addition, walleyes need relatively cool (maximum summer temperatures not exceeding 80° F or so) clear waters with gravelly bottoms on which to spawn.

Spawning takes place soon after ice-out, with the water temperature between 45° and 50° F. No nest is built, but a particular spawning area is sought—usually an area with a current over gravel or other bottom debris. The female releases 25,000 to 50,000 eggs per pound of her body weight, which are fertilized as they fall by any accompanying males. The eggs settle into the gravel and hatch with no parental care. Upon hatching, the tiny fry live off their egg sacks for several days and then turn to a diet of microorganisms. By the time they attain a length of a few inches, they have moved to deeper water and are feeding largely on other fish.

Like largemouth bass, the most commonly caught walleyes are in the one- to three-pound class; six- to eight-pounders are bragging size, and anything 10 pounds or over is trophy-size.

Like their smaller cousins the yellow perch, walleyes tend to congregate in schools on the bottoms of lakes or rivers. But unlike perch, they tend to feed more heavily in the evening and at night.

Walleyes are not the ideal fish for the absolute beginner. Because of the size and type of lakes in which they are found, and because of their feeding habits, depths, and locations, finding them is difficult. I mention them here only because they may be quite prevalent in your area, and you may hear a great deal about walleyes. Start with some of the other fish, though, until you have attained a level of fishing expertise and enthusiasm that will allow you to sit for hours without catching anything, yet still enjoy yourself. Then try walleyes.

Walleyes are fished for deep with live worms and minnows (baitcasting, spinning, and spincasting tackle) on special walleye jigs.

Walleye. Drawing by Ernest Lussier.

These species constitute the gamefish I consider the most likely to be encountered by the absolute beginner. There are plenty of other gamefish in North America—like salmon, steelhead, and muskellunge—but most are even less suited to the beginner than the walleye. And then there are trout, which deserve their own chapter.

8

Trout

In the two previous chapters, you learned about the most common types of panfish and gamefish. What they all share in common is that all are found in what we call warmwater habitats. Their individual temperature preferences may vary (largemouth bass will tolerate higher water temperatures than smallmouth bass or walleyes, for example), but they all live in warm-water environments.

Trout, on the other hand, are coldwater fish. They thrive only in clear, cold, oxygenated waters. Most trout have a preferred temperature range of roughly 55° to 60° F. They inhabit fast-moving rivers and streams and deep, cool, spring-fed lakes and ponds.

Although many species of trout occur naturally throughout the continent, the absolute beginner is most likely to encounter only three kinds that are widely raised by state hatcheries and are com-

monly used to seasonally stock local streams and ponds: rainbow trout, brook trout, and brown trout. Without such stocking, large numbers of trout would not normally be found in those waters, and they normally do not survive to overwinter and establish native populations.

Apart from their preference for cold-water environments, trout are distinguished from the panfish and the other gamefish in another way: they can be considered both panfish and gamefish, depending upon their size. It is as common to go fishing for delicious little pan-size trout as for big, fighting, monster trout.

RAINBOW TROUT

Rainbow trout were originally found only in waters from the Rocky Mountains to the Pacific Ocean from Mexico through

Typical eastern trout water. Red Ball photo.

Typical western trout water. Wyoming Travel Commission photo.

Alaska. Now, however, they are one of the commonly stocked species throughout the country.

As the name implies, rainbows are colorful—a narrow red band extends from the fish's cheek to the base of its tail. Above the red band, the fish is usually dark greenish and covered with solid black spots that continue into the tail. The area beneath the red band usually is silvery to white with fewer, if any, spots. Coloration, however, is extremely variable, depending on age, environment, and other factors. In the rivers of the Pacific Northwest, where rainbows occur naturally and make migrations to and from the sea, these trout acquire a uniformly silvery coloring and are called steelhead. Steelhead fishing is beyond the ken of the absolute beginner. The rainbow's main distinguishing feature is the presence of the solid black spots and the absence of any other colored spots.

The beginner is likely to encounter *stocked* rainbows, in a wide range of sizes. Different hatcheries provide fish of different sizes for stocking, and you are as likely to encounter small fish of just a few inches as hefty battlers of well over a foot in length. In my favorite home stream, a small woodland brook no wider than a narrow street, some 17-inch rainbows

Michigan Travel Commission photo.   Red Ball photo.

A couple of bragging-size rainbows.

Rainbow trout. Drawing by Ernest Lussier.

Brook trout. Drawing by Ernest Lussier.

Brown trout. Drawing by Ernest Lussier.

were stocked one year that were nearly impossible to land on the light tackle customarily used to fish that stream.

A hooked rainbow will generally put on a more impressive aerial display than any of the other trouts and will also be found in faster water than the others. Rainbows eat mainly aquatic insects.

Rainbow trout are fished for with dry flies, wet flies, and nymphs (fly fishing tackle); live bait such as worms, small insects, and salmon eggs (fly fishing and light spinning tackle); small artificials such as spinners and spoons (light spinning tackle); and, too often (it irks me to have to mention it), with such baits as cheese, marshmallows, corn, and bread.

BROOK TROUT

Also widely stocked, brook trout were once found only in northeastern North America. They are not a true trout, as are the rainbow and brown, but are actually in the char family—a fact of no importance to most anglers, beginning or not. However, a distinguishing characteristic of all members of the char family—and one that will therefore help you identify brookies from the others in this chapter— is that the leading edges of the fins on the fishes' undersides are always white. In the brook trout, that leading white edge is immediately followed by a line of black; the remainder of the fin is usually orange.

Brookies are even more colorful than rainbows. The back is usually a dark green covered with black, wavy lines that extend up into the dorsal fin. The belly may be brilliant orange in the males or creamy yellow to white in the females. All brookies will have red spots, each surrounded by a ring of blue.

Brook trout are usually small, in many locations never getting larger than 10 inches. Yet they are, in ideal habitats, quite capable of reaching several pounds in weight. They are generally regarded as being easier to catch than the other trouts because of their almost totally indiscriminate diet, which consists of any organisms that will fit in their mouths. They are, however, much more sensitive to environmental factors than are the other trouts and will not survive in waters that lack a high oxygen content and low temperatures.

Brookies are more likely to be found in spring-fed lakes than are the other trouts, often occurring in such numbers there that they remain quite small throughout their lives due to the rigors of overpopulation.

Brook trout are fished for with worms (fly fishing and ultralight spinning tackle); dry flies, wet flies, nymphs, and streamers (fly fishing tackle); and many types of artificials such as tiny spinners and spoons of one-eighth ounce or less (ultralight spinning tackle).

BROWN TROUT

Brown trout, natives of Europe and Asia, were introduced to North America in the late 1800s. They are now widely distributed throughout the world and are commonly stocked in the streams and rivers of North America.

The brown trout needs well-oxygenated water but is more tolerant of warmer, slower-moving waters than is the brook trout, and so it thrives in some streams where brookies cannot survive. It also tends to prefer the deeper, slower portions of streams, often being found beneath undercut banks and in the deep holes.

Brown trout are wary—they are not fooled easily. Dry flies must be presented well. Smaller browns—under 12 inches—feed mainly on aquatic insects, while the larger ones are more interested in a diet of small fish.

Because they are true trout like the rainbows, browns lack the white leading edges on their underfins that characterize the brookies, which are chars. Browns—appropriately enough—are generally brownish in color, fading to yellowish and then white on the belly. They are covered with black spots, many of which are surrounded by light halos. Browns are distinguished from rainbows, which also have black spots, by the light halos and by the absence of any reddish band. Where the spots on rainbows extend into the tail, browns have very few spots on the tail, if any. Also, rainbows are usually quite silvery and browns are distinctly coppery.

In streams where populations of brown trout are established, the absolute beginner is not likely to catch them. Where they are seasonally stocked along with rainbows and brookies, however, even the absolute beginner has a good chance of catching a brown. As with all stocked trout, size is quite variable, but browns of a pound are not uncommon. In more natural situations, brown trout can reach weights of several pounds.

Brown trout are fished for with dry and wet flies, nymphs, and streamers (fly fishing tackle); live bait such as worms, frogs, minnows, crayfish, and hellgrammites (fly fishing and spinning tackle); and spoons, plugs, and spinners (spinning tackle).

You have now been introduced to some of the most popular panfish, gamefish, and trout in North America. Many others exist, though most are not within realistic reach of the absolute beginner—because of the specialized techniques used to catch them, or the angler's need to first obtain some basic experience on more easily caught species. It is not prudent, for instance, for a beginning angler to go off with several hundred dollars worth of special tackle and stand for hours in swollen rivers casting 50 feet of heavy fly line to 30-pound Atlantic salmon before ever having caught a bluegill. Certainly there are beginning salmon anglers, but they are rarely, if ever, entirely new to the sport of angling.

So stick with those fish mentioned here, at least several of which will be found in your area no matter where you live or spend your vacations. Fishing for them will give you the experience and sense of angling that will soon lift you out of the absolute beginning stage and carry you into a deeper understanding and appreciation of what fishing is all about.

9

Where to Fish

This section has provided you with a great deal of information about the habits and habitats of the fish you are likely to catch. You now know where in a lake or stream each fish should be sought. But where do you find the lakes and streams that are worth fishing? How do you know if a body of water holds fish? And how do you go about finding those bodies of water that hold the specific kinds of fish you would like to catch?

The answers are simple: fish where there is water. That may sound facetious, but it is basically true. Many inconspicuous waters have yielded some surprisingly conspicuous fish. A friend of mine who lives in southern Florida has an enormous largemouth bass mounted on the wall of his den. The trophy weighed nine pounds when he hauled it out of a water trap of a local golf course. I have caught worthwhile trout in a stream so small that I straddled it as I fished. Untold numbers of anglers with an eye for productive waters have taken trophies or dinner from little roadside streams and ponds that seduced them into stopping and making a few casts while on their way to work or a meeting. And, of course, there are dozens of larger lakes, streams, and rivers, well-known to local anglers, that can be relied upon to provide consistent sport in your area.

To go about finding those spots, you must seek information. Whenever you come upon a body of water that is being fished, even by youngsters, stop and make inquiries. Ask the fishermen what they are catching. Most anglers are eager to exhibit proof of their success. If you meet an especially loquacious individual, you may even extend your inquiry to include types of bait, specific areas of the pond or stream that are best, and other good places he knows about in the area. If the angler seems reluctant to share information, do not press the issue. Many people fish for the solitude it provides and resent intrusive conversation. In any case, though, it rarely hurts to ask.

An excellent way to find local waters is to purchase U.S. Geological Survey (USGS) topographical maps of your area. These "topo" maps are very small-scale, highly detailed maps that are indexed according to quadrants, which are areas of just a few square miles (your house will likely be on the map). Many good camping stores carry topos, or they can be ordered directly from the USGS Branch of Distribution, Eastern Region, 1200 S. Eads St., Arlington, VA 22202 for states east of the Mississippi River, or USGS Branch of Distribution, Central Region, P.O. Box 25286, Federal Center, Denver, CO 80225 for states west of the Mississippi. The topo maps will show all the lakes and streams of fishable size in your immediate area, many of which you may have passed within 100 yards of without knowing of their existence. It seems incredible, but a 100-acre lake just off the main road can remain unknown to you for years—until you discover it on a topo. Once you have found such places on the maps, go out and explore their accessibility. Some may have no public access, while others may turn out to be the town swimming and fishing hole that everyone but you has known about for years.

Yet another good source of information is your state's Division of Fisheries and Wildlife (or some similar name). That governmental department often has a person called the Chief Information and Education Officer who is responsible for providing just the kind of information you are looking for. Here, at last, is an opportunity to see your taxes at work. Call the Division and ask away. Tell them you are new to the sport of fishing and would like a list of lakes and streams in your area that provide good fishing. Ask if lake maps are available. Those may be anything from rough approximations of the lake's shape to detailed surveys, but they usually show the general shape and contour, points of access, locations of any boat-launching ramps, inlets, outlets, and depths at various points. Often, they will include a list of the fish species found in them as well. If lake maps are not available, the Division should be able to provide some of that information in other forms.

The types of places available for fishing depend largely on the area of the country in which you live. The East and Midwest are particularly rich in natural lakes, ponds, rivers, and streams, most of which are worth trying. The South has its bayous, rivers, ponds, and impoundments, and parts of southern Florida are uniquely riddled with canals of all sizes. The West and Southwest have rivers, impoundments, and farm tanks. And the Northwest and Mountain states enjoy streams, rivers, and glacial lakes. In *all* parts of the country, local reservoirs may be open to fishing. And be on the lookout for water-filled quarries and mining excavations. Swimming holes, water obstacles on golf courses, and landscaping ponds at large malls and developments also should be explored.

You can find previously unfished bonanzas in the most apparent places, simply because everyone before you has looked at that body of water and passed it up, saying: "How could any fish possibly have gotten in there?'' Yet fish get into places by any number of natural and unnatural means, not the least likely of which is that fish eggs stick to the legs of wading birds and are literally airlifted to new waters.

My only warning as you seek places to fish is to respect private property. If a body of water is posted with ''No Trespassing'' or ''No Fishing'' notices, obey them—no questions asked. If a pond or stream is entirely on private land but is unposted, however, try asking the owner for permission to fish the water. If you get permission, respect the owner's hospitality—do not litter; close gates; offer him part of your catch. Do everything to ensure that others who seek permission will not be shut out because of your poor example.

Experienced anglers sometimes go to great effort and expense to fish world-class salmon rivers or bass lakes in far-off places. I do that myself from time to time and always get a great thrill from such experiences. But I also cherish a 100-acre neighborhood pond and an obscure local woodland stream that are sources of limitless pleasure. If you can find such waters within a few minutes of home—and if you follow my suggestions, that should not prove too difficult—consider yourself lucky indeed, and fish them as often as you can. They may be all you ever need.

Section III

THE METHODS

How to Get the Fish and Tackle Together

10

Live Bait

At least some form of live bait can be used to catch every type of fish described in Section II of this book. In fact, a live, garden-variety earthworm will attract every species mentioned—although other forms of live bait may be more effective for some species at certain times.

Live bait includes any living organism that can be fastened to a hook and used to induce a fish to bite. But it may also refer to selected parts of previously living organisms that are no longer alive. Such things as crayfish tails and salmon eggs fall into that category.

Live bait's biggest advantage is that it is natural. The things you attach to your hook either are or closely resemble the actual natural food of your quarry. They have a natural smell, taste, and feel in the fish's mouth. They also move under their own power—most of them. Thus, a living bait such as an earthworm or a minnow may be left suspended beneath the surface in one spot while it wiggles and swims and attracts attention to itself with no help from the fisherman.

The disadvantages of using live bait are that it must be kept alive during the period of use—for example, minnows must be kept in water in a bucket of some sort, worms in moist bedding, frogs in an appropriate container—and must be replenished for each outing (few live baits keep well). Another disadvantage is that fish have a tendency to swallow live bait much more deeply than they do artificials, making it impossible to release your catch unharmed—a practice followed by many anglers. So the use of live bait is inadvisable when planning to release fish.

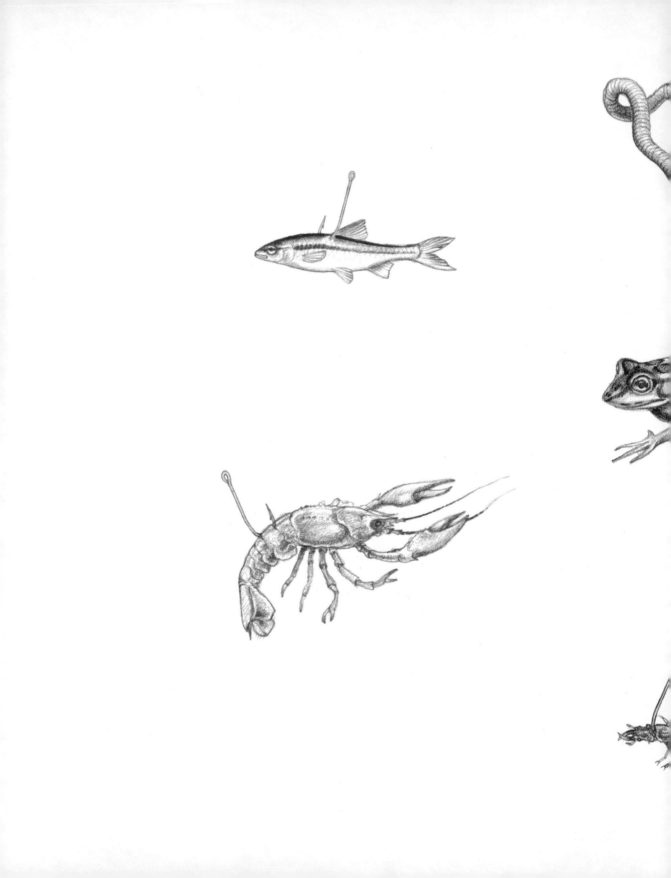

Some of the most common live baits, and how best to secure them on a hook. Drawing by Ernest Lussier.

If you are planning to keep your catch for eating, however, this concern is academic.

Strangely, many fishermen look askance at the use of live bait. They claim that it is either unsporting or artless. Neither is true. There are times when the use of live bait is preferable to the use of artificials, and times when the reverse is true. You should become familiar with both methods and select whatever method gives you the greatest success or the most enjoyment at any particular time. Fishing is pretty much a process of combining fun with problem-solving, and you will succeed best at both by knowing several techniques to apply.

This chapter will first introduce you to the most common forms of live bait available. Then, because the usual order of things is to decide on the type of fish to try for and then acquire the appropriate baits, I will suggest the proper choice and rigging of baits, organized according to the types of fish. (In the next chapter, on artificial lures, this order is reversed, since you will undoubtedly first stock a tackle box with a variety of lures before deciding on a specific quarry.)

WORMS

Two types of worms are commonly used for fishing. Angleworms, which are the small, skinny earthworms found in most gardens, are perfect for panfish and small trout, while nightcrawlers, the large, fat worms that emerge from burrows in lawns on moist nights, are excellent for big bass, walleyes, and large trout. Both types of worms may be purchased from bait stores, or may be dug up by the fisherman. They are best kept in a can or box filled with damp (not wet) sphagnum or loose soil.

MINNOWS

Several types of small fish are used as live bait. Many are the natural baitfish upon which the larger predators normally prey. Such baitfish include shiners, dace, and chubs—all members of the minnow family—though small fish of other families may find their way into bait buckets as well. One popular minnow sold in bait shops is the golden shiner, which is a distinct shiny, metallic gold. Minnows are usually available from bait shops in lengths of two to four inches as bait for crappies and yellow perch, largemouth bass, pike and pickerel, walleyes, and large brown trout. Those who fish with live shiners for trophy largemouth bass may use bait measuring nearly a foot in length. Minnows are usually kept in a specially made bucket that may provide aeration or may be hung in the water wherever you fish.

CRAYFISH

Crayfish are freshwater crustaceans that resemble small lobsters. They are quite common in the ponds and streams of nearly every section of the country and make excellent bait in whole or in part for both largemouth and smallmouth bass and large trout. Crayfish in sizes of one to about four inches can be caught by the fisherman or purchased from bait shops. They are best kept in a minnow bucket with a good supply of moist sphagnum.

FROGS

Small frogs are excellent live bait for both largemouth and smallmouth bass and for pike and pickerel. By "small" I mean those that measure no more than about two inches from nose to rear-end when sitting. They can be caught by the fisherman or purchased from bait shops, although I have found that fewer shops carry frogs now than did in the past. Frogs can be kept in a minnow bucket with a little water or moderately moist sphagnum in the bottom.

GRASSHOPPERS AND CRICKETS

Live grasshoppers and crickets, sometimes sold in shops but more often collected by the angler, are fine baits for bluegills and sunfish, crappies, smallmouth bass, and all trout. They can be carried in just about any container without need of moisture or bedding. A stoppered bottle is just fine.

HELLGRAMMITES

There is an extremely large, winged insect called the dobsonfly that is sometimes attracted to lights at night. It can reach a length of four inches. Its larva, called a hellgrammite, is an aquatic nymph that lives under stones at the bottom of streams and grows to a length of about two or three inches before changing to the winged adult. The hellgrammite is a predacious larva with large jaws and a hard, chitinous body. Handled carelessly, it can inflict a painful pinch on your finger. As a child fishing with my father, I always hated it when he decided to pick up some hellgrammites at the bait shop. Nonetheless, they are indisputably deadly on smallmouth bass. They can be gathered in cold streams by the fisherman (a time-consuming proposition) or purchased at many bait shops. Keep them in a minnow bucket with cold water and a bedding of damp sphagnum. It may be necessary to add ice cubes to the water to keep it cold enough for the larvae's survival on hot days.

MISCELLANEOUS

At one time or another, nearly any living insect, mature or immature, can be used effectively for bait. Panfish love the white grubs found in garden soil. Small

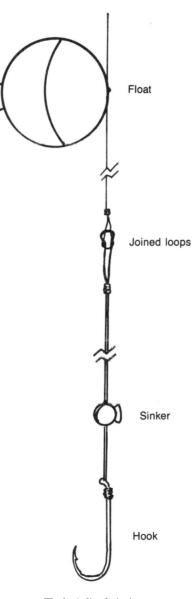

The basic live-bait rig.

caterpillars, which often fall in abundance from shoreline trees, can make excellent bait. Larvae found in plant galls, acorns, or right in the water can be used with success. Salmon eggs, usually sold in jars at bait and tackle shops, are excellent bait for trout.

Entire books are written about all the possible ways live baits can be fished. Nearly infinite combinations and permutations exist, each the potential solution to a specific problem. None of that falls within the needs of the absolute beginner. For you, there is a single, simple setup that will suffice for most of the situations you will encounter. A couple of variations

will also be mentioned. Once you feel experienced enough to go to other information sources, you will not lack the literature necessary to complicate this relatively simple form of fishing.

The basic live bait setup consists of a hook, a sinker, a float, and some bait. The bait, of course, goes on the hook. The hook is attached to the end of your line. The sinker is attached to the line some short distance above the hook. And the float is attached to the line some distance above the sinker.

What you are doing is creating a rig that suspends the baited hook a given distance above the bottom (or below the sur-

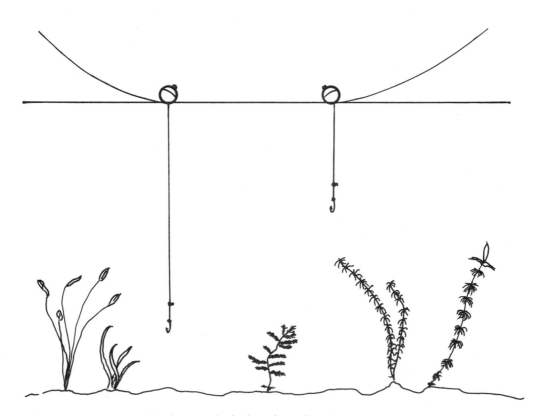

By changing the position of the float, your hook (shown here unbaited) can be made to hang deeper or shallower.

face, depending on your perspective). The sinker's weight causes the baited hook to hang straight down, while the float keeps it from falling all the way to the bottom. By varying the amount of line between the hook and the float, you determine at what depth the hook hangs. The float also serves as a visual indicator, showing you when a fish is on your line.

The size of the hook to use is determined by the type of fish you are after and the size of the bait you will use. The size of the sinker is determined largely by water conditions (a heavier sinker is required to keep your bait down in a strong stream current than in a stillwater pond). And the size of the float is determined by the size and weight of your terminal tackle (hook, bait, and sinker). Generally, you want to use the smallest float that will do the job. Sometimes you will want your bait to lie right on the bottom and will therefore need no float at all.

The proper way to attach each of the common types of live bait to a hook is shown on pages 124, 125. These methods allow the bait to move naturally but keep them from getting off the hook.

Now I will briefly suggest the best bait, hook size, sinker, and float configurations for each of the fish mentioned in Section II. For a more detailed explanation of hook and sinker sizes and types, see Chapter 13.

BLUEGILLS AND SUNFISH

These fish have small mouths, so small hooks and small baits are called for. The best rig for bluegills and sunnies involves a size 10 or 12 hook. Squeeze a split-shot sinker onto your four- or six-pound-test monofilament line about two inches above the hook eye. The split-shot should be midway between a BB and a pea in size. Somewhat farther up the line—the exact distance is going to be determined by the depth of the water you will be fishing, but for now let's say about two feet above the sinker—attach a round plastic float about the size of a Ping-Pong ball.

For sunnies and bluegills, the very best bait to attach to this rig is one or two small earthworms. A small cricket or grasshopper is also effective, and white grubs or small caterpillars can also be used.

CRAPPIES

The mouths of crappies are larger than those of sunnies and bluegills, so a size 6 or 8 hook should be used. Six-pound mono is a good line weight for crappies. A sinker is not necessary if you are using minnows; with worms or other small baits, use the same size sinker as for bluegills. Use the smallest float that will keep the bait from sinking (probably the size of a Ping-Pong ball or slightly smaller). The float should be attached at the proper distance above the hook to allow the bait to hang at the depth where the fish are located, which will vary.

The very best bait for crappies is a minnow 1½ to 2½ inches long, never larger. Hook the minnow through the back as shown. Earthworms, crickets, and hellgrammites are also effective.

YELLOW PERCH

Yellow perch favor deeper water in summer than do the other fish discussed above. In order to use the same float-sinker-hook rig, the float would have to be so far above the hook as to make the rig awkward or impossible to cast. Therefore it is usually best to leave the float off when fishing for yellow perch. Use a No. 6 or 8 hook on six-pound mono line, and attach a pea-size split-shot about eight inches above the hook. Attach to the hook either a two-inch minnow, hooked through the lips, or an earthworm or two, and cast the bait out into deep water, allowing it to sink to the bottom before reeling it in at moderate speed.

BULLHEADS

The rig for catching these bottom-feeders also requires no float. In fact, the same setup can be used for bullheads as for yellow perch. Bait the hook with a couple of good-size earthworms or one fat nightcrawler, cast it out, and let it sink. After it sits for a few minutes, reel it in very slowly, allowing it to rest a minute or two every few feet.

LARGEMOUTH BASS

Largemouths have very large mouths, so you will want to use a good-size hook. Let's assume that you are not starting out to catch a trophy, and that you will most likely be encountering small to average-size bass in the one- or two-pound class. In that case, a hook size of 2 or 4 is about right. Attach a small float about three feet above the hook when using a minnow or frog. A float may be omitted when using a nightcrawler, but a small, BB-size split-shot may be used.

Best bet for largemouths is a minnow hooked through the back or a frog hooked through the leg and allowed to swim below a float near the edge of a weedbed. A single large nightcrawler, hooked through the head with the remainder trailing be-

hind, is also very effective when cast out and retrieved slowly along the edges of weeds.

SMALLMOUTH BASS

A No. 2 or 4 hook is good for smallmouths as well, and the same rig used for largemouths is fine. Many of the same baits, too, will work well on smallmouths, particularly nightcrawlers, minnows, and small frogs, all fished as for largemouths but in the rocky areas preferred by smallmouths.

Even more effective baits for smallmouth bass are hellgrammites and crayfish. Hellgrammites are hooked under the collar and crayfish through the tail, as shown. Small sinkers should be used just above the hook, especially in streams and rivers. It is particularly important, when using hellgrammites and crayfish, to adjust the position of your float so that the bait hangs close to—but not on—the bottom. Both baits, if allowed to reach bottom, will crawl under a rock and be out of sight of the gamefish.

NORTHERN PIKE

Northern pike are large and powerful. Fish for them with eight- or 10-pound mono at least. A No. 2 or larger hook will be necessary for accommodating the large minnows used as bait. Still, all you need is the basic rig of a float—in this case one about the size of a tennis ball—a few feet above the baited hook. Because of the pike's sharp teeth, though, many fishermen attach their hook to a six- or eight-inch wire leader, which they then attach to their monofilament line. Others feel that the leader causes fewer strikes, so the practice is optional.

In any case, the best live bait for pike is a large, shiny, and lively minnow about four inches in length, hooked through the back. A sinker may be necessary to keep the minnow deep.

PICKEREL

Pickerel are much smaller than pike, so use lighter line—about six-pound—and a smaller hook such as a No. 4. The same rig you use for bass will work well for pickerel.

The best baits for pickerel are small minnows and small frogs. Fish them as for largemouth bass.

WALLEYES

Walleyes are not really an absolute beginner's fish, but if you find yourself with the opportunity to fish for them, use live minnows hooked through the back with a hook of about size 2 or big nightcrawlers. Walleyes are deep-water fish, and it is essential that you fish for them on or near the bottom, which may be down 40 feet or more. Clearly, a float is out of the question, and a good, heavy sinker is necessary to get your bait down and keep it there. Often special jigs are used to hold the bait and provide the weight.

TROUT

All three trouts can be fished similarly with live bait. Usually, no float is used, and only enough weight is needed to get the bait down in the stream current. Sometimes, when the bait is cast upstream, the current will take it down without the need of any additional weight at all. That is ideal, for sinkers tend to get hung up on the bottoms of streams and you end up losing your hooks.

So the rig is simple. Attach light line, such as four- or six-pound mono, to a No. 10 hook. Thread on an earthworm or two, or a cricket, or grasshopper, and toss it out into the stream upstream of your position, letting it drift downstream with the current. If you have trouble keeping the hook off the bottom, a small, clear-plastic bubble-float may be used to suspend the bait above the streambed. Anything more obtrusive will generally spook the trout.

Here is a list of items the absolute be

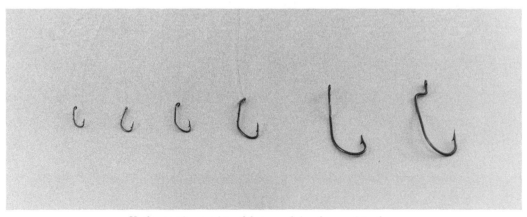

Hooks come in a variety of shapes and sizes for a variety of uses.

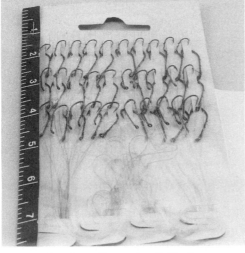

A package of assorted snelled hooks.

ginner should have in order to be basically equipped to fish live bait for a variety of fish:

• An assortment of snelled or unsnelled ("snell" is leader material) hooks in sizes 12, 10, 8, 6, 4, and 2 (see Chapter 13 for details). These are usually sold on cards. If an assortment of sizes can be found on a single card, you are all set. Otherwise you will need one card of each size.

• An assortment of variously sized split-shot sinkers. These come in small plastic bags or boxes, usually holding shot of one size. If possible, get a sectioned container that holds a variety of sizes. Many other types of sinkers are suitable, but split-shot are the most versatile.

• An assortment of floats. Get five round, plastic floats. These are usually red and white, and have a small button on top that, when pressed, causes a small metal hook to protrude from the bottom. Wrap your line four or five times around the hook, let go of the button, and the hook snugs back against the bottom of the float, holding your line securely so that the float cannot move up or down the line. These floats come in a variety of sizes. Your smallest

On one common type of float, pressing the button on top . . .

. . . exposes the hook at the bottom around which you wrap your line.

should be about the size of a large acorn, the next about the size of a Ping-Pong ball, the largest the size of a tennis ball. Also get a small clear-plastic bubble-float for trout. You may also want to try a bobber stop with a sliding float. These allow you to fish deeper without making casting impossible. (See Chapter 13.)

That is all the information the absolute beginner needs in order to go into a bait and tackle store and purchase the tackle he will need for using live bait on a variety of fish. More details about how to actually fish them will be presented in Chapter 12, when we actually go fishing. First, though, you must also learn about artificial lures.

11

Artificial Baits

Since ancient times, it has been known that fish can be fooled into taking baits that look and act like their natural foods but are made of materials not normally eaten by the fish. Such materials have included hair, feathers, wood, and bone. With the exception of bone, those materials are still used today, as are metal, plastic, and rubber.

Artificial baits are commonly called "lures" or "artificials" to distinguish them from live bait. There are myriad types of lures, running the gamut in design from highly realistic imitations of real creatures to impressionistic suggestions of life. And to paraphrase Abraham Lincoln—some artificials will fool some of the fish most of the time, and some will fool many of the fish some of the time, but none will fool all the fish all the time.

Some, however, will fool none of the fish all the time.

Artificials solve all the problems associated with live bait. You do not have to keep them alive, and you do not have to continually buy fresh ones. A single artificial can be used to catch fish after fish, rarely wearing out or losing its efficacy. Many are lost, of course, but they do not die after being clamped in the jaws of a large fish, as do minnows, frogs, and other live bait.

The disadvantage of artificials is that they are not alive. They have no movement of their own. You must impart an impression of life to them while they are in the water. That usually entails retrieving them in a manner attractive to fish. Unlike live bait, an artificial cannot simply be hung overboard at the end of your

A display of antique plugs.

line and be expected to do its own advertising. Artificial lures of all designs and types must be cast out and retrieved, trolled (pulled behind a moving boat—see Chapter 15), or activated by way of water currents. Those are the only ways they can be made to look alive. And if they fail to look alive, they will not impress fish as something worth striking.

Generally speaking, lures are designed to imitate the natural foods fish eat. They may or may not look much like those naturals, but they somehow trigger in the fish enough hunger, aggression, or curiosity to make the fish bite. Sometimes the

lure accomplishes that by the way it moves; by its color, shape, or sound; or by the way it reflects light. Most lures are designed to combine several of those factors. It is commonly agreed, however, that the majority of lures are designed more to catch fishermen than fish. The true test of a lure is in its ability to catch fish when used the way it was designed to be used. How it looks to you is of little consequence. Years of experience have taught me that some of the most realistic-looking lures, and some with the fanciest actions and doo-dads, hold a nearly perfect record of being ignored by fish, while many of those with the simplest designs, looking like nothing a fish would be interested in, have been reliable producers year after year. Years of experience have also taught me that the exact opposite is also true.

Some lures are designed for specific types of fish; there are lures for bass, lures for crappies, lures for pike, etc. But because lures are meant to imitate food, and most fish share the same basic diet of minnows, frogs, insects, etc., many lures may be used for many types of fish, with size being the major variable.

Because live bait and lures involve such different methods, there are strong feelings among fishermen about which is better. The fact is that neither is better; both have their advantages and disadvantages, and those may change with conditions, fish species, and situations. It is really a matter of personal preference. Generally, I prefer to use live bait for panfish and artificials for gamefish and trout. Yet there is no question that at times the opposite is preferable. Catching panfish with flies can be an action-packed, fun experience, while catching trophy bass on live shiners is often the only way to go. The bottom line, however, is to become familiar with as many fishing techniques as is necessary to bring you success and enjoyment. The only truly objective factor to keep in mind when choosing between live bait and lures is that fish tend to swallow live bait deeper than artificials. So if you are planning to release your catch, use artificials.

In order to use artificials intelligently, it is necessary that you become familiar with some of their many basic designs. That is best handled by categorizing lures into the kinds of foods they imitate.

LURES THAT IMITATE MINNOWS

This category is by far the largest. Minnows of one size or another make up the diet of nearly every fish you will be trying to catch. Even sunnies and bluegills will go after the fry of other fish.

Many design elements may go into a lure that suggests a minnow. There is a characteristic shape that is rounded in front and tapering behind. There is a certain amount of flash from shiny, metallic "scales." There is a wiggly-wobbly movement or "action" that suggests a minnow swimming. And even more enticing is the off-kilter, erratic, exaggerated wobble that suggests an injured, disfigured, or sick minnow, one that is easy prey for a hungry predator. There may also be a sound associated with minnows—perhaps a flutter, gurgle, or plop. The lure may have additional fluttering or flashing appendages to suggest fins and provide more attraction.

Different lure designs seek to exploit different combinations of those features. In doing so, some seek to actually imitate a minnow, while others seek only to suggest one. At a given time or in a certain situation, the "suggesters" work as well as the "imitators." And lures painted with the most peculiar and unnatural markings and colors may work as well as or better than those made to look absolutely realistic.

Crankbaits and Plugs

These are commonly made of wood or plastic. They are more or less cylindrical, suggesting the basic shape of a minnow, and are often characterized by having some sort of underhanging lip. The lip may be quite short or amusingly long,

Lures that imitate minnows. Top row: *surface disturbers;* second row: *floater/divers;* third row: *streamers;* fourth row: *spoons;* fifth row: *spinners;* sixth row: *jigs;* seventh row: *spinnerbaits.*

and is made of either plastic (often clear) or metal. In the absence of an underhanging lip, plugs may have a scooped or dished face or wings or other outstretched appendages that accomplish the same purpose, which is to give the plug a characteristic swimming or wobbling action when retrieved through the water. Those with lips are designed to dive and wiggle when retrieved. Some crankbaits float when at rest and dive only when retrieved. Others float under all conditions. Some sink at rest and wiggle and dive deep when retrieved. Others float on the surface and make popping or gurgling sounds when twitched. Some have propellers that emit sounds when retrieved.

Crankbaits and plugs are categorized by the way they are meant to be worked in the water, and by the actions they exhibit. As described above, there are surface lures (those that stay primarily on the surface of the water, also known as topwater lures) and subsurface lures (those that either sink at rest or dive to depths of more than a few inches). Within those two basic categories can be found poppers, darters, stickbaits, and many other surface disturbers; and floater/divers, sinker/divers, deep divers, sonic (noise-making) plugs, and other subsurface crankbaits.

The basic strategy is to cast the plug near the edges of lily-pad beds, over subsurface weedbeds, or along dropoffs and submerged creekbeds and let it sit still

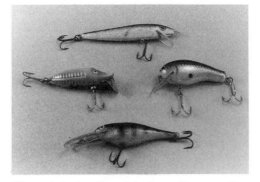

Minnow-imitating plugs of the surface-disturbing type. Top row, left to right: Zara Spook and Jitterbug; bottom row, left to right: Crazy Crawler, Lucky 13, and Tiny Torpedo.

Minnow-imitating plugs of the floater/diver type. Top: Rapala Original; middle row, left to right: River Runt and Wee R; bottom: Shad Rap.

until all the rings of disturbance from its landing have dissipated. Then the lure is moved, either by a combination of twitches of the rod and cranking of the reel handle or by cranking continuously, until it is fully retrieved.

Crankbaits come in a wide variety of sizes, from ultralight (less than one-quarter ounce) for trout and panfish to heavy-duty (three-quarter ounce or more) for big bass and pike. Sizes of one-quarter to one-half ounce are usually best for average-size bass, pickerel, and the larger panfish like crappies and perch.

Spoons

Spoons are pretty much what they seem—spoon-shaped pieces of metal with a hook on one end and a hole or loop for tying line on the other. When the spoon was first invented, it was actually made from part of a teaspoon. When pulled through the water, spoons wobble in such a way that they resemble the action of an injured minnow. Because of their weight and design, they always sink—no spoons sit on the surface while at rest. Designs

do vary, however, so that spoons of different shapes and weights swim deeper or shallower when retrieved. Spoons rely on action and flash to attract fish and are rarely shaped to be realistic imitations of minnows. Spoons are either shiny metal on both surfaces, or painted on the convex side and shiny on the concave side.

Spoons are most often trolled (see Chapter 15) or cast and retrieved in relatively deep water. The spoon is cast out

Spoons. Top row, left to right: Johnson's Minnow and WeedWing; second row, left to right: Dardevle and Al's Goldfish; third row: Kastmaster; bottom row: generic and Wob-L-Rite.

and allowed to sink, fluttering as it does, cranked in for a short way, allowed to sink again, etc. An exception, explained in Chapter 12, is when a weedless spoon is fished on top of a lily-pad bed.

Spoons in the quarter-ounce size are very good for pickerel and bass. Large spoons of one ounce or more, especially in red and white, are traditional favorites for pike. Tiny spoons weighing less than a quarter ounce are effective on panfish and trout.

Spinners

Spinners are spoon-shaped blades that revolve around a stationary shaft to which your line is attached. A hook trails behind. Unlike spoons, which wobble, spinners actually spin, creating a great deal of flash and commotion. Alone, they suggest a struggling fish that is expending a great deal of energy without making much progress. Spinners are often combined with other materials, including bucktail and realistic plastic minnows. Spinners usu-

ally incorporate built-in weights to keep them below the surface. The blades may be shiny or painted.

Small spinners are great for trout and panfish. Larger spinners can be effective on bass but tend to collect weeds.

Spinners are generally cast out and reeled in with a steady retrieve, keeping the blade spinning. In streams they may be held in the current so that the action of the water keeps the blade in motion.

Jigs

These devices incorporate a hook and a lead-head weight in one element. The fisherman may buy jigs naked, dressing them himself with molded, soft-plastic, wiggly critters that resemble minnows, or he may purchase already dressed jigs that combine feathers and other materials into minnow imitations. Crappie jigs (yes, for crappie fishing) are very popular and effective types of ready-made jigs. Jigs are relatively heavy and are fished down below the boat like live bait, except they

Spinners. Top: *Mepps Aglia Long;* middle: *Mepps Black Fury;* bottom: *Swiss Swing.*

Jigs. Top: *Sting Ray Grub on jig;* middle: *Augertail Grub on jig;* bottom: *Sonar.*

must be jigged up and down by the angler to give them the suggestion of life. They may also be cast out and retrieved like other lures.

The nature of jigs usually necessitates their being fished in fairly deep water.

Spinnerbaits

Spinnerbaits combine a spinner with a jig dressed with rubber or vinyl strips. In some the spinner is in line with the hook (in which case it is called an in-line spinnerbait), and in others the two are at opposite ends of a safety-pin-shaped wire that causes the spinner to rotate above the hook, keeping it relatively weedless. The strips, called the "skirt," come in a variety of colors; the spinner may be a single or double blade, usually of shiny metal. The lure is extremely versatile and combines flash, action, sound, and the suggestion of a minnow's shape to attract fish. It can be worked close to the surface or allowed to sink deep.

In shallow water near shore, spinnerbaits may be fished to imitate a fleeing baitfish. They will usually not get hung up in the shoreline weeds and snags. In deeper water, they can be cast out, allowed to flutter down while sinking, then cranked in for a short distance and allowed to fall again.

Spinnerbaits are usually too large to be used for average trout or panfish. They are most effective for gamefish, especially bass, and are most commonly sold in weights of one-quarter to one-half ounce.

Streamers

Streamers are flies that are made to suggest fish rather than insects. They are

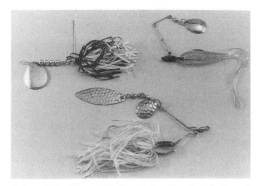

Spinnerbaits: Top row, left to right: *Snagless Sally and rigged Augertail Grub;* bottom: *No-No.*

used with flycasting tackle and are traditionally made of either feathers or bucktail. Nowadays, however, streamers (and other types of flies as well) often incorporate useful new synthetic materials.

There are hundreds of streamer designs, and the appropriate ones in the appropriate sizes can be used to catch crappies, yellow perch, bass, pickerel, pike, and trout.

In streams, streamers are usually cast across and at about a 45° angle down-

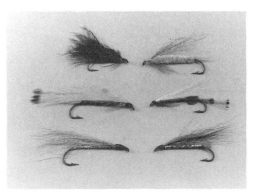

Streamers. Top row, left to right: *Black Marabou and Light Edson Tiger;* middle row, left to right: *Black Ghost and Royal Coachman;* bottom row, left to right: *Mickey Finn and Black Nose Dace.*

stream. The current will swing them downstream toward the center of the current. Then they are stripped in in short spurts and cast again.

LURES THAT IMITATE FROGS

Most lures intended to imitate frogs actually have to look like them—at least, more so than those that seek to suggest minnows have to look like minnows. Yes, some lures only suggest "frogginess," but even those look enough like a frog to be obviously a frog lure. There are very few basic types.

Rubber or Plastic Floaters

These generally realistic frog imitations have at least a frog-shaped body and long, dangling hind legs. Made of rubber or plastic, these lures float both at rest and when twitched or retrieved. There is usually a design attempt to make them weedless—either by the position of the hooks or by use of a wire deflector of some sort to protect the hooks—because of the extremely weedy places in which these lures

are best fished. They come in a variety of frog-like colors and sizes.

These frog lures are best fished in relatively shallow water near and among weeds and lily pads. Cast them out and let them sit for a minute or so. Then give them a tiny, preliminary twitch. After another long pause, swim the lure a foot or so with a short sweep of the rod. Continue alternately swimming the lure and letting it sit until it is back to your rod. The lures are meant primarily for bass, pickerel, and large trout.

Pork-Rind Frogs

These vaguely frog-shaped chunks of pork skin are often used as trailers for other lures, usually spoons or jigs. They come in jars of liquid to keep them from drying out and turning into stiff leather. Placed on the hook of a spoon or jig and allowed to trail along behind, pork-rind frogs have an action so liquid and lifelike that they have suckered all types of fish for decades. These frog imitators are subsurface lures, for all the spoons and jigs on which they are meant to trail are sink-

Lures that imitate frogs. Top row: *Super Frogs;* middle row, left to right: *Uncle Josh Pork Frog and Snag Proof Frog;* bottom row, left to right: *Hawg Frawg and twin-tail grub.*

Two great frog-imitating lures: a Johnson minnow with a pork-frog trailer and Super Frog.

ing lures. (An exception to this rule is explained in Chapter 12.) Imitation pork frogs made from soft plastics are also available. They don't need to be kept moist, but are not nearly as durable. They are used the same way.

The best pork-rind frogs, made by the Uncle Josh Bait Company, come in a multitude of sizes and colors. They can be used for trout, bass, pickerel, and pike in the appropriate sizes. Work them along weed lines.

Deerhair Frogs

These fly-rod lures are too light to be cast with any other type of tackle. Deerhair frogs come in very large sizes for bass, and in small sizes for trout. They are used much like the rubber or plastic floaters described above, but with flycasting tackle.

Crankbaits

These are the same lures described above under the headline "Lures that Imitate Minnows," but with markings and colorings that are supposed to suggest frogs. Many are excellent minnow imitations; none are worthwhile frog imitations, no matter how green and spotted they are. What is a fish supposed to make of a lure that looks and acts like a minnow but is colored like a frog? Forget frog-colored crankbaits.

LURES THAT IMITATE CRAYFISH

There are few worthwhile designs that seek to imitate crayfish, though the good ones are valuable additions to your tacklebox. They suggest crayfish by action,

Deerhair frog for flycasting.

coloration, detail, or a combination of features.

Crankbaits

There *are* worthwhile crayfish lures among the crankbaits. They are the ones designed either to sink at rest and dive and wiggle when retrieved, or to remain, when at rest, nearly suspended at the level to which they dive when cranked.

Lures that imitate crayfish. Top: *Uncle Josh Pork Frog;* middle row, left to right: *Deep Wee Crawfish Floater and Wiggle Wart;* bottom row, left to right: *Killer Craw on slider hook and twin-tail grub.*

They do not pop to the surface like corks when at rest. Real crayfish do not do that.

The danger with crayfish-imitating crankbaits is that in many cases manufacturers have simply replaced the minnow bodies on their crankbaits with crayfish bodies—without caring that crayfish and minnows do not look or act alike. Crayfish stay well below the surface, near the bottom, and should be fished there. Use only those crayfish crankbaits that stay near the bottom when at rest, or rise only very slowly when you stop retrieving.

A line of excellent crayfish crankbaits with a variety of diving characteristics is made by Rebel. They are perfect for bass, particularly smallmouths, when retrieved over and through rockpiles in cool, clear lakes. Sizes of one-fifth to one-half ounce are appropriate.

Soft Plastic Crayfish

These lures come in a variety of designs from extremely realistic to impressionistic. All are meant to be used with either a lead-head jig or a slider hook (a lead-head jig shaped to slide along the bottom in a way that will keep the bogus crayfish upright), for they are all simply crayfish-shaped, soft plastic "toys" with no hooks or weight of their own. Once such a lure is rigged on the slider or jig, it is up to you to impart the appropriate crayfish action that will entice and fool fish. Fished correctly, some can be very effective. Keep in mind that crayfish crawl forward but swim backward with quick, powerful snaps of the tail.

Soft plastic crayfish rigged on slider hooks are good for bass, particularly smallmouths. They come in a vast and confusing variety of shapes and colors, but if you stick to the most realistic of both, you will not go far wrong. A slider hook with a weight of one-eighth or a quarter ounce is recommended.

Pork-Rind Frogs

No, this is not an error. Pork-rind frogs, when used in conjunction with a jig or spoon, can be made to suggest crayfish as well as they can be made to suggest frogs. It is simply a matter of changing their action. A frog is easily suggested by a fat body and two trailing legs. A swimming crayfish is also a chunky body with two trailing claws. When a pork-rind frog is trailed slowly behind a jig or spoon so that it stays on or within inches of the bottom, fish will take it for a crayfish. Use Uncle Josh black, brown, or orange pork frogs in the appropriate sizes: No. 101 for trout, No. 11 for bass. Use a jig or spoon that is proportionate in size to enhance the suggestion of a crayfish.

LURES THAT IMITATE INSECTS

As far as I am concerned, the only worthwhile lures meant to imitate insects are flies: dry flies (intended to float on or in the surface film), wet flies (subsurface flies), nymphs (subsurface flies that imitate larval insects), and terrestrials (flies meant to imitate non-aquatic insects such as ants, crickets, grasshoppers, beetles, moths, bees, leafhoppers, etc. that fall onto the water by accident).

Flies are fished with flycasting tackle because they are too light to be cast with any other form of tackle. Even the largest bass bugs, which may be a couple of inches long and are deadly on bass under the right conditions, must be cast with flycasting tackle. Flies from the size of barely visible midges to large grasshop-

Lures that imitate insects. Top row: *bass bugs;* second and third rows: *dry flies;* fourth row: *wet flies;* fifth row: *nymphs;* sixth row: *terrestrials.*

pers are traditionally used on trout but can be equally effective on most panfish, especially sunnies and bluegills. Trout flies are often fashioned, in traditional patterns, after real insects of several aquatic groups, including mayflies, caddis, and stoneflies. Dry flies imitate the winged adults, wet flies the emerging nymphs as they swim toward the surface, and nymphs the immature larvae that live underwater. Bass bugs may imitate real aquatic insects like dragonflies, real terrestrial insects like grasshoppers and moths, or may be entirely fanciful.

The size of a fly is traditionally determined by the size of the hook used to make it. For the absolute beginner, trout flies between No. 16 (small enough) and No. 6 (large enough) will suffice. Bass bugs should be between No. 2 (small enough) and No. 2/0 (big enough). The smaller bass bugs and all of the trout flies will be fine for panfish. On streams, dry flies and terrestrials (which also float) are usually cast upstream and allowed to drift

Bass bugs are surface flies used mainly for bass.

Dry flies are surface flies used for trout, panfish, and bass.

back toward you. Wet flies and nymphs, like the streamers discussed earlier, are usually cast across and downstream and then stripped in after they have swung straight downstream in the current.

LURES THAT IMITATE WORMS

The plastic worm is arguably the most effective bass lure that has ever been developed. In the hands of an experienced fisherman, these lures can be used under

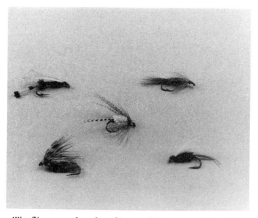

Wet flies are subsurface flies used for trout and panfish.

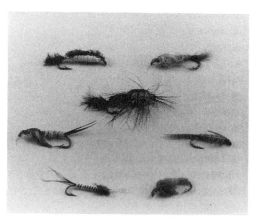

Nymphs are subsurface flies used for trout and panfish.

Terrestrials are surface flies that imitate non-aquatic insects and are used for trout, panfish, and bass.

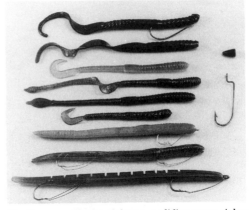

Plastic worms. To the right are a sliding worm sinker and one type of plastic worm hook.

a variety of conditions to produce consistent bass-catching success. The key word here, however, is "experienced." Because of the patience, touch, feel, and know-how involved in working plastic worms effectively—for example, knowing when a bass has taken the lure, and how to strike the fish properly—I think that the absolute beginner should not use these lures until he has gotten a bit more mileage out of the many other fine artificials available to him.

Here is a basic list, categorized by lure types, of the artificials the absolute beginner should have in order to try for the widest variety of fish under the widest variety of conditions. In most cases, I have indicated a range of sizes that necessitate a variety of tackle. If you are planning to use only one type and weight of tackle, use only those types and sizes of lures that will be appropriate to and in proper balance with your equipment. The actual brand and model names may be taken verbatim or used as examples of the design they represent, though I believe that these lures are the best of their kind. Where not specified, colors are up to you.

Crankbaits: Rapala Original in the two-inch, 3½-inch, and 5¼-inch sizes. This

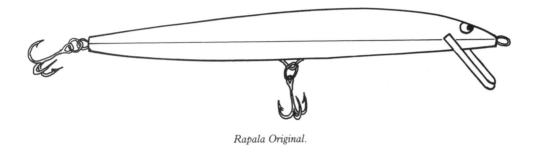

Rapala Original.

Heddon River Runt.

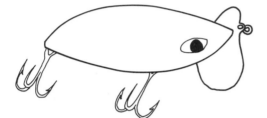

Arbogast Jitterbug.

Arbogast Hula Popper.

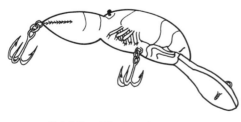

Rebel Deep Wee Crawfish Floater.

lure is a long, skinny, floater/shallow diver, minnow imitation.

Heddon River Runt in the ¼-ounce and ½-ounce sizes. This minnow-shaped floater/diver dives to about seven feet and wiggles like crazy.

Arbogast Jitterbug in the ¼-ounce size. This is a classic surface disturber. All you need do is reel it in.

Arbogast Hula Popper in the ¼-ounce size. Another classic. This one floats on the surface and can be twitched and popped as desired.

Rebel Deep Wee Crawfish Floater. This ¼-ounce crayfish imitation has the right characteristics to get down to about eight feet and stay there.

Spoons: Dardevle spoons in sizes ¹⁄₁₆, ³⁄₁₆, and ¼ ounce. As for color, start with a red/white, a nickel, and a brass in each size. Cast it out, allow it to sink several inches or feet—depending on

Dardevle.

Johnson Silver Minnow.

the water depth—and reel in, stop, let it sink, reel in, etc. Pork-rind trailers may be attached, but are not necessary.

Johnson Silver Minnow in ¼-ounce size, in silver, black, and gold finishes. This weedless spoon works best with a pork-rind frog trailer. It rides with its hook upward and is arguably the finest spoon available. A classic.

Spinners: Mepps Aglias and Black Furies in sizes from ¹⁄₁₂ ounce to ¼ ounce. These are among the best spinners made and can be used for trout, panfish, and gamefish in the appropriate sizes. Just cast them out and reel them in, pausing every so often to allow them to fall.

Spinnerbaits: Mister Twister and Bass Buster soft-bodied spinnerbaits in ¹⁄₁₆-ounce through ¼-ounce sizes. These are lead-head jigs rigged with an overhead spinner. The soft-plastic grub bodies are changeable. These lures are good for trolling or for casting through submerged weedbeds.

Generic hard-bodied, skirted spinnerbaits with either single or tandem spinners, in ¼-ounce size. Dozens of manufacturers produce similar offerings. Extremely versatile.

Jigs: An assortment of marabou crappie jigs (no particular manufacturer) in several color combinations including all white, all black, black/white, red/white, yellow, and chartreuse. Cast and retrieve, or jig them straight down into brushpiles.

A couple of skirted bass jigs in the ¼-ounce size to be used with a pork-rind frog trailer. Fish them slowly on

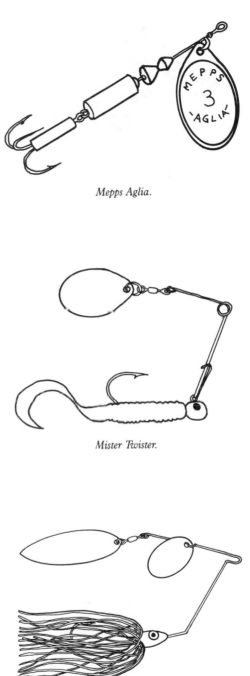

Mepps Aglia.

Mister Twister.

A generic tandem spinner bait.

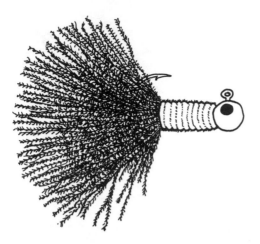

A generic crappie jig.

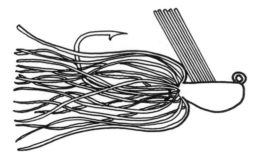

A generic skirted jig.

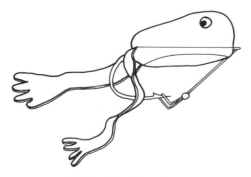

Harrison Hoge Super Frog.

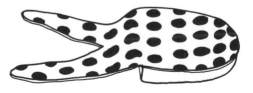

Uncle Josh's Pork Frog.

the bottom to imitate crayfish. Black, brown, or brown/orange.

Frog Lures: Harrison Hoge Super Frog in green. This is an outstanding, life-like, and extremely weedless floating frog. Easy to cast. Cast it out, let it sit, then make it act like a frog.

Uncle Josh Pork Frogs in size 11. These come four to a jar. For use with Johnson spoons, get the white frog with green spots. For use with a bass jig as a crayfish imitation, get black, brown, or spotted crawfish. There is a precut hole near the front of each chunk. Insert the hook from below so that the frog will swim upright. How to get the hook out again is something you will have to figure out for yourself.

Trout Flies: A basic selection in sizes from No. 8 to No. 16 should include such patterns as Adams, Royal Coachman, Black Bivisible, and Brown Bivisible dry flies; No. 8 to No. 12 Royal Coachman, Light Hendrickson, and Coachman wet flies; a few No. 10 weighted nymphs in light, medium, and dark shades; an assortment of No. 4 to No. 10 crickets, grasshoppers, beetles, and woolly worms; and a few No. 4 to No. 10 streamers in such patterns as Mickey Finn, Black-Nose Dace, Muddler Minnow, and Black Ghost.

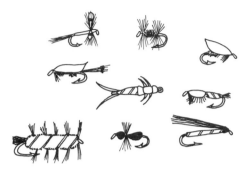

A selection of flies.

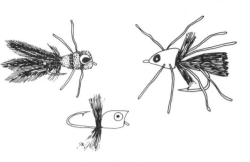

Assorted bass bugs.

Bass Bugs: A small assortment of deer-hair, cork, or balsa bugs and poppers in sizes 2 or 4. The very bushy ones become difficult to cast.

Clearly, the absolute beginner will most likely not want to run out and buy every one of the lures and sizes listed here. Their types and sizes range over all the kinds of tackle discussed in Section I. Most beginners will be using only one or two of those kinds. If you have decided to use only a midweight spinning outfit at this stage of your fishing, you will be interested only in those lures that weigh between one-quarter and one-half ounce, approximately. You will not need flies or bass bugs at all. Conversely, if you have decided to try flycasting tackle, you will be interested only in flies and bass bugs, to the exclusion of all spinning and baitcasting lures. Those with ultralight spinning tackle will be interested in the lightest and smallest lures (not flies), and those using baitcasting tackle will want to look into the lures of about one-quarter to five-eighths of an ounce.

Keep in mind that my lure suggestions are a drop in the bucket. I have not even mentioned all my own favorites. Your experienced friends will have their favorites to recommend as well. Before long, though, you will be making your own informed decisions, based on your own experience of what works, what does not, what is pleasant to use and easy to cast and has good action—plus at least a dozen prejudices, many of which have little or nothing to do with whether the thing actually catches fish. Now, let's go fishing.

12

Let's Go Fishing

Up to this point, you have been absorbing a great deal of fishing fact and theory. You now know about the most important pieces of equipment, about what fish are most often sought, and about the lures—both live and artificial—used to catch them. There are still a few topics that should and will be discussed in the next section of this book before you can actually go away as a reasonably well-informed absolute beginner. Nonetheless, I offer you a choice in how you continue your education.

Each of us can absorb only so much theory before we must go out and apply those theories. You may feel that it is about time you put your new knowledge to actual use, or you may not mind taking in a bit more information first. Take your choice. You can skip this chapter for now, coming back to it later after reading the additional chapters in the next section, or you may read it now and refer to those later chapters as I mention the information they contain. Either way, in the long run you will learn it all. I am simply giving you the opportunity to structure your education to your personal learning preference.

You are about to embark on three imaginary fishing outings. Clearly, the possibilities are far more numerous than that, what with 13 species of fish, four types of tackle, and several modes of fishing (Chapters 13 and 14). But I have decided that these three outings will serve to demonstrate the variety and general experience of fishing as you will most commonly experience it.

You will first be fishing for panfish with both live bait and artificials, using spincasting and flycasting tackle. Then you will try for bass from a boat, using both live bait and artificials with spinning tackle. And lastly, you will go wading in a small stream for trout, using flies and live bait. Whether or not you intend to use all those methods in your real fishing, our imaginary outings will orient you to their use so you can get a good feel for the possibilities.

A PANFISH OUTING

You are standing on the shore of a small pond whose banks rise only a foot or two above the water and drop off rapidly to a depth of five or six feet. The pond is only about 50 acres in surface area, yet you have seen anglers here in the past, sitting or standing on the banks in those spots that are now worn to bare ground. Large trees line the shore, but there are many shaded, open spots along the banks that allow unhampered casting. The surface of the water is calm, and you can see an occasional ring of a rising sunnie as it snatches something from the film. Beyond your feet, the lake's bottom is visible as a light, sandy area, but it quickly deepens and darkens until no detail is discernible. Then, about 10 feet out, you can see that a weedbed has started, and the tops of the weeds are just visible a few inches below the surface. Farther out, about 20 feet from you, a few lily pads dot the surface.

You have brought your spincasting tackle, rigged for use with live bait. A No. 10 snelled hook (see Chapter 13) is

Bank fishing.

tied to your line (see Chapter 16 for knots), and a split-shot is pinched onto the snell above the hook. You also have an assortment of floats in your tackle box, and a coffee can full of juicy worms lies on the ground by your feet.

Start by placing a Ping-Pong-ball-size float on your line about three feet above the hook. Next, thread a worm onto the hook as described in Chapter 10. Now, do you see where that weedbed is, about 10 feet out? There is a clear spot just off to the right between the edge of the weeds and another bed a little farther down the shore. That's where the sunnie rose to feed on top. Cast your worm right into that hole. You have learned how to do that in Chapter 4. Nice cast. Now just crank the handle once to get it out of freespool.

The float is now resting quietly on the water, and the worm is hanging below it at a depth of three feet from the surface. Now, just wait—and keep an eye on the float. When the water is calm like this, it is easy to tell when something is going on. When the wind is blowing and the float is bouncing on the water, things are not so simple. Just let that float sit there.

Aha! Did you see the way it kind of nodded three times? Now it is quiet again. That commotion was a little fish pecking at your worm. It is possible that he may have sucked it right off the hook. Wait a couple of minutes, and keep watching the float.

Well, there has been no further action in the last few minutes. Reel in your rig and check your bait. Just as I thought . . . that little fellow stripped off your worm. Okay, that happens all the time. Put on a new worm, and push the float six inches farther up the line—let's see if the bigger fish are a little deeper. Cast back into that same general area by the edge of the weeds. Good. Remember to give the handle one crank to get the reel out of freespool.

Let it sit. Oops! Something has pulled it down. Quickly wind the slack out of your line, and strike by lifting the rod tip sharply and bringing the rod up toward your shoulder. Do you feel that solid resistance at the end of your line? He's on! Great! Reel in, and let's see what you've got.

It is a nice bluegill. Just lift it right out of the water with your rod, and grab the snell to lift it the rest of the way. Notice where the hook is—way inside the fish's mouth, indicating that you let him swallow it before you struck. The hook should be just in the lip. Next time, try striking as soon as you see that float jump. Now you will have to injure the fish in taking out the hook, so you are going to have to keep it. Injured fish should not be released. It's a good thing you were planning to eat today's catch anyway. Just take him off the hook, and put him on your stringer or in the bucket full of water you brought along. Grasp him firmly around the middle with one hand, being careful of the dorsal spines. If you smooth them back as you place your hand around the fish, they will lie down and not stick you. With the other hand, work the hook out as best you can. That is easy when the fish is hooked in the lip, but it takes a good deal more effort when it is that far down in his throat. Unfortunately, you will cause a fair amount of bleeding during this operation. There should be no blood at all from a properly hooked fish. Now put on another worm and try for another fish.

Okay, you have been fishing here with worms for an hour and have done pretty well. There are eight or nine fish in your bucket, two of which look to be yellow perch. Not bad. You have been changing the position of the float to make the bait hang at different depths, and you have been casting to several different spots within your range. Very good. You certainly seem to have the hang of it. But now things are beginning to slow down. How about trying something else?

Take off the float and the snelled hook with the split-shot attached, and put them in your box. Now tie on that little Mister Twister, the soft plastic wiggly thing with the overhead spinner. Tie your line to the loop in the elbow of the spinner arm, using an Improved Clinch Knot (Chapter 16). Now you are going to do some casting. You could not reach the lily pads with the live-bait rig because of its awkwardness, but you should have little trouble reaching beyond it now.

Try casting as far as you can, straight out toward those pads. Excellent! You had no idea you could cast so far, did you? Okay, now let the lure fall for a count of three, and begin reeling it back in slowly, stopping every few cranks to let it fall again for a second. Do you feel the lure crossing through the weedbed? The sensation feels like it may be a strike but is kind of dull and lifeless. Before long, experience will teach you the difference between weeds and a strike. Here comes the lure. Crank it back up to within a few inches of the rod tip, and cast it out again. This time, try a little farther to the left, just off the leftmost edge of the pads. Good cast.

Let it fall a few seconds, then start reeling slowly. Did you feel that bump or tug? That was probably a fish. It felt more sudden and solid than the resistance caused by weeds. If you feel that tug again, strike back. Just make sure there is no slack in the line. Ahhh! There you go. Snap that rod back. You've got him. Keep your line tight and maintain constant pressure on him while reeling. Bring him in. That's it. Oh, a nice crappie. They have a bit more fight than the perch and bluegills, don't they? And you'll notice that you struck him just right, too, because the hook of your lure is right through the membrane behind his lip. Perfect. If you wanted to, you could release this fish entirely uninjured. But I suggest you add him to your catch. The crappie is a good eating fish.

Okay, try again. Crappies run in schools, so where there is one, there ought to be more. Put that lure right back in the same spot. Good. Let it fall as you did before, and be prepared to strike immediately. Nothing yet? Start reeling, let it fall again, reel a little, stop. There you go; another one is on. This is good panfishing action—just what you had hoped for.

Now you have been covering this whole area with that Mister Twister for a while. You have enough fish for a meal or two, and the action has slowed down again. But I've got one more thing for you to try—just for the sport of it.

See that little boat dock down the shore a way? How about going out on it and giving your fly rod a quick workout? Fishing from the end of that dock will get you away from the trees so you won't have to worry about your backcast, and it will allow you to reach new water as well.

Okay, you have your trout/panfish fly tackle rigged as recommended in Chapter 5: DT-6-F line and a 7½-foot leader with a 4X tippet. Tie to the end of the tippet a green, sponge-rubber spider with live-rubber legs, and let's see what happens. Before you cast it out, squeeze the spider and hold it underwater as you let it expand, thus allowing it to soak up water. That will make it sink very slowly when it lands.

Now pull some line from the reel with your free hand and, waving the rod overhead, rhythmically work out the line until you have about 15 feet (not counting the leader) in the air. Then cast it out onto the pond. Do not worry about finesse; practice will provide that refinement eventually. Right now, just concentrate on getting the fly out onto the water a reasonable distance. When the spider lands, grasp the line between the reel and the first guide with your free hand, and strip it in with short jerks, letting it simply fall on the dock at your feet. The first couple of fingers of your rod hand should catch the line between jerks so you can reach up with your free hand for another tug. Keep the rod pointed at the fly. When something hits, just hold onto the line with your free hand and lift the rod tip.

Well, you have gotten the spider back to within a couple of rod lengths of your tip top, so just lift the rod, throw the fly back into a backcast, and let the extra line that has fallen on the dock sail back out on the forward cast. You can false-cast one more time, pulling yet more line from the reel and letting it increase the amount of line you have out, or you can continue with the initial 15 feet of line and just cast to a new spot.

There's a nice cast. Wait a few seconds to let the spider sink a couple of feet. Now start stripping it in again. Whoa, you've got a hit. Raise that rod. Wow, look at that bluegill jump! Just keep pulling the line in with your free hand and let it fall on the dock. When you get the fish near the dock, hold the line against the grip with your hand, kneel down, and lift

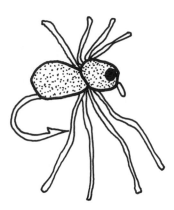

A sponge-rubber spider.

the fish out of the water with your free hand.

Now just unhook it and put it back. Fun, eh? Fly fishing for panfish is great. You might want to take that spider off and put on a dry trout fly just to see how much fun it is to watch the fish hit on the surface. You probably will not get as many strikes as on the sinking spider, but it is worth the experience. Have fun.

A BASS OUTING

For this trip you have use of a friend's rowboat, and the friend has even volunteered to do the rowing so you can just fish and not worry about anything else. I sure wish I had friends like that. So just climb into the boat and take along your spinning outfit, that minnow bucket full of shiners, and your tackle box. Sit right up there on the front seat.

The lake you are on now is a good-size one of about 300 acres. Houses crowd the shoreline in some areas, but in others, where marshy ground makes building unsuitable, there is nothing but woods. In one undeveloped cove, a dense blanket of lily pads extends out from the shore and

Bass fishing from a johnboat.

suddenly stops as the water deepens. Your friend heads into that cove and drops the anchor right at the edge of the pads. As you look down over the side of the boat, you can see that the water is only about three or four feet deep where the pads end, but it deepens quickly to a subsurface bed of furry, dense weeds that extend in a vast expanse as far as you can see out into the lake. The tops of those weeds reach up to within a foot or two of the surface.

Rig up your medium-weight spinning outfit, and tie onto your line a Johnson Silver Minnow. That weedless spoon is perfectly suited to prospecting for bass in this cover of lily pads. On the hook of the spoon place an Uncle Josh Pork Frog in such a way that when the spoon rides

with its hook upward, the frog's colored side is upward as well.

Now cast the lure right down one edge of the pads so that it lands on the pads themselves about three feet in from the open water. Begin reeling as soon as it lands. The idea is to keep the lure on top of the pads—do not let it fall through. If you keep the lure moving, it will stay on top and bass underneath will be able to track its movement. If an interested bass is down there, you will know it—believe me.

Okay, when the lure gets back to the boat, toss it out again, but about eight feet in from where it landed last time. Eventually, you will want to cover the area in a semicircle with you at the center, until you are casting along the edge 180 degrees from where you started. That is called "fan casting" because the area you cover is in the shape of a fan.

Oh! Did you see that—or, rather, hear it? Something punched at the lure from under the pads, about 20 feet out at about 10 o'clock. Don't stop retrieving. The only way the fish can find it again is by the sound and motion the lure makes while it's moving. The fish may follow and try again. Nope. No dice. But toss the lure back in that area again. Chances are good that you will draw another strike.

Good cast. Now just keep it moving over the spot where you got the hit before. Right about . . . THERE! Wow! Strike that fish hard. You've got him. Now reel like crazy. You don't want him to get down in those pads and tie you up in there. Keep reeling. That's it, just haul him right over the pads. Beautiful. Now get him right up near the boat, but don't try to lift him out of the water with the rod or you may break your line. A bass is a heavy fish when it's not buoyed by water. Instead, reach down with your free hand and put your thumb right in his mouth, picking him up by his lower lip.

That's it. That is how you pick up a bass. It quiets them right down, and you do not get your hands all over them and risk injury to the fish. Nice job. You see how the hook is right in the corner of his mouth? A perfect hook-set. Now you can either keep him or put him back. Good choice. Just gently lower him back into the water.

Okay, now finish working this lily-pad area, casting and retrieving just the way you did for that first fish. Exciting, isn't it? Bass come right up through there without any warning at all. Puts a little strain on the old ticker every once in a while, eh? Hey, there's another one. Set that hook. Now bring the fish in quickly before it gets down in the stems. Ho, look here—you've got yourself a real nice pickerel! That is very common, for much of the cover that bass prefer is prime pickerel habitat also. And nothing is more attractive to a big pickerel than a fast-moving prey running for its life. But don't pick this fellow up by his lower lip. If you stick your thumb in that mouth full of teeth, you will learn a whole new definition of pain and bloodshed. Grasp a pickerel around the middle with a wet hand,

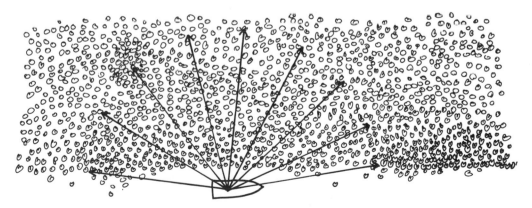

Working an area in a methodical, semi-circular pattern is called "fan casting."

A largemouth bass of average size.

and work the hook out with the other. These fish have tough mouths and a habit of driving your own hook through your own thumb if you let them. Be careful, and put him back uninjured (both you and the fish, that is).

Now for another technique. Snip off that spoon-and-pork combination, and put the frog back in its jar so it doesn't dry out. Now tie on that yellow River Runt. This lure is a floater/diver crankbait that floats while at rest and wiggles and dives to about six feet when reeled. You will be fishing it over and through those subsurface weeds away from the pads.

Cast the lure out straight toward the main body of the lake. When it lands, let it sit. Crank your reel once to close the bail, and take up any slack line. The lure will float on the surface. Keep an eye on it. You never know when something will hit it. After about 15 seconds, give the rod tip a little twitch to make the lure jerk a bit. If a bass is eyeing it, you will get a strike right now. Otherwise, start reeling slowly and steadily, and the lure will begin wiggling and diving. You can feel the vibrations of its action. You will inevitably bump some weeds. When you do, stop reeling and let the lure float back up to the surface. If it does not come up, give it a yank and free it from the weeds. Then let it float up. Reel some more. Feel it wiggle? Let it float up again. If something hits, it will be a good, solid bump and a good struggle will follow. Bass usually hit a crankbait with certainty and then try to swim off with it. You will know a fish from a weed after a very short while.

When you have swum the lure back to the boat, cast it out again, a little farther to the left or right of your previous cast, and let it sit for 15 seconds again. Then twitch it, pause, start reeling, let it float up, reel, stop. WHAM! Set that hook. Oh, boy, this one is a big one! You can tell by the way it's taking out line. Do not reel against the drag. You will only put a zillion twists in your line. If the fish is taking line against the drag, let it. When it stops, regain the line. Bass tire pretty quickly. There, it's coming in now. Whoops, there it goes on another run. Just let it go. Okay, now reel in some more line. Here it comes. Nice fish! Look at the size of that mouth. Don't rush it, and don't try to grab that lip until you're sure the fish is tired. Oh, no! It threw the lure. Awwww, that's a shame. You just didn't have it hooked well enough. That happens sometimes. The hook hits bone or just does not penetrate the membrane in the lip well, and the fish makes a good shake of its head and throws the lure. But wasn't that some thrill anyway? You bet. And now you know that fish is still in here, just waiting for you to fool him again. That ought to get you back out here pretty soon.

Let's try one more technique on these bass. Have your friend row you out to deep water, maybe at the mouth of this cove where the subsurface weedbed falls off into even deeper water. The deep edge of the bed should be a perfect spot to try some live shiners. Snip off the crankbait, and tie on a No. 4 hook—a good size for the three-inch shiners you brought along. Since you don't really have to cast far, and the water is deep here, place a two-inch-diameter float about six feet up your line. Now grab one of the shiners—a nice lively one—and hook it through the back, just ahead of the dorsal fin (see Chapter 10). Now toss the rig out along the weedline. If you want to get farther away from it, move the boat.

Let the rig sit. Remember that a live shiner will cause a lot more movement of the float than there would be from a worm. Expect to see it swim around pretty freely. If it stands still too long, it may mean that the shiner has found a hid-

ing spot in the weeds or has hung the line on a weed. Give a tug and pull the float about a foot. That should set things right again.

Watch the float for any peculiar action. You may see it suddenly take off or bounce erratically. If a big bass is eyeing your shiner, you can bet that shiner is going to get very upset and try to disappear one way or another. Just be patient. Look! Your float is moving away. There it goes down. A bass has taken your bait. *Let it go.* Leave your bail open, and let the line run out freely. Just let it go. The bass has not yet got it in its mouth in such a way that the hook will catch its lip. You must wait until the bass turns the bait to swallow it, which it will do when it stops. It is still running with the bait. Let it go. . . . There—it stopped. It is now turning the bait in its mouth. Wait until it starts moving again. Don't do anything yet. Just wait. Okay, it's moving again. Crank the reel once to close the bail, and carefully take up the slack. Feel the pull of the bass? Rear back and strike that fish hard. Make believe you are trying to throw the

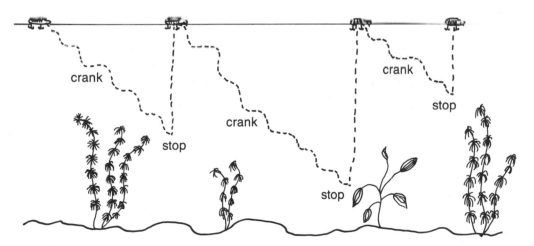

The River Runt, like most floater/diver plugs, is most effective when retrieved by a stop-and-go technique.

bass over your shoulder with the rod. There you go. Keep that line tight. Don't let the fish have any slack or it may throw the hook again. Keep reeling as long as the bass is not pulling out line against the drag. Keep it coming. Nice fish! Get it by the lip, and lift it into the boat. Beautiful.

A TROUT OUTING

You are going to fish a pretty little brook that runs through the woods. In most places it is no wider than a two-lane road, and it spills among boulders in swift runs, then slows in deep pools for stretches of 50 yards or so before once again shoaling and speeding up over gravel and stone riffles. The brook is stocked each season with rainbow, brown, and brook trout 10 to 14 inches long, and there are plenty of places, away from the bridges and easy access spots, where an angler can get away by himself and think he is in the wilderness.

You have just walked a mile up the abandoned railroad tracks that follow the brook, carrying your fly outfit and your ultralight spinning gear. You are wearing chest waders (see Chapter 14) and a fishing vest (Chapter 13) in which is stowed your collection of trout flies and some ultralight tackle. At the cutoff to the spillway pool, you turn down the path through the woods until you reach the

Fly fishing for trout. Michigan Travel Commission photo.

brook. There you put down your rods, sit down on a streamside boulder, and watch the pool.

The spillway pool is 30 yards long and about 15 feet wide from the point where it comes bubbling through the boulders and fallen trees at the head of the pool to the point where it curves around and gurgles through the old stone spillway at its tail. In between, large boulders litter the pool's bottom and trees and shrubbery hang over the stream. There is no place to cast from shore, and there are no obvious signs of fish.

Your fly rod is rigged as described in Chapter 5: DT-6-F line and a 7½-foot tapered leader. The tippet is 4X. From your vest you take a box containing wet flies. Among them is a No. 10 Royal Coachman. You tie it onto your tippet with an Improved Clinch Knot (see Chapter 16), and carefully ease into the stream. The bottom here is somewhat mucky and wading is difficult, but you ease out to midstream and face the tail of the pool. Pulling some line off the reel with your free hand while waving the rod over head, you work out about 12 feet of line and cast it downstream and across the pool so that the fly lands near the far bank, slightly downstream from your position.

Slowly the current catches the fly and the line and swings them downstream and back toward the middle of the pool. As the line straightens out below you, you hold the rod low and parallel to the water while stripping line back in short jerks, catching every other coil of line in the palm of your stripping hand so the line does not fall on the water and get swept downstream. Meanwhile, your rod hand catches the line against the grip with the first two fingers each time you reach for more line with your stripping hand. In

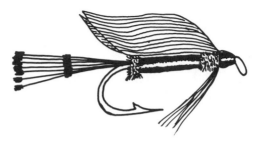

A Royal Coachman wet fly.

this way, you swim the wet fly upstream toward you in short glides. If a trout hits it, you will feel a sudden bump and you must hold the line with your stripping hand and raise the rod tip sharply with your rod hand.

But nothing happens. When the leader is six or eight feet from your rod tip, wade carefully downstream a few feet, lift the fly into a backcast, and cast it once again down and across, again allowing it to swing with the current before stripping line in. Ahh! Was that a bump? Maybe so. Try letting some line back out and allowing the current to just carry the fly back down a few feet. Now strip it in again. Anything? Okay, try another cast to the same spot. There's a hit! Hold onto the line and sharply raise the rod. You've got him. Hoo, boy, look at that rainbow jump! And he's putting quite a strain on the rod, too. Don't try to horse him in. Just hold him there if you can, and keep him from running up under the bushes. When he begins to weaken a bit, try stripping him in. You can let the line fall on the water now. Just make sure you don't get all fouled in it. Here he comes, but watch it—once he sees you, he'll probably panic and take off again. Just try to hold him. If you feel there is too much strain on the tippet, let some line slide through your fingers, then snub him up again when you can. Here he comes. Nice rainbow. If you want to keep him, he'll make a fine meal. Just grasp him around the middle and take out the hook. Then knock him on the head and slip him into your creel.

Now come on out of there and sit back on that rock for a moment. Look around. Notice anything? A lot more insects are in the air than when you first arrived, and a lot of splashing sounds are coming from the head of the pool. Oh, and there's a rise upstream. See that ring? Now is the time to cast dry flies to individual, rising trout. There is no better thrill in the entire sport of fishing.

Clip off your wet fly, and tie on a No. 14 or 16 Adams dry fly. Treat it with floatant and let it dry to ensure a nice, high float. Now ease back out into the pool, and face upstream this time. Plip! See that ring about 15 feet straight ahead of you? That is your trout, and you are going to offer him your fly. For this presentation you need a little finesse. The idea is to drop the fly, with very little disturbance, about three feet above that rise. You want the fly to drift naturally over the fish without the least bit of drag (drag results when the current pulls on your line and causes an

unnatural drift of the fly), and you want to strip line in at the same rate of drift so that no slack forms between yourself and the fly. But you also want to avoid causing the fly to move faster than the current. There is a certain amount of practice needed here—a certain "touch" must be developed. But the only way to get it is to do it. So go ahead.

Work some line out in the air. When you think you've got the range, let it go, making sure to stop the cast well above the water so that the fly does not slap down. That will kill your chances as surely as throwing a rock at the fish. Nice cast. Now keep an eye on that fly, and slowly strip line in to keep up with the slack that is forming by its float downstream. You can let the stripped line fall on the water—it will stay downstream, out of your way. He rose! But not to your fly. He took a real fly right near yours. That's okay. It means your cast did not put him down. Just keep stripping in line until you can backcast again. Now put that fly right down in the same spot. Great! Keep an eye on it, and take up the slack. Right about there. Hmmm, no rise. It may just be too soon after he ate the real one. Try again. Good. Here it comes again. He took it! Hold the line and raise the rod. Solid hook up. Now there's a jumper! Hold him with the line. Try to work him downstream. Uh-oh, he's headed for that snag; put on a bit more pressure and see if you can turn him. If he gets your tippet around that branch, forget it. Oops! He broke you off. Too bad, but that's the way it often goes in these wooded streams. Nice action, though, eh? You don't get to see aerobatics like that too often. Tie on another Adams, and try for that riser over there. Same method. Better luck this time. In

An Adams dry fly.

the meantime, I'm going down below the spillway to have a look at the lower pool.

Well, I see you've been doing well over the past few minutes. Plenty of trout rising up here, eh? Looks like you have, what, three in the creel? And you say two others broke you off? You can't ask for more action than that. But let me show you something, just for the sake of your education, because I don't think you are going to be too impressed by this after the kind of time you've been having with dry flies. Anyway, grab your spinning tackle and follow me down to the lower pool.

Tie that little Mepps spinner you brought along in your vest to the end of your spinning line, and toss it out into the fast water below the spillway there. Good. Now let it sweep down into the pool, and start reeling very slowly. Can you feel the vibration from the rotation of the spinner blade? The moment that vibration stops, strike. Hah! There you go. Now just reel her in. Nice trout. But not as much of a thrill as the challenge of casting a dry fly to rising fish, is it? Still, if you've promised somebody a trout dinner, this is your best bet for filling your limit, I think. Another possibility is to hang a worm a few inches below a clear bubble-float and let it drift through this run. It's the same kind

Trout fishing. Michigan Travel Commission photo.

of thing. When the float does down, strike.

Now, what do you say we go back to the upper pool and do some real fishing while the trout are still rising?

Section IV

EXTRAS AND FINE POINTS

13

Additional Tackle

In Section I, you learned about the different forms of freshwater tackle available. The discussion, though, was limited mainly to rods, reels, and line. As you learned in Section III, tackle also includes hooks, sinkers, floats, and lures. In this chapter, I will give you a little more information on hooks, sinkers, and floats (enough so that you can make an informed choice when you walk into a tackle shop), and some additional background on other items of tackle that you may or may not need but will no doubt encounter. Remember that there is a good deal more to be learned about these things as your interest and expertise increase.

HOOKS

What could be simpler than a hook? Well, if I were to tell you everything there is to know about the different types, designs, and subtleties of fish hooks, this book would be several hundred pages longer than it already is, and you might decide that fishing is not the thing for you. Luckily, an absolute beginner—and even an experienced angler—need not know all that much about hooks.

What you *should* know about hooks includes the following facts: there are different types for different purposes (some are for tying flies, some are for bait fishing, some are for lure making, etc.). There are different designs within each type—Aberdeen, Sproat, Kirby, Limerick, O'Shaughnessy, Carlisle, and Eagle Claw are hook designs that have characteristic bends, for example. There are differences in the length and design of a hook's shank, bend, barb, point, and eye (there are turned-down eyes, turned-up eyes, ringed eyes, flat eyes, ball eyes,

There are hooks for every purpose under heaven.

needle eyes, tapered eyes, and brazed eyes). And there are differences in size, differences in the diameter of the wire used to make the hooks, weedless and non-weedless varieties, and snelled and unsnelled hooks. You do not, at this point, need to know much about what those differences mean—just as long as you are aware that you cannot go into a tackle shop and just ask for any old hook.

Although a good standard is lacking, the sizes of hooks are more or less consistent from one manufacturer to another. That is, a No. 10 hook made by one company will be about the same size as a No. 10 hook made by another company. However, because of variations in design, for one thing, two hooks that are the same length may differ in the size of their gaps, making one more suitable for your pur-

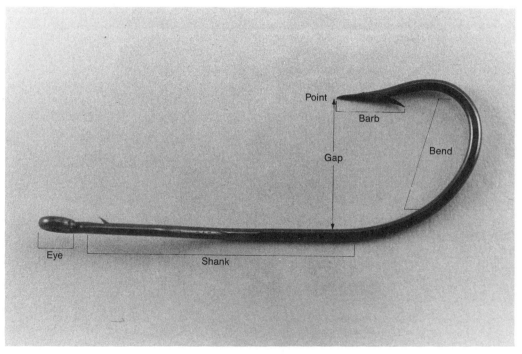

Anatomy of a hook.

poses than the other. But generally, sizes are fairly uniform, and when I suggest a hook size in this book, the hook you find in any tackle shop will be very close to what I have in mind.

The size of a hook is indicated by a number. The tiniest fly-tying hook that is commonly used is No. 28. It is barely visible and is used for tying imitations of midges. As hook sizes get larger, the numbers get lower. Mosquito imitations are tied on No. 20 or 18 hooks; average mayflies on No. 16, 14, and 12 sizes; large flies on No. 10 and 8 hooks; and bass bugs on No. 2. After No. 2, the hooks keep getting larger but the numbering system changes. The numbers begin going up again, but with a /0 after the main number: No. 1/0, 2/0, 3/0, etc. This numbering system is true of all hooks, not just fly-tying hooks.

Hooks also come snelled or unsnelled. A snell is simply a length of heavy monofilament that is permanently tied to the hook. The snell has a loop tied in the end opposite the hook to which you can tie or clip your line. Snelled hooks usually are packaged several to a card; sometimes a card holds hooks of the same size, sometimes an assortment of sizes. Unsnelled hooks usually come in a small plastic box, again either all one size or as an assortment.

Rather than confusing you with a surfeit of hook arcana, let me simply tell you what to look for when you buy hooks. For live-bait fishing, buy Sproat or Eagle Claw hooks (oops, this is confusing already—Eagle Claw is not only a design, it is also the name of a manufacturer), either snelled or unsnelled, in the sizes I have already recommended for specific fish and baits. Snelled hooks are my personal preference. Because of the length

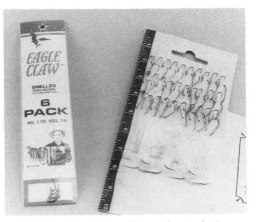

Hooks come in packages of assorted or single sizes.

of heavy mono snell (usually about six inches), you can use much lighter line on your reel without worrying about a fish's jaws abrading the line and possibly breaking it. The snell acts as a protective leader. Another advantage to snelled hooks is that you can attach your sinker to the snell, so that when you remove the hook from your line, the hook and sinker remain as a single unit. Otherwise you must remove the hook from your line and then remove the sinker separately each time.

To clear up the Eagle Claw confusion: Eagle Claw is a design, but you will no doubt encounter Eagle Claw (the company) snelled hooks on the pegboard of any tackle shop you are likely to visit. This maker's Series 31 (Plain Shank) Snelled Hooks or Series 139 (Baitholder) Snelled Hooks in the appropriate sizes are exactly what you are looking for, so you cannot go wrong there.

That simplifies your hook-buying for bait fishing. When you buy lures, the hooks are, of course, already part of the lure. Most crankbaits and plugs use treble hooks, as do many spoons and spinners. Spinnerbaits usually employ single hooks, as do jigs, weedless spoons, and most flies and bass bugs. Plastic worms for bass fishing are most commonly rigged on special weedless worm hooks that are pushed through the worm's head and then turned back into the body of the worm to make them weedless. These are known simply as worm hooks and come in the most popular sizes of 1/0, 2/0, 3/0, and 4/0.

SINKERS

As with hooks, there are a surprising number of sinker types. Most popular for freshwater fishing are split-shot, egg sinkers, bass casting (dipsey) sinkers, and a variety of twist-on types. All have their advantages and disadvantages under various circumstances, and here is another potential area for me to overwhelm and confuse you. So I will back off and tell you this: use the type of sinker that is easiest to put on and take off, as long as it comes in the right sizes and weights.

My preference—because they come in a variety of useful sizes and are inconspicuous, inexpensive, and easily manipulated—are split-shot sinkers, small spheres of lead with a notch cut through them. You lay your line in the notch and squeeze the sides of the shot together,

pinching your line. Somehow a split-shot stays pretty much where you put it. Water Gremlin, a tackle company in Minnesota, has improved the split-shot sinker by adding little tabs that make it easy to reopen. Thus the sinker can be easily repositioned or removed and reused.

The sizes and weights of sinkers are indicated by a variety of methods that are neither necessarily helpful nor uniform. The simplest method gives the weight of the sinker in ounces. Egg and dipsey sinkers are generally rated by weights ranging from $\frac{1}{16}$ ounce to one ounce. That system does not tell you how big the sinker is, however, so you still must select your sinker by sight. Clinch-on and twist-on sinkers are designated by numbering systems that have nothing in common with either the numbering system used for hook sizes or those for other types of sinkers. So forget about understanding those. They generally run something like 000, 00, 0, 1, 2, 3, 4, and 5, from smallest to largest.

Split-shot sinkers have yet another numbering system that may once have related to the system used in sizing shot for shotgun loads, but it doesn't anymore, so knowing the buckshot system will not help you much, either. Basically, the smallest split-shot is called B, of which 1,700 are required to make a pound. That

Sinkers. Left to right: *clinch-on, egg, dipsey, and split-shot.*

means that each B-size split-shot weighs about 1/100 ounce. The next size is BB, of which there are 825 to the pound, making each one about 1/50 ounce. Then follow 3/0 (approximately 1/25 ounce), 7 (1/16 ounce), 5 (1/10 ounce), 4 (1/8 ounce), 3 (5/32 ounce), and 2 (1/4 ounce). A sectioned box of five assorted sizes (usually BB, 3/0, 7, 5, and 4) is a handy thing to have. Otherwise, I find the 3/0 size to be the most useful; one of them is usually the least weight you will want if you want any weight at all, and if you want more weight, you can keep adding shot without creating a bulky mass that would pick up weeds.

FLOATS

Floats are also called bobbers. Those two names neatly identify the dual purposes of these highly variable devices. First, the float keeps the bait at the proper depth, suspending it a specific distance from the bottom or the surface, depending on your point of view. Second, it provides a visual strike indicator. When the bobber bounces and finally goes under, you have a fish on your line. That being the case, it is necessary that the float stay where it is fastened and be highly visible to the angler while staying as inconspicuous as possible to the fish.

Probably the most popular type of float is the snap-on. It is spherical, plastic, and two-toned, usually red-and-white or orange-and-chartreuse. Either color combination is highly visible under most conditions. The snap-on float connects to your line by way of a tiny metal hook, normally hidden within the bottom of the float. When a button on the top of the float is pushed down, the hook protrudes from the bottom. You make a few turns of your line around the exposed hook at the

Split-shot sinkers may be bought in a dispenser that houses an assortment of sizes.

point you want the float to stay, then let go of the button. The hook retracts against the body of the float, holding your line securely. Snap-on floats come in several sizes from 3/4 to 2 1/2 inches in diameter. As with all floats, use the smallest one that will stay afloat under the weight of your bait, or that will remain visible in rough water.

Another popular float design, especially for panfish, resembles an egg pierced lengthwise by a pencil. This design is particularly effective for telegraphing nibbles while remaining inconspicuous to the fish.

Both designs can be found in models that can be slid up and down your line. Why would you want to do that? Well, imagine fastening a float about four feet above your hook. After you reel in as much line as you can (that is, until the bobber hits your tip-top rod guide), you still have four feet of ungainly line, sinker, hook, and bait to cast. But suppose the float were allowed to slip down

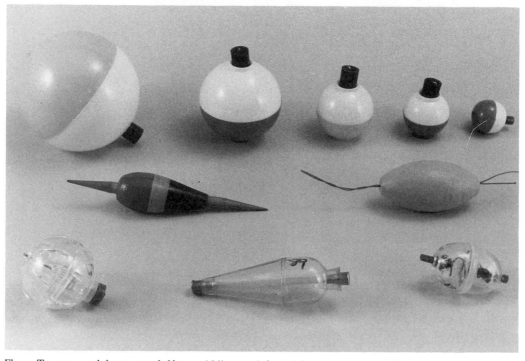

Floats. Top row: *push-button type bobbers;* middle row, left to right: *antique wooden float and foam plastic float;* bottom row: *clear plastic bubble-floats.*

the line until it was stopped by your sinker. Then you could reel in nearly all the line you needed to cast efficiently. So, you cast. Your hook, sinker, float, and line hit the water, and the weight of your sinker pulls the line down through your float until a small bead attached to your line—a bead small enough to have passed through your tip-top but too big to pass through the float—hits the float and stops the hook from sinking farther. This arrangement appears in various guises under many trade names, but basically it may be described as a sliding float with a bobber stop. If you are fishing at depths of less than four feet or so, sliding floats are unnecessary. They are essential, however, in order to fish deep with a float.

There are also clear-plastic bubble-

floats that remain nearly invisible to fish in clear water. These are particularly good for use in baitfishing for trout. They may also be used to cast a fly with a spinning outfit. Normally, flies are much too light to cast with anything but flycasting tackle, but if a bubble-float is attached a couple of feet up the line for weight, the rig can be cast with spinning or spincasting tackle. Only the nearly invisible bubble-floats should be used with this technique, however.

SNAPS AND SNAP SWIVELS

Each time you want to change your lure or hook, you have to cut off the old one and tie on a new one, requiring a new knot (see Chapter 16) each time. Doing so will quickly make you proficient at tying the Improved Clinch Knot, and you will probably not mind tying it several times each day. However, you do have an alternative. You can tie on a snap or snap swivel once and simply unsnap your old lure or hook and snap on a new one.

Basically, a snap is like a safety pin. You tie your line to the loop on one end, and hook your lure onto the clasp at the other end. A snap swivel adds to the snap a rotating ball or barrel that prevents line twist.

As with sinkers, snaps and snap swivels have no consistent numbering system to indicate sizes. Some manufacturers use the hook system of having the numbers get smaller as the snaps get bigger, while others have the numbers get bigger as the snaps get bigger. If you want to use a snap swivel, find a brand that is numbered by the hook system—the bigger the snap, the lower the number—and buy No. 10 or 12 snap swivels.

My stronger recommendation, however, is that you not use snaps at all. I believe they have several disadvantages. First, they represent another possible source of tackle failure when playing a fish; I feel better having my line tied directly to my hook or lure. Second, snaps interfere somewhat with the proper action of many lures. Third, there is evidence that they may scare finicky fish.

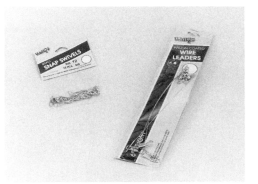

*Snap swivels (*left*) and leaders (*right*) come in packages like these or in plastic boxes.*

Fourth, they make it too easy to change lures. I find it worthwhile to stick with a lure until I am certain I should change. People who use snaps have a tendency to change lures too often, simply because it is so easy to do.

By not using snaps, you are forced to learn how to tie at least one knot well. Soon you will get good enough and fast enough so that you will not mind tying it. However, if tying knots troubles you and impairs your enjoyment of fishing, by all means use snaps.

LEADERS

A leader is a piece of monofilament or nylon-coated stainless-steel wire with a snap swivel on one end and a loop or swivel at the other. Leaders come in lengths from about six inches to as long as three feet. They are generally rated at 20- to 50-pound test.

Leaders are used between your regular line and your hook or lure when fishing for species that have big, sharp teeth. They are much more popular for saltwater fishing, but are regularly used in freshwater fishing for northern pike. You

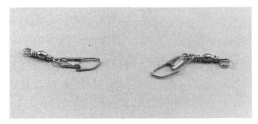

Snap swivels.

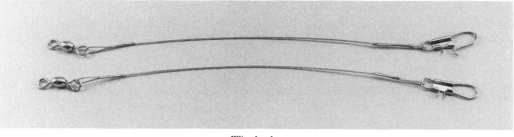

Wire leaders.

will probably not need a leader for most of your fishing, other than the heavy monofilament snells that come permanently attached to snelled hooks.

LANDING NETS

Some people like to use nets, and some do not. It is a matter of both personal preference and heated debate. That makes it typical of many things in fishing. Some anglers claim that using a net on a fish you are planning to release does more harm to the fish than does holding it in your wet hand. Others claim it a far less damaging way of holding a fish than squeezing it in a hand. The battle rages on. With fish you intend to keep, some are more easily landed with the help of a net, while others are not.

You seldom need a net for panfish. Just swing them up on the bank or into the boat, hold them in your hand, and extricate the hook. Bass, even very large ones, can be easily subdued by grasping them by the lower lip and lifting them out of the water. I rarely use a net for bass, although I have sometimes regretted losses that occurred when a partner recklessly lunged at my hooked fish before it was ready to be netted. Pickerel and pike, I believe, are more easily landed with a net. You cannot stick your thumb in their mouths without injuring yourself. Trout that you intend to keep are best netted. They are incredibly slippery and hard to hold otherwise. I suggest you do not net trout that are to be released.

Traditional trout nets have a teardrop-shaped frame of laminated wood and a mesh bag of cotton or nylon. Gamefish nets are usually framed in tubular aluminum and have a mesh bag of polyethylene netting. Trout nets generally have six-inch handles; gamefish nets often have handles as long as three feet.

STRINGERS

You are not likely to go home as soon as you catch a fish. As you continue to fish for more, what are you going to do with the fish you have caught? Most often, sunnies and bluegills are tossed into a large bucket. All other fish should be placed on a stringer. A stringer may be as simple as a length of nylon rope with a ring on one end and a spike on the other. Or it may be a length of chain with large safety-pin-like clips attached along its length. A stringer allows you to safely and securely attach your fish, alive and in the water, to your boat or a bankside shrub until you are ready to go home.

Fish are attached to the stringer by threading the spiked end of the simple design, or the hook of the clip type, into the fish's mouth and out its gill opening, or through the thin membrane just inside the fish's lips. Then the clip is snapped shut, or the spike is passed through the ring at the other end to form a closed loop. The number of fish you can attach to the simple design is limited only by the length of the rope. The clip type is limited by the number of clips, commonly eight to 10.

TACKLE BOXES

You are going to need some way to carry all your hooks, sinkers, floats, lures, and the other assorted fishing paraphernalia that you will be accumulating over the years. Depending on your personality and the amount and type of tackle you have, that job can be turned over to a shoebox with a rubberband wrapped around it, or to a $100 tackle box with neatly compartmentalized drawers, tiers, and shelves.

There is a style of tackle box to suit every taste and everyone's concept of order. If you like the idea of being able to see right through the cover so you can locate a lure before even opening the box, you can have it. If you like deep, roomy, cavernous boxes, they are available. Perhaps you would prefer flat, easy-access cases, or boxes with drawers in the side or rows of shelves that fold out, or boxes specifically designed to hold jars of pork rind or spinnerbaits or plastic worms. No problem. They all exist.

Just keep in mind a few important things before deciding on a tackle box: it should be large enough to hold all the tackle you want to take along; it should

Tackle boxes. This small selection of Plano boxes includes, top row, left to right: *Model 727, Phantom Model 1466, Phantom Model 1468;* bottom row, left to right: *Model 2200; Magnum 1123; Stowaway 3448 (sitting on 1123); Mini-Magnum Pocket Pak 3213; and Model 6300.*

help you keep your equipment organized; it should help you find what you are looking for; it should be made of wormproof plastic (metal rusts, and any box made of a plastic that is not wormproof will melt when it comes in constant contact with plastic worms and other soft-plastic lures); and it should have a good clasp that reveals at a glance whether or not it is fastened (there is nothing worse than inadvertently picking up an unlatched tackle box and dumping its entire contents all over the boat, the dock, or into the lake).

For a start, get a fairly small and simple box, a wormproof plastic model that opens from the top and contains two or three fold-out shelves divided into about 15 compartments. The belly of the box will hold your floats, larger lures, and your stringer. Such a box is the Plano No.

2200, for example, but there are dozens of similar makes and models.

Resist the urge to plan too far ahead. Part of the fun of being a fisherman is to periodically find it necessary to move up to a larger tackle box.

For the fly fisherman, the tackle box is usually replaced by the fishing vest, a multi-pocket garment that can be worn in midstream where the angler would be unable to put down a tackle box. Fly fishermen will also most likely want to invest in a pair of waders, which are discussed in the next chapter.

That should be about all the additional tackle you will need for a while. And even some of the items mentioned are expendable. Yet you may be amazed at how much additional, questionably useful stuff you will accumulate from now on.

14

Boats and Not Boats

There are basically only three places you can be while fishing: on shore (bank-fishing), on the water (fishing from a boat of some sort), or in the water (wading).

The most limiting situation, of course, is to be on shore. You can reach fish only as far from shore as you can cast your bait or lure. You can cover water only near those spots from which casting is possible. And you can gain access to the water's edge only in those areas where vegetation, solid ground, and public access allow. On some ponds and streams, that situation does not leave much room. Despite those limitations, however, bank-fishing is a popular, rewarding, and unencumbering way to go. You need haul only your tackle and lures or bait. Sunfish, bluegills, perch, bullheads, bass, pickerel, and trout are all commonly caught from shore with both live bait and artificials.

There is no question, though, that having access to some form of watercraft will put you in touch with a lot more fish, or at least a lot more water that potentially holds fish. Your fishing is no longer limited to the length of your casts, and even shallow-water areas that are inaccessible from the shore can often be reached by boat. And such areas are often perfect habitat for bass and pickerel. Having a boat also allows you to troll, a technique by which bait or a lure is towed behind a moving boat (discussed in depth in Chapter 15).

The most common small boats for freshwater fishing are canoes, johnboats, rowboats, and bass boats. All should be equipped with a good anchor. Canoes, of

Fishing from a canoe.

Johnboats are flat-bottomed and square-ended.

course, have been around for a long time. They are certainly a favorite on northern lakes, and are commonly used for all kinds of lake and river fishing. They are highly maneuverable, can get into extremely tight and shallow places, and can even be driven by small gas or electric motors. If they have a disadvantage, it is that their stability may be less than perfect during the playing and netting of a big fish, and standing up in them—often a desirable thing to do while fishing—is not advisable.

Johnboats, on the other hand, are quite stable while still being fairly maneuverable and able to float on very shallow water. Additionally, johnboats have a flat bottom, which allows you to comfortably store tackle on the floor of the boat. Johnboats can be rowed or driven by small gas or electric motors. You can stand up in a

johnboat as well. Some are small enough to carry on top of a car, while even the larger sizes can be trailered behind a small car with ease.

Rowboats are similar to johnboats in many of their advantages. The V-hulled ones, however, though better able to cut through rough water than a johnboat, lack the advantages and comfort of a flat bottom. Still, rowboats are roomy and stable and can be rowed or driven by electric or gas outboards. They can also be easily trailered or cartopped—depending on the relative sizes of the boat and the vehicle, of course.

Bass boats are specialized craft that usually include such features as pedestal seats and a raised, carpeted casting deck. The better-equipped ones also come furnished with aerated live wells, rod lockers, electronic depth gauges, a bow-

Fishing from a rowboat. The Walker Agency photo.

Bass boats are specialized craft characterized by pedestal seats.

mounted electric trolling motor, and a large outboard motor capable of moving the thing at speeds of up to 65 m.p.h.—to name just a few features. It is clearly a boat made for the effective and comfortable catching of bass. It is not particularly appropriate for fishing small lakes and ponds.

Another way to reach fish is to wade or walk in the water. Much fishing for trout or smallmouth bass in streams and shallow rivers is done by wading. Wading is also practiced along the edges of ponds and lakes. Wading allows you to cast your lure over fish that cannot be reached from shore, and it gets you away from the shoreline shrubbery so you can cast at all. Trout streams are inevitably lined with trees and shrubs that prevent the shorebound flycaster from even attempting to fish properly.

In order to stay dry while wading, anglers wear nylon or rubber overalls, called waders, that go on over their pants. There are three common styles of waders. Stocking-foot chest-high waders are worn with a separate pair of wading shoes. They are like heavy nylon or rubber stockings that extend all the way up to

your armpits and are held up by suspenders. Boot-foot chest waders have rubber boots attached. You slip your feet into the boots and pull the rest of the pants up to your armpits. They, too, are

Fly fisherman wearing chest waders. Red Ball photo.

Fisherman wearing hip waders. Red Ball photo.

Belly boats are propelled by flippers or paddles worn on the angler's feet. Bass Pro Shops photo.

held up by suspenders. Hip waders are boot-foot waders that extend only up to the upper thighs. They are held up by attaching each separate leg-top to your belt. Obviously, they are for shallow streams.

Somewhere between wading and boating comes the belly boat. This is simply an innertube equipped with a canvas seat. Wearing waders and foot paddles, the angler sits in the tube and floats around in the water. Belly boats are best used relatively near shore. They are very handy and transportable and can certainly increase your range in lieu of a boat. Their main disadvantage is that they do not provide a really firm base from which to solidly strike and play a big fish. Belly boaters have been known to be towed around by good-size fish.

Those are the most common options for freshwater fishing in average-size lakes, ponds, streams, and rivers. Most experienced fishermen enjoy all of these methods at one time or another and for one species of fish or another. The absolute beginner should try each one as soon as practicable.

15

Trolling

Trolling is basically the technique of towing a live bait or artificial lure behind a moving boat. It is an excellent way to expose your lure to a large number of fish while learning the lake, finding out where the fish are, taking in the scenery, going for a nice ride, lessening the feeling that you are fishing in the wrong place, staving off boredom, and otherwise enjoying a nice day. You can also catch plenty of fish. Trolling is not particularly effective for catching sunnies, bluegills, or bullheads, but yellow perch, crappies, bass, pickerel, pike, walleyes, and trout—all of which are in the habit of chasing fast-moving prey—will respond to the technique.

For the absolute beginner with access to a boat of some kind, trolling is the way to go on slow rivers and on lakes of, say, 50 acres or more. If you are alone, you will need a small gas or electric outboard, for it is difficult to row and troll properly by yourself. But if you have someone along who will paddle or row while you fish, trolling can be accomplished effectively from an unmotorized canoe or rowboat.

The basic principle is simple: instead of sitting in one spot and casting your lure out and then reeling it back in to give it action, you cast it out, leave it out there, and move the boat, dragging the lure behind. At the proper speed, the lure will display exactly the same actions as if you were reeling it in, except that it never gets reeled in. It just travels around the lake behind your boat, in view of all the hungry fish in all the spots you pass. Only when you actually get a strike—or pick up weeds—is it necessary to reel in your line.

You can imagine how effective this technique might be for locating good

Trolling is the technique of towing a lure or bait behind a moving boat. The Walker Agency photo.

areas in which to anchor and cast. (The one limitation of trolling, of course, is that you are always just passing through. If you think you have located a productive fishing area by trolling, you will want to fish it more thoroughly by anchoring near the spot and casting to it.)

But trolling is effective only if done correctly, and that involves using the right types of lures and following some simple techniques.

You can troll with any type of tackle. If you have a fly rod, you will probably do best to use streamers or live baits such as a nightcrawler, minnow, or crayfish. With baitcasting, spinning, or spincasting tackle, many of the standard artificials

will work well, including some crankbaits, spoons, spinners, jigs, spinnerbaits, and plastic worms. You can also use a nightcrawler or other live bait.

Trolling is done at a fairly uniform speed, usually about as fast as a person can walk, which is around five miles per hour. That factor being more or less constant, the lure's characteristics and distance behind the boat are going to determine how deep it swims. The depth of the lure is very important when trolling. Quite honestly, it is difficult for me to tell you at what depth you should troll. Different species of fish are often found at different depths. Water, temperature, weather, season, light, and numerous other conditions will determine at what depths various fish are likely to be found at any particular time. Part of the process of trolling—and of fishing in general—is to find out where the fish are, not only in what area of the lake but at what depth as well.

But I can advise against two conditions: you do not want your lure to be water-skiing on the surface, nor do you want it running so deep that it is constantly grabbing weeds and bottom debris. Therefore, do not use surface lures for trolling, and do not use lures that dive extremely deep or that are very heavy, unless you are trolling a very deep lake. With crank-baits, do not troll with surface disturbers, poppers, stickbaits, or other buoyant lures that are designed to stay on the surface. Floater/divers are fine, however, because they dive under the surface when in motion. Some spoons and spinners also have a tendency to rise to the surface when trolled, but others work quite well and run at a good depth. You will have to experiment with lures to be certain they stay down at a reasonable depth.

Running too deeply is just as bad. If a floater/diver or sinker/diver crankbait is designed to dive to a depth of 10 feet and you are trolling in water that is only eight feet deep, your lure will be constantly dredging the bottom and will soon be so loaded with weeds that fish will see nothing but a moving salad. The same is true when trolling a jig or spinnerbait; if the weight of the lure is too heavy for the speed you are travelling, it will drag bottom and be ineffectual, not to mention a complete nuisance.

To a certain extent, the depth at which your lure rides as you troll can be controlled by how much line you let out behind the boat. This is a little tricky,

though, because some lures are designed to run deeper as you let out line—until a certain point. Then they begin to rise as more line is let out. Even experienced trollers can be fooled by this phenomenon and may have their lure running just inches below the surface while they think it is running near the bottom. Nonetheless, up to a point, you can assume that your lure will run deeper as you let out line. That point will vary with the lure, but you will usually still be okay at 50 feet. Now let's take a test run, and you can learn how to do it.

Let us assume that you are using bait-casting, spinning, or spincasting tackle and that you are sitting on the stern seat of a johnboat or rowboat while running the outboard motor with your left hand. To your line you have tied a Mister Twister-type spinnerbait, the soft-plastic part of which is about two inches long. Your line is tied to the small loop in the overhead spinner arm's elbow. Because of the way you have to sit—turned slightly toward your left—in order to steer and control the motor, it will be most comfortable for you to fish off the left side of the boat.

When you get to know the lake better, you will know in which areas you want to troll, but for a start, try an area that is relatively quiet (where few other boats are anchored and there are no swimmers, water skiers, or rocks) and perhaps where you can run parallel to an expanse of lily pads or other surface weeds. While running along the edge of the weeds and about 10 or 15 feet out from it (keep the weeds on your left side), slow the boat to walking speed, and cast your lure out behind. A short cast of about 20 feet is fine.

When the lure hits the water, let it fall for a second or two, and then snub the

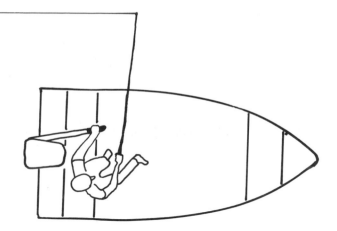

An overhead view showing the proper solo trolling posture.

line with your finger or thumb, depending on which type of reel you are using (if you are using a baitcasting reel, stop the spool with your thumb; with a spinning or spincasting reel, stop the line with your index finger). You can, of course, stop the line from coming off the reel by giving the crank a turn, but you will be letting more line out in a moment, so leave the reel in its freespool or open-bail position.

Point your rod straight out from the side of the boat so that it is parallel to the water. Rest your elbow on your knee if you wish, but never let any part of the rod or line rest on anything. It is through the rod and line that important information will be telegraphed to your hand from the lure, so you don't want anything dampening those signals.

Now relax, watch the tip of your rod, and feel the signals that are reaching your hand. If your lure is running freely through open water, your rod tip will have only a little bend in it, and you will feel nothing much. If that is the case, lift your thumb or finger from the reel just enough

to allow a controlled amount of line out—about five feet—and snub it again. Wait a second or two. If nothing changes, let out another five feet and snub it again. What you are waiting for is the sensation of intermittent, gentle taps and the sight of your rod tip momentarily bending and then straightening out again. That signal will mean that your lure is travelling freely along through the very tops of subsurface weeds. That is where you want it, and when you see and feel that happening, crank your reel the one turn needed to take it out of freespool or close the bail.

If, however, your rod tip has taken on a moderate but pronounced bend that does not intermittently straighten out, and there is a dull weight or frequent heavy tugs on your line, your lure is running too deep and picking up weeds. Reel it in, pick off the weeds entirely, and cast again, but do not make quite so long a cast, and do not let the lure fall too far after it hits the water. You want to feel the light, intermittent taps described above.

It is difficult for the beginner to tell the difference between weeds and fish. When in doubt, strike back. If it is a weed, it will either let go or hang on with a dead, dragging weight. A fish, on the other hand, will usually let you know that there is something alive on the end of your line that very much objects to the direction in which it is being led. A fish will also hit quite solidly, feeling as though the lure has bumped into something much less yielding than any flexible plant material could ever be. A real strike feels exciting and sends great gushes of adrenaline pumping through your drowsing brain.

When you do get a real hit, it is best to throw the motor into neutral or kill it altogether. That way, you are not fighting the fish against the added drag of your forward motion through the water.

Now, unfortunately, it is also possible to troll the entire extent of your chosen area and not get a hit. In that case, try this: reel in your line and turn your boat around so that the lily pads are now on your right side. Cast over your left shoulder again, just as you did before, and follow the edge of the pads back along the same path you took coming up. Because your rod is now pointed *away* from the pads, your lure is now travelling 10 or 12 feet (twice the length of your rod) farther from the pads than it was before. That may make a lot of difference. Again, find the depth at which your lure is just tapping the tops of the subsurface weeds without getting hung up. With practice, you will learn to accurately picture what your lure would be seeing if it were alive.

If an area proves unproductive, try moving closer to shore or farther out into deeper water, or try an entirely new area.

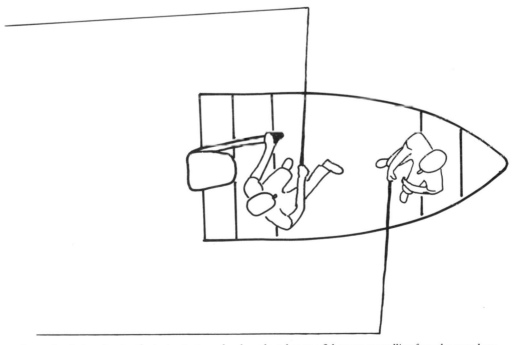

An overhead view showing the proper posture of each angler when two fishermen are trolling from the same boat.

Try a similar lure of a different color, or try another type of lure entirely. You will soon learn which lures are nightmarish weed-collectors and which are pleasant to troll.

Once you get a strike, you may wish to anchor and cast to the area, exploring it more thoroughly than is possible while trolling. I have seen times, however, when the fish would strike only a trolled lure. You never know.

By the way, in case you are not the one running the motor, you should sit up in the bow of the boat and face the stern, again fishing toward your left side. For righties, anyway, this is the most comfortable position. More importantly, though, if the person running the motor is also trolling, he has no choice but to fish his left side, so you will want to fish the other side to avoid getting in your partner's way. If you are in the bow of a canoe with someone else paddling from the stern, face forward and fish off the left side; the paddler will probably not be trolling at the same time.

If you intend to troll with flycasting tackle, follow the same procedures as I have described for the other types of tackle. The only real difference is that you may need to use a sinking-tip line to get your streamer down to the proper level.

I find trolling to be a wonderful way to keep slow days from getting boring. At least you are on the move, constantly exploring new territory. You are putting your lure within sight of more fish than is possible while casting or stillfishing during the same amount of time. And when a fish hits a trolled lure, it always feels bigger than it really is. All of those factors make trolling a fun technique for introducing beginners—especially youngsters short on patience—to fishing. And often it is the most productive way to fish a body of water.

16

Knots

The most common cause of lost fish is knot failure. Nothing else I can say could possibly underscore more strongly the need for you to learn how to tie a few good knots properly.

There are hundreds of fishing knots, and serious anglers maintain a working knowledge of many of them, for all have their proper uses in specific situations. Entire books are written about knots. The knot enthusiast can spend the rest of his life learning new variations; those less zealous can quickly master a good repertoire of about a dozen knots that will handle all their fishing needs.

The beginner need not master more than six—but those six must be mastered. Bad knots will ruin your fishing and frustrate all the effort you have put into learning this new pursuit. That may sound like

an overstatement, but I am trying to stress the fact that knots, though seemingly inconsequential in comparison to rods and reels and zillions of lure designs, are to be taken seriously.

The most important concept for you to accept is that all knots are not equal. Some knots slip; they do not hold in monofilament nylon line. Some knots are too bulky; they get hung up in your rod guides, which may cost you a fish or make casting a nightmare. But most important, some knots lower the breaking strength of your line to such a degree that the 10-pound test on your reel may actually be able to withstand only five or six (or even fewer) pounds of stress—just because of an improper knot.

Knots have specific applications. There are different knots for tying line to your hook or lure, for tying line to your reel, for making a loop in line, for joining two pieces of mono, and for many other purposes beyond the scope of this book. Even a well-tied knot used for the wrong application can cost you a fish. And the correct knot poorly tied is always a disaster waiting to happen.

So learn the following six knots carefully. Practice and master them *before* you go fishing. The place to perfect your knot-tying skill is at home, in good light, while you have plenty of time and patience to try, try again. The place *not* to do it is in a boat or waist-deep in a stream, in the failing light of evening or the full heat of day with sweat dripping into your eyes, while fish are splashing all around you and all you want to do is get your hook into the water as fast as possible.

These six knots should serve you for a while. When you are no longer an absolute beginner, you may find applications that call for the learning of new knots. In all cases, take them seriously, and choose the ones that come recommended by experts.

And here's a warning: there are plenty of benighted individuals out there with fishing rods who will tell you that the best way to keep a knot from slipping is to melt the end of your mono with a match or cigarette. Never do it. First of all, the knots included in this chapter, if properly tied, do not slip. And second, the heat of a match or cigarette may well weaken the knot so it is no longer reliable.

Six Knots for the Absolute Beginner

Reel Knot

This is a simple and secure knot for tying the end of your mono or braided line (in the case of fly-line backing) to your empty reel spool. The following illustrations show you how.

Reel Knot: Make a simple overhand knot in the end of the line.

Pull the knot tight.

Feed the end around the spool. Using the end of the line containing the knot, tie another overhand knot around the main part of the line.

Pull the knot tight.

Pull steadily on the main line until the knot tightens around the spool. Then keep pulling until the first knot jams up against the second. Trim the excess with a nail clipper, and reel the line onto the spool.

Improved Clinch Knot

   This knot is used to tie your line snugly to the eye of a hook, to the line-tie ring of a lure, or to the loop of a snap swivel. You can also use it to tie your line to the loop on the snell of a hook, but there is a better method (see the Double Surgeon's Knot, below). For the sake of verbal economy, let us assume you are tying your line to the eye of a hook. This knot has a breaking strength equal to 95 percent of that of the unknotted line. The illustrations will guide you through the Improved Clinch Knot.

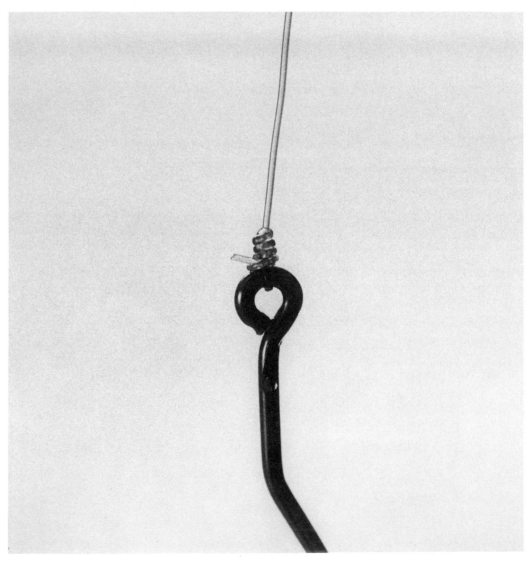

Improved Clinch Knot.

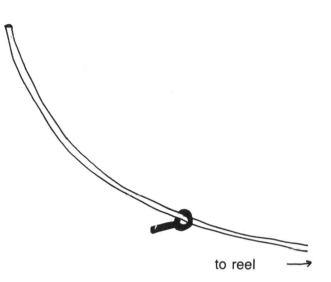

to reel →

Holding the hook in your left hand, thread about six inches of line through the eye. With your left thumb and forefinger, hold the line firmly against the eye.

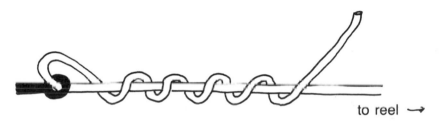

to reel →

With your right hand, hold the main line taut while winding the short end back over the main line exactly five times, using your right thumb and forefinger.

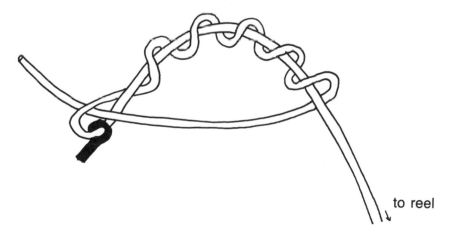

to reel

Poke the end back through the first loop, nearest the eye, and grab it with your left thumb and forefinger.

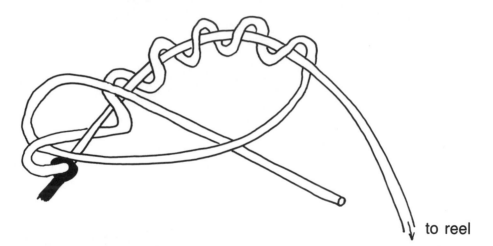

to reel

Now poke that end through the big loop just formed by the end and the twisted part. Grip the end in your front teeth, and lick all parts of the knot thoroughly to help it tighten smoothly.

Pull slowly, steadily, and equally in all three directions with your teeth on the end, your right hand on the main line, and your left hand on the hook until the knot is snug. Trim the end closely with a clipper.

When the knot is properly tied, it should look just like the illustration. If it does not, do it over.

Jansik Special

This knot serves the same purposes as the Improved Clinch Knot, above, and is suggested as an alternate for those who find the other too difficult. Children especially may find this one easier to tie. My father taught it to me when he first took me fishing at about the age of five. The Jansik Special has a breaking strength equal to 98 to 100 percent of that of the unknotted line. The following illustrations will help you learn it.

Jansik Special.

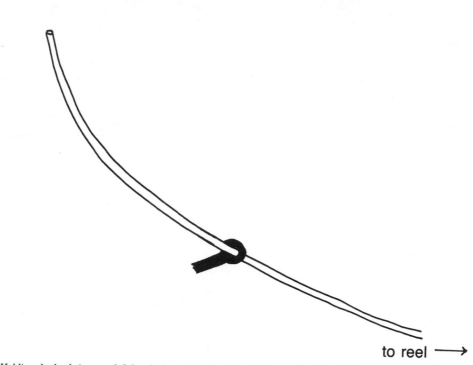

to reel →

Holding the hook in your left hand, thread the line through the eye for about eight inches. With your left thumb and forefinger, pinch the line firmly against the eye and hold it there.

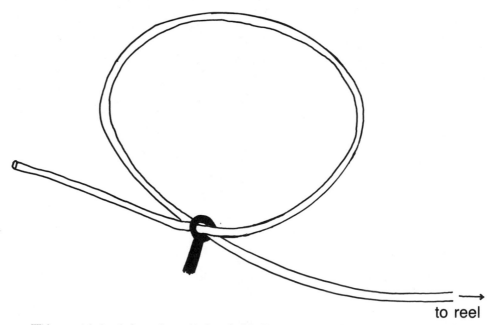

to reel →

With your right hand, form a loop with the end of the line, and thread it through the eye a second time.

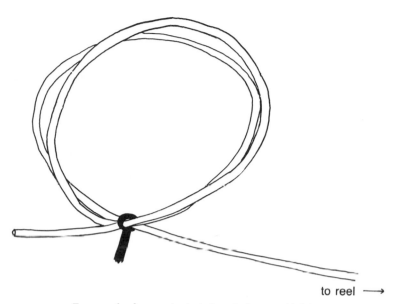

to reel ⟶

Form another loop, and poke it through the eye a third time.

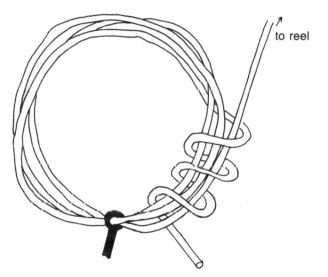

to reel

Form another loop, but instead of pushing the end through the eye for a fourth time, wrap it three times around the three strands of mono that form the side of the big loop. Grip the end in your front teeth, and lick all parts of the knot to help it tighten down smoothly.

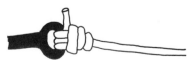

Pull equally, slowly, and firmly in three directions with your teeth on the end, your left hand on the hook, and your right hand on the main line. Trim the end closely with a clipper.

Double Surgeon's Knot

This knot makes a quick and easy job of forming a loop in the end of a line. The beginner may want to do that in two possible situations. First, you may wish to interlock two loops—the one already provided at the end of a snell and the one you will be tying in the end of your line—rather than tying either an Improved Clinch Knot or a Jansik Special to the loop on the snell. Second, when attaching a tippet to a fly-line leader, the interlocking-loops system is strongest and easiest. You will therefore need to know this simple knot.

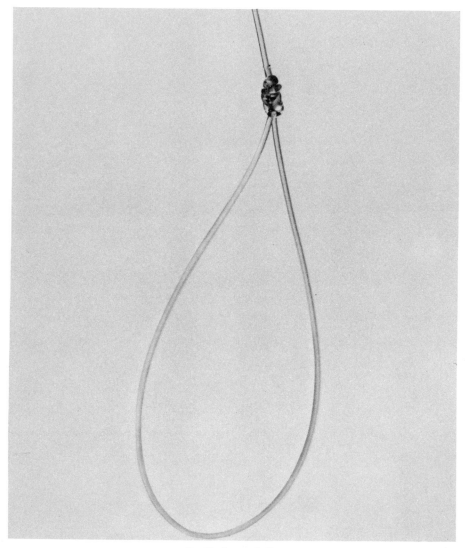

Double Surgeon's Knot.

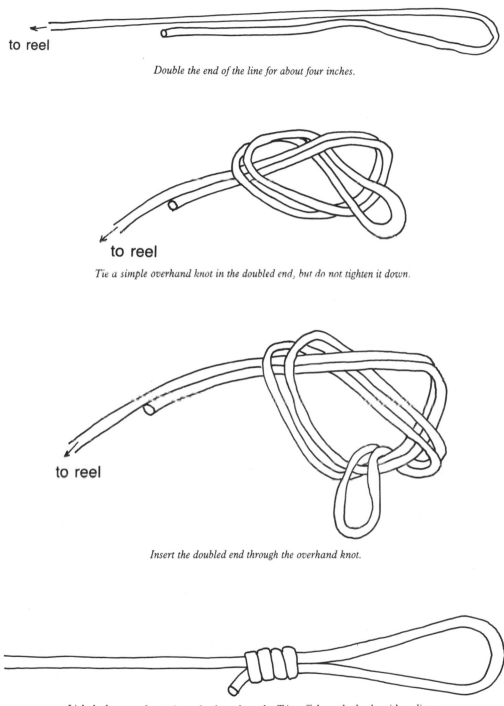

to reel

Double the end of the line for about four inches.

to reel

Tie a simple overhand knot in the doubled end, but do not tighten it down.

to reel

Insert the doubled end through the overhand knot.

Lick the knot, and snug it up slowly and evenly. Trim off the ends closely with a clipper.

Now, join two loops together (the loop of a snelled hook and the loop you have just made on the end of your line).

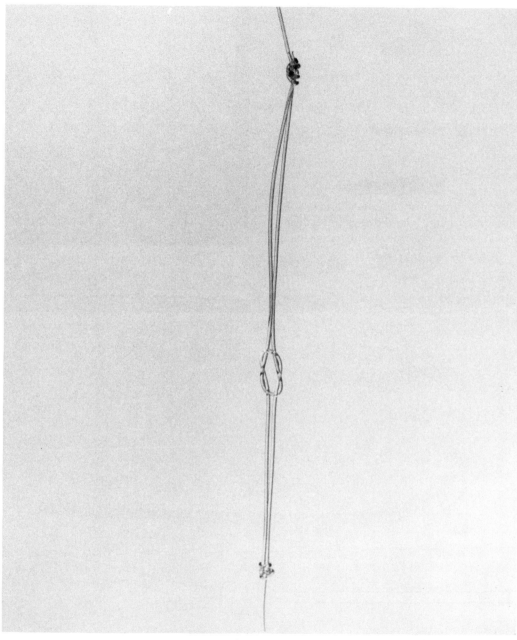

Joined loops.

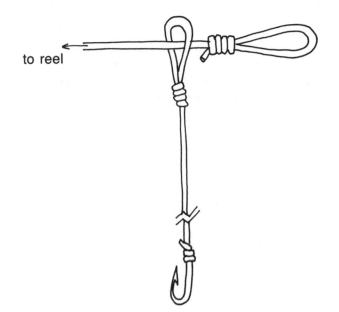

Insert your line-end loop entirely through the loop in the snell.

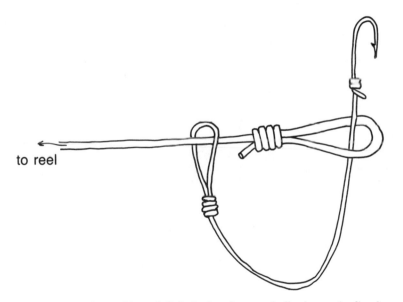

Insert the hook up through your line-end loop. Pull the hook and your main line in opposite directions until the loops interlock.

This method lets you remove and replace snelled hooks and tippets in seconds, without retying knots.

Duncan Loop Knot

When you tie a lure to your line with either the Improved Clinch Knot or the Jansik Special, the knot is pressed snugly against the line-tie ring. For some lures that have a wide-swinging, side-to-side action, that kind of knot is restrictive and may interfere with the lure's proper action. The solution is to use a knot with a sliding loop. During retrieval of the lure, the loop is open and nonrestrictive, but when a fish strikes, the knot slides down and tightens against the ring. Follow the step-by-step illustrations.

Duncan Loop Knot.

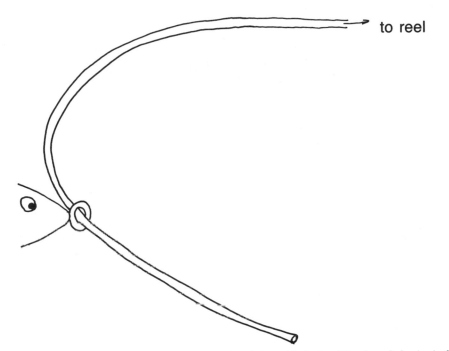

Holding the lure in your left hand and the line in your right, thread about eight inches of line through the ring in the lure.

Bend the end of the line back and under the main line so that it lies parullel to it. Hold both strands with your left thumb and forefinger.

Bend the end back toward the lure once more so that the line forms an S.

to reel

Holding all three strands with your left thumb and forefinger, wrap the end five times around the two upper strands together, but not the bottom one. Hold both the end and the main line with your right thumb and forefinger, and start pulling the lure with your left hand. Stop pulling when the windings tighten up but before the knot closes down on the ring.

At this point, use your teeth or a pliers to pull on the end to tighten the knot, which will be able to slide up and down the line, leaving a loose loop around the ring.

Take care that the knot does not slide *too* easily, for you do not want it to tighten down during the cast, only on a strike.

Blood Knot

This knot is for the purpose of joining two pieces of mono of either the same or dissimilar diameters. It is used extensively in the building of knotted, tapered fly-line leaders, for tying a tippet to a leader when the interlocking-loop system is not used, and for emergency repairs on line used for baitcasting, spinning, or spincasting. It retains 90 to 95 percent of the unknotted line's breaking strength. The absolute beginner may not use this one much, but you had better know it. It is a good one.

Blood knot.

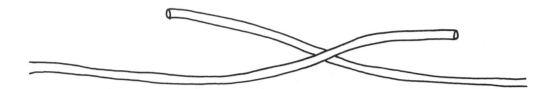

Hold about eight inches of one line and eight inches of the other line in each hand, and cross them to form an X. With your right thumb and forefinger, squeeze the intersection of the X firmly.

With your left hand, working only on the left side of the X, wind the short end five times around the other main line.

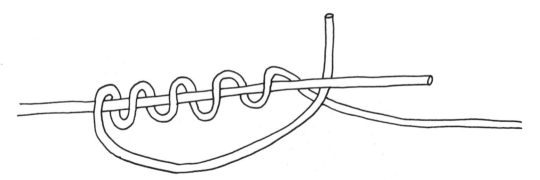

Bend the short end back toward your right hand, and insert it up through the crotch of the X on the right side. Switch hands carefully so that you now hold the strands in your left hand.

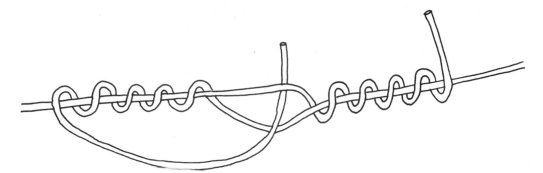

Using your right hand, and working on the right side of the X, wind the remaining short end five times around the other main line.

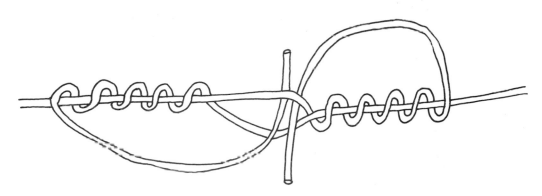

Bend the end back and tuck it into the same space as you did the other end, but from the opposite direction. *If the first end comes* up *through the space, the second end must go* down *through the same space.*

Lick all the windings thoroughly, and pull the two main lines in opposite directions until the windings all snug up. If both lines are 10-pound test or stronger, tighten the knot with a quick yank. Weaker mono must be pulled slowly to avoid breaking it. Trim the ends closely with a clipper.

17

Fishing High-Tech

Sooner or later, you are going to realize either that fishing is not going to become a significant part of your leisure activities or that you are hooked. In the latter case, you will sooner or later pick up an outdoor magazine, open a fishing-tackle catalog, or browse through a tackle shop and be struck by the realization that there is considerably more tackle on which to spend your money than I have mentioned in this book.

Today's tackle comes in almost infinite variations of colors, sizes, and designs of lures; designs and action characteristics of rods and reels; strengths of line; and designs of tackle boxes. But beyond that variety—beyond what I consider to be the "necessities" of fishing—are the gizmos, the doo-dads, the gimmicks, and the gadgets. And in this age of miniaturization and microchips, some of them exhibit the most fascinating assortment of features ever seen within 10 feet of a minnow bucket.

This abundance of high-tech fishing paraphernalia coincides with the emergence of tournament bass fishing. There are today a number of professional fishermen who, like golf and tennis pros, make six-figure incomes by landing more or bigger bass than anyone else. Naturally, those pros become national celebrities within the fishing community, and so they also become valuable advertising vehicles to every company that has a fishing-related product to sell. And because the mail-order outfits that publish large catalogs, the tackle shops, and the companies that advertise in outdoor magazines are all in business to sell products, there is a high profile to a competitive fishing mentality. Even the casual angler

The age of electronic fishing has arrived.

cannot help but get the message that catching more and bigger fish is somehow critical to his enjoyment of life and his worth as a human being.

People who fish for a living—on the tournament circuit or commercially—do have a need for the most advanced technological gizmos available. Their reputations and livelihoods depend on the edge they can get by whatever means are legally allowed. But you and I do not. We can fish with a bent pin, if need be, and have a good time. Yet all the advertising and hype attendant to the new high-tech fishing gimcracks are directed largely at *us*. The pros are *given* the stuff gratis by the manufacturers with the hope of future

endorsements. *We* are the ones who are being asked to buy.

With all that in mind, you will ultimately have to decide for yourself what kinds of fishing toys—or tools, depending on your perspective—will make your angling more enjoyable. All I can do is offer you a brief and incomplete review of the kinds of things you will be seduced by and to suggest those things that really do have merit for simple, old-fashioned, non-competitive fishing.

GRAPHITE RODS

Not all high-tech advances involve electronics. In the case of rod design and manufacture, improvements are material- and design-related. Graphite has far surpassed fiberglass as the current material of choice, for it is lighter, stronger, and more sensitive. No doubt there will be yet a newer twist in rod manufacture before long, and the fishing public will be asked to shell out more money for the new development.

My experience has taught me that any technological advances that increase the sensitivity of a fishing rod are to be welcomed. Even the casual angler can appreciate the increased enjoyment of being able to feel more information being telegraphed from his lure to his fingertips. It is not just a matter of catching more fish; it is a matter of more intense and perceptive experiences in general.

In achieving greater sensitivity, rod manufacturers have not only adopted the more sensitive materials but also have developed a trend toward more sensitivity in rod design. That factor is manifested mainly in one-piece rods and in rods in which a section of the rod-blank is exposed to the angler's fingertips through the grip. A one-piece model has a characteristic pool-cue shape in which the rod gradually broadens from the tip to the butt until the rod itself becomes wide enough to be the handle. Because you are actually holding the whole rod in your hand, uninsulated by a separate grip, sensitivity is maximized. The design in which an exposed section of the blank is in contact with your fingertips through the conventional grip is also highly sensitive, but looks more traditional.

If you have dollar bills burning holes in your pocket, this is one area in which to invest them. A good rod is highly worthwhile.

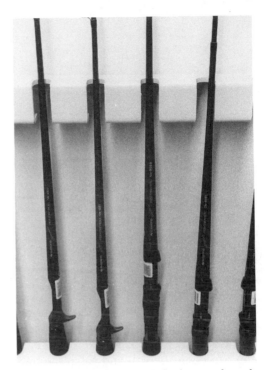

Shimano's Fightin' Rods, one make that uses the pool-cue design.

HIGH-TECH REELS

Reel designs have been changing like crazy, particularly in baitcasting but to some extent in spinning reels as well. The focus for baitcasting reels has been to eliminate the inherent backlash problem, and technological advances have mainly taken the form of mechanical rather than electronic solutions. Magnetic anti-backlash adjustments in conjunction with deeply V-ed spools have significantly changed the look, if not actually the operation, of baitcasting reels.

I own and use some of those new baitcasting reels, but I am still not convinced that they are enough of an improvement

Shimano's Speedmaster, the first of the high-speed reels.
The Walker Agency photo.

over the older designs to justify the price differences.

Spinning reels need no such improvement, so the manufacturers have focused on different features. Now spinning reels are available with one-hand operation; you can open the bail and catch the line on your finger in one step, with one hand. Unless you only *have* one hand, I'm not sure I fully appreciate the genius in that. But as the French say: *"Chacun a son goût."*

Both types of reels are also being manufactured with high-speed gear ratios for faster line retrieval. Gear ratios of 4:1 to 5:1 were once the norm, but today ratios of 6:1 and higher are being introduced. It is always essential to keep a tight line on a hooked fish, so fast retrieves can be a real boon. Such reels may, however, make it difficult to crank a lure slowly enough to get the fish to strike in the first place. They are worth checking, though.

The electronic additions to both baitcasting and spinning reels are little short of outrageous. Models now exist with built-in microcomputers that tell you the length of your cast, how much line you have out, and your rate of retrieval,

among other data. That kind of information may be important, but it is information that every good angler develops a feel for all by himself, without doubling the cost of his equipment.

LINE

The major companies that manufacture fishing lines are in a constant race to come up with something to make their line the one of choice. Occasionally, a new development is more than simply cosmetic. DuPont, for example, has developed a cofilament (as opposed to monofilament) line—a low-stretch polyester core within an abrasion-resistant nylon sheath—that represents a truly high-tech change in line design. The company claims the new line is significantly less stretchy than standard mono, thereby improving its hook-setting capabilities. As of this writing, though, some anglers claim that the two filaments tend to separate. They refuse to use the stuff for that and a variety of other reasons.

Berkley, another leader in line manufacture, has developed a new TriPolymer process for uniting three complimentary polymers into a monofilament line. It

Two new lines.

claims that the new line, TriMax, is stronger, has a higher degree of dry-to-wet stability (standard mono lines are strength-tested dry but lose significant strength when wet), casts farther, and is more sensitive than both standard mono and cofilament lines. Whether those claims are totally valid is less significant than the breakthrough in packaging that has been introduced along with the new line. TriMax comes in a dispenser that hangs on your rod and has an adjustable drag so that you can wind new line onto your reel without the help of a second party (someone to hold the spool of new line while you reel), while maintaining precise tension on the line. It is the sort of ingenuity that is sure to be copied soon, but Berkley deserves praise for the idea.

Such developments should be tested first-hand by the angler, for line is one of the most important components of tackle. The small investment in a spool of new line is a good one to make in the pursuit of increased fishing enjoyment.

DEPTH GAUGES AND RECORDERS

This category of gear is where microchip circuitry really comes into its own. There are so many advancements coming so fast in this field that nearly anything I might write here could be obsolete by the time you read it. Most of these devices are more than their names imply. No longer do they simply gauge or graph the depth of the water beneath your boat. Most are now capable of displaying on a screen an accurate representation of the bottom contour, weed growth, structure, and fish within a 15 to 20 degree cone angle beneath your boat. With most, you can operate on different depth ranges, get

A depth-sounder/fish-finder using a liquid crystal display (LCD).

A flasher-type depthsounder.

digital readouts of various data, and even in some cases zoom in for a closer look at details. Some even indicate fish in color. Such units provide almost a closed-circuit TV picture of what is going on underwater.

Most pros have these devices aboard their boats, yet they do not catch every fish they locate, meaning that finding fish and catching them are two different things—something I have known all along. Certainly these devices are far from necessary for the beginning angler.

WATER-CONDITION METERS

These devices include temperature gauges, oxygen-level gauges, and pH meters. A slew of these electronic instruments are now on the market, and each has a professional advocate who swears that one or another water-condition factor is the most important criterion for catching fish.

The truth, of course, is that all water factors have their effects on fish behavior—after all, the fish have to live in the stuff. But unless you lug around an entire water-analysis laboratory and study changing conditions in specific locations over long periods of time, you have not a prayer of understanding what your readings will mean in terms of a day's fishing. Random readings of any one isolated factor will not tell you much, with the possible exception of pH.

I have used a pH meter while fishing, mainly because I am involved in the monitoring of the effects of acid rain in my area, and I have found a direct relationship between high acidity and lousy fishing. That finding holds true even when acidity is part of the natural, seasonal cycle of a lake due to plant chemistry and other temporary, natural factors. In areas where I get readings lower than six, I no longer bother to fish. A pH meter can help you to quickly eliminate unproductive water if your time is too precious to allow simple trial-and-error methods.

LURE-COLOR INDICATORS

As of this writing, I am short on hard fact but long on opinion about these gizmos. I have used one for a couple of seasons and cannot say that I did any better by using a lure of the color suggested by the indicator than by using one of my own choosing based on intuition. Sometimes, though, my own choice worked better than the machine's.

These electronic indicators generally consist of a light-reading probe connected by a very long wire to a meter. The wire is marked off in feet, so you can easily determine the depth of the probe. By noting at what depth the probe is still visible, you can determine the clarity of the water, and the meter will indicate the most visible color at the depth of the

Lake Systems Division's pH Guide.

Lake Systems Division's Color-C-Lector.

probe under the current degree of clarity, angle, intensity of light, etc.

There is nothing wrong with the theory behind this instrument. In fact, it is ingenious. I just wish the fish were better informed of it. Perhaps the problem is that the most visible color is not necessarily the color that is the most appetizing.

If you must have a toy to monkey around with, this one is kind of fun. But it is a long way from necessary.

CHEMICAL FISH-ATTRACTANTS

A number of brands of squirt-on, rub-on, or spray-on goop are claimed to make your artificial lures more attractive to fish. After using many of them for reasonable amounts of time, I can say that they necessitate the carrying of a towel or rag to wipe the stuff off your hands, and they seem, if not quite to *attract* fish, at least not to *repel* them. I cannot say for certain that any one of them improved my fishing. Yet there are fishermen—including some whose opinion I respect—who swear by these chemicals.

The best I can say in favor of these products is that they do serve the useful purpose of masking the fish-repelling

Two types of fish attractants.

odors of gasoline, motor oil, deodorant, after shave, insect repellent, and others that we tend to transfer from ourselves to our lures. That may be reason enough to use them on occasion.

The bottom line is simply this: fishing is for fun. If a gizmo or gimmick will increase your fishing fun and you can afford it, buy it. If it turns out to be more of a burden than an asset, get rid of it. Just remember that none of these extras is necessary unless you are a professional—no matter what the media might like you to believe.

Conclusion

It may be that I have given you more information about freshwater fishing than some people would deem appropriate for the absolute beginner. And there are probably other areas in which some people would deem the proffered information insufficient. So be it.

I have tried to take you from a state of total or near-total ignorance about freshwater fishing to a point at which you can actually do some successful fishing and enjoy it. You now know at least the basics.

If you decide that fishing appeals to you—as I truly hope you do—you'll find that resources for furthering your education are nearly unlimited. Not only are there many fine books that cover the general subject of fishing to a more detailed and sophisticated degree than this beginner's guide, but there are also hundreds of books that go into exquisite detail on the catching of specific fish; the use of specific tackle, lures, boats, electronics, and peripheral equipment; and arcana that you may not even suspect. On trout or bass alone, there are enough books to keep you in debt for the rest of your life. Many of those books are highly readable and informative.

There are also magazines full of columns and articles by knowledgeable anglers. Some, like *Field & Stream*, *Sports Afield*, and *Outdoor Life*, are national monthlies that offer well-written and useful information at many levels of expertise (though usually not for the absolute beginner, which is one reason I wrote this book).

Now that you have the basics under your belt, some on-the-water experience will enable you to understand and benefit from most of the pieces in such publications.

You may encounter self-proclaimed ex-

Need I say more? The Walker Agency photo.

perts among your friends, acquaintances, and relatives. Many of them will be ever eager to pass on their fishing theories, invited or not. Some of those advisors will know of what they speak. Others won't. What you've learned in this book should put you in a pretty good position to assess the quality of their advice. You already know more than some of them. A truly knowledgeable fishing companion, however, is an invaluable find at this stage of your education. If one comes your way, listen and learn.

There's another thing I should leave you with. I put it at the end because it seems not to fit anywhere else. There are laws governing freshwater fishing, and usually you need a license. Make sure you know the laws and buy a license. License fees and requirements vary widely from state to state. The laws—which define when, where, and with what equipment you may fish, which species you may keep, how many, and what size they must be, among other things—are also widely variable. Often, different regulations apply to different bodies of water in the same state. And a state's regulations may change from year to year or even season to season.

Most states give out an abstract of angling laws when you buy a license. It's important to know the score. Also variable are the kinds of places where you can buy a license. In some states, licenses are readily available at any tackle shop. Other states sell their licenses only at city and town halls. A license valid in one state is most likely invalid in any other state or province.

If the laws of your home state require you to have a license, buy one. In doing so, you are not only complying with the law (and avoiding fines and the possible confiscation of your equipment) but also contributing to the proper management of the fisheries resource. Your license fees contribute to the state's implementation of fish management.

Finally, remember that fishing is for fun, relaxation, personal fulfillment, ecstacy, or whatever else you want. It can even be for competition, if you want it to be. The important thing is that it be pleasurable.

By taking care of your equipment, you'll keep it in proper working order. By learning how to use it, you'll ensure its cooperation (as fully as fishing tackle ever cooperates). And by learning about fish and fishing, you'll better your chances of routine success. With those factors under your control, you'll usually find fun and pleasure in fishing. And that is no more or less than anyone can ask of anything. Good luck.

Index

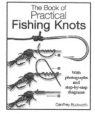
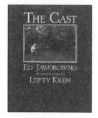

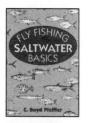

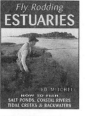

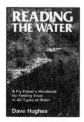

S'HOMO DES BE

GUIDE
Menorca

A TOUR OF THE ISLAND

▼ TRIANGLE POSTALS

© 1997

TRIANGLE POSTALS S. L. Sant Lluís, Menorca

Photography

Jaume Serrat

Ricard Pla
Lluís Bertràn
Iñaki Relanzón
Melba Levick
Pere Sintes

Text

Joan Montserrat

Imma Planes *(Information and suggestions)*

Acknowledgements

Lluís Plantalamor (Museu de Menorca)
Fernando Contreras (Ecomuseu de Cap de Cavalleria)
Aeroclub Sant Lluís

Translation

Jina Monger

Grafic concept

Joan Barjau
Ricard Pla

Illustrations

Perico Pastor

Layout

Triangle Postals. S. L.

Cartograpy

Triangle Postals. S. L.

Colour separations

Tecnoart

Printed by

Industrias Gráficas Viking S.A.

Depósito legal

B.: 30.518 - 1997

ISBN

84-89815-18-6

Contents

Cala Macarelleta

An island of surprises

Even the briefest visit to Menorca tends to provide the curious traveller with an insight into the unique and surprising nature of the island's character.

This element of surprise has become a rare commodity in this day and age and is, therefore, for the visitor, one of the most rewarding first impressions.

The second largest and most northeastern of the Balearics, Menorca differs from the other islands in both climate and morphology. Throughout the course of history, successive changes of fortune have left their mark here, as have the diverse cultural influences of the many races who have occupied the island over the centuries. This turbulent past history has endowed Menorca with an original, distinctive character about which much has been written. The island not only of-

fers a wealth of things to see, but also much food for thought and discussion.

Here, in the past, a high degree of independence existed between one township and another and, on occasions, this even degenerated into conflictive rivalry. Each centre of population sought to protect itself against loss of identity and living space by keeping its distance from its neighbours. In modern times, both the need for a more global territorial policy and improvements in transport and communications contributed to a rapprochement between them which put an end to the exaggerated insularity of these "islands" within an island.

In total contrast to this attitude, and perhaps as a result of the cultural and ethnic melting pot from which they descend, Menorcans have always been open and generous in their dealings with outsiders. Suffice it to say that, until quite recent

Grazing land

Cala Galdana

times, it was customary for front doors to be left unlocked at all times and this is, indeed, significant of the tranquil way of life, the *calma*, that has always been one of Menorca's main attractions.

It is not easy to maintain such a life-style when faced with the massive influx of tourists during the summer months, although the people of Menorca do strive to share it with their visitors and bear with good grace the difficulties that inevitably arise when the seventy thousand inhabitants of the island find their numbers more than doubled. If the service industries sometimes appear inadequate, it can only be attributed to the disproportionate demands made upon them. The island's resources must be administered with care in order to ensure the continued survival of these privileged surroundings.

In recent years, the inhabitants of the islands have become increasingly preoccupied with the protection of their environment. Until a few years ago, opposition to development projects in Menorca had been almost exclusively limited to minority groups who foresaw the irremediable damage that could result from indiscrimate urbanization. (The *Grup Ornitològic Balear*, a local group dedicated to the conservation of nature and the environment, is one of the oldest and most active organizations of its kind in the country). Now, however, there is a unanimous desire to reconcile the interests of the conservationists with those of the tourist industry. Some sectors remained unconvinced of the importance of a protected environment until the recent concession by the United Nations of the **Reserve of the Biosphere** denomination.

Another decisive step, along the same lines, has been the *Llei d' Espais Naturals* legislation which guarantees different levels of protection for almost the entire island. Between those classified as *Àrees Naturals d' Especial Interès* or *Àrees Rurals d' Interès Paisatgístic*, (local equivalent of Sites of Special Scientific Interest), altogether nineteen zones have been included which gives a clear indication of the extent of the natural wealth of the island.

Geophysical features

In the south of the Gulf of Lyon, Menorca is situated practically in the centre of the western Mediterranean, at a point almost equidistant

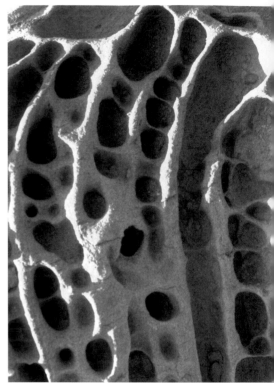

Erosion by wind

between Marseille and Algiers in a north-south direction, and Castelló de la Plana on the Spanish mainland and Oristano on the isle of Sardinia in an east-west direction. The area of the island measures 701 km²., the perimeter 290 km., and 48 km. is the longest distance between one end of the island and the other. The four most extreme points are, to the north Cap de Cavalleria; to the south Illa de l'Aire; to the east Cap de Sa Mola; and to the west, Cap de Bajolí. The distance between Ciutadella and Alcúdia, the closest point on the island of Mallorca, is 50 km.

An imaginary line drawn from Maó harbour, across the island, to Algaiarens would coincide with a natural division of the land which varies greatly between the north and the south. Above this line we find the island's oldest terrain which, in part, pertains to the Paleozoic insular shelf and partly to the Triassic, Jurassic and Cretaceous eras. This combination results in an interesting contrast of colours and textures. It is an area of gently rolling hills, including Monte Toro (358 m.), S'Enclusa (274 m.), and Santa Àgueda (264 m.), the three highest points on the island.

Rural scene

A wide strip of Miocenic terrain overlapped the southernmost extreme of this area, forming a flat limestone surface. Later, torrents from the north eroded the soil and formed channels that remain today as the small, but deep, ravines or gorges that are characteristic of this part of the island. Here in the *migjorn*, the south of Menorca, the rock is calcareous and the sand white, whereas, in the *tramuntana*, or north, the rock is siliceous with traces of sandstone, slate and shale.

Water, light and wind

The animal and vegetable life of the island has adapted to the conditions of the subsoil and to the availability of water. The supply of drinking water has preoccupied Menorcans since the beginning of time, as is demonstrated by the prehistoric *cocons*, shallow niches excavated in the rock, and the cisterns and tanks of more recent times. The collection of rain water has always been imperative as there are few natural sources. Principally, they are found in the south of the island, where the more permeable subsoil permits the formation of underground reserves.

Fortunately, the climate is very humid as compared to the rest of the archipelago. The visitor who has only seen Menorca during the dry summer months can hardly imagine the intense verdancy of the rest of the year. Except for years of generalized drought, the regularity of the rainfall and the abundant winter dews compensate for the summer dryness. Autumn, unknown here as a season, is replaced by the *primavera d'hivern*, or winter's spring. The mildness of the temperatures and the virtual absence of the deciduous trees that, in other latitudes, are the first indicators of the proximity of winter, add to the spring-like atmosphere that can be enjoyed here in October and November.

Another decisive characteristic of Menorca's climate is the constant presence of the wind. As there are no natural obstacles to stop it, the island is at the mercy of gusts from all directions. Those from the north are the most dominant and, among them, the fierce *tramuntana*, the strongest and most insistent, reaches speeds of between 35 and 90 km. per hour. It has spectacular effects on the environment: bowing and reshaping trees and bushes in its path, hampering

Monte Toro

AT 358 METRES ABOVE SEA LEVEL, MONTE TORO IS
THE GEOGRAPHIC CENTRE OF THE ISLAND AND A
PLACE OF PILGRIMAGE. ITS LOCATION MAKES IT A
PERFECT VANTAGE POINT FROM WHICH THE ENTIRE
COASTLINE OF THE ISLAND CAN BE SEEN AND, ON
CLEAR DAYS, MALLORCA IS VISIBLE ON THE HORI-
ZON TO THE SOUTH-EAST. ONCE IT WAS FORTIFIED
TO PROTECT THE ISLANDERS FROM THE INCUR-
SIONS OF BERBER PIRATES AND TODAY IT IS A
SPIRITUAL REFUGE DEDICATED TO OUR LADY DEL
TORO, PATRON SAINT OF MENORCA WHOSE IMAGE,
SO LEGEND HAS IT, WAS DISCOVERED HERE BY A
FRIAR FOLLOWING THE SIGNS PASSED ONTO HIM BY
A SILVER-HOOFED BULL. THE MONASTERY IS INHAB-
ITED TODAY BY FRANCISCAN NUNS. THE HILL-TOP IS
SOMEWHAT CLUTTERED WITH A PROFUSION OF
COMMUNICATION AERIALS AND ANTENNAS, AND A
RATHER PERPLEXING MEMORIAL TO THE DEAD OF
THE NORTH-AFRICAN WAR.

THE MOUNTAIN'S NAME IS DERIVED FROM THE PRE-
ROMANESQUE NOUN *TOR*, ORIGIN OF THE CATALAN
TURÓ OR HILL. THE ARABS CALLED IT *AL THOR*
WHICH HAD THE SAME SIGNIFICANCE. IT IS POSSI-
BLE TO WALK TO THE TOP FOLLOWING A FOOTPATH
ON THE NORTH SIDE AND, ON THIS SAME SLOPE, AT
THE SITE OF THE ENZELL SPRING, MENORCA'S ONLY
MINERAL-WATER BOTTLING PLANT HAS RECENTLY
BEEN INSTALLED.

work on the land and at sea, and depositing
harmful salt on crops and orchards. In compensation, the *tramuntana* brings with it an abundance of blue skies, clean atmosphere and brilliant sunshine...and the cows seem to thrive on
the salty fodder.

Extreme temperatures are unkown here and
records of significative snowfalls must be
sought in the archives. In summer, the average
temperature is 25ºC and in winter 12ºC and this
temperate climate is an added attraction for the
considerable number of retired people, British
in the main, who choose Menorca as their residence.

Flora and fauna

We have already mentioned the almost total
absence of deciduous trees on the island. This
is another consequence of the shortage of water which, in this instance, favours the growth
of the evergreen varieties. Among these, the
most common species are the carob, the al-
mond, the fig and the wild olive, genetic prede-
cessor of the olive tree. The prickly pear also
abounds and is known to the Menorcans as the
figuera de moro or Moor's fig. For use as building material or firewood, the well-established
wild olive or evergreen oak are used and, to a
lesser extent, the two varieties of pine that are
found in the central and northern woodlands,
and the sabines that grow close to the beaches
and marshlands.

Other types of vegetation include the mastic
bush, buckthorn, madronas, heather, myrtles,
broom, oleander, bramble, juniper and wild as-
paragus. A multitude of wild flowers exist on the
island: asphodels and orquids, gladioli, poppies
and convolvulus.

Many species of small wild animals, reptiles,
insects and birds are to be seen all over the island: martens, ferrets, weasels, rabbits, bats,
field mice, hedgehogs, lizards and Mediterranean tortoises being the most common. There
are also a few non-poisonous snakes. The fact
that pairs of majestic red kites, and other birds
of prey, are still a relatively frequent sight says
much for the state of Menorca's wildlife, as
their presence indicates the survival of many
lesser species that form the lower echelons of
the ecological pyramid.

Pig's ear (Dracunculus muscivorus)

Sawfly orchid (Ophrys tenthredinifera)

Mediterranean tortoise.

Common egret (Egretta garzetta)

Each of the different topographic areas of the island is host to many species of birds. In the gorges: turtledoves, wood pigeons and blackbirds. On the cliffsides and harbours: seagulls, storm petrel, shearwaters and cormorants. In the woods and on cultivated land: woodcocks, goldcrests, nightjars, flycatchers, partridges and quail. In more open spaces: larks, Thikla larks, corn bunting, hoopoes and crows. During the winter, robins and orphean warblers are to be seen, along with great flocks of thrush and starlings that stop here on their way south and, during the summer, swallows, swifts, crag martins and bee-eaters arrive from North Africa.

Some parts of the island play such an important role in the migrative and reproductive cycles of these species that development projects in the vicinity have been prohibited. In the Albufera d'Es Grau where, apart from an important resident colony, thousands of birds gather each year to breed, planning permission for an urbanization was withdrawn even after building had been started. As a result, the Albufera is an ornithologist's paradise where mallards, coots, water rails, aquatic warblers, grebes, egrets, pochards and stone curlews can all be observed undisturbed in their natural habitat.

Various predatory and scavenger species can be observed all year round, although man's invasion of their nesting areas has led to the drastic reduction in the number of these larger birds. This is the case of the osprey, the booted eagle and even the red kite, but falcons, kestrels, hawks, Egyptian vultures, buzzards, marsh harriers and owls are still plentiful along with many types of small, insectivorous birds.

The sea and its riches

As befits an island, the enjoyment and appreciation of nature extends beyond the confines of the coastline to the surrounding sea where another, constantly changing panorama awaits us. The visitor who attempts to follow the perimeter of the island by land will find it a difficult task. The **Consell Insular** has started work on the restoration of the *Camí de Cavalls*, the bridle path dat-

nother bird of prey, the buzzard (Buteo buteo)

npressive aspect of the Egyptian vulture (Neophron percnopterus)

Lizards

THE MANY SUBSPECIES OF LIZARDS TO BE FOUND
ON THE ISLETS AROUND MENORCA ARE SUBJECT OF
INVESTIGATION BY BIOLOGISTS AND NATURALISTS.
THE FACT THAT THEY ARE BLACK HAS CREATED A DE-
MAND FOR THEM AS CURIOSITIES EVEN THOUGH, IT
IS SAID, THEY CHANGE COLOUR ONCE REMOVED
FROM THEIR NATURAL HABITAT. OVER THE YEARS,
THE NUMBER OF SPECIMENS TO BE FOUND ON THE
ILLA DES SARGANTANES, ILLA D'EN COLOM, AND
PARTICULARLY ILLA DEL AIRE, HAS DROPPED
ALARMINGLY. NOW THEY HAVE BEEN DECLARED A
PROTECTED SPECIES AND LAWS HAVE BEEN PASSED
TO ENSURE THAT, IN FUTURE, THOSE WHO WISH TO
CONTEMPLATE THEM MUST DO SO IN SITU.

Brown cows, black horses

THE VISITOR WHO HAS SEEN THE HERDS OF BLACK
AND WHITE FRIESIANS THAT ABOUND ALL OVER THE
MENORCAN COUNTRYSIDE MAY BE SURPRISED BY
THIS HEADING. IT IS, INDEED, RARE TO COME
ACROSS EXAMPLES OF THE ISLAND'S NATIVE BREED
OF HANDSOME, REDDISH-BROWN CATTLE, BUT AT-
TEMPTS ARE BEING MADE TO REVIVE INTEREST IN
THEIR BREEDING AND, HOPEFULLY, THEIR PRESENCE
WILL INCREASE IN THE NEAR FUTURE.

THERE IS, HOWEVER, NO ROOM FOR DOUBT AS RE-
GARDS THE COLOUR OF MENORCA'S INDIGENOUS
BREED OF HORSES. IN ALL THE LOCAL FESTES AND
FESTIVITIES THE MAGNIFICENT JET BLACK HORSES
PLAY A LEADING ROLE. THEIR MAINS AND TAILS
ADORNED WITH COLOURED RIBBONS, THEY ARE
THE CENTRE OF ATTRACTION AS, INDEED, ARE THE
SKILLFUL JOCKEYS WHO RIDE THEM.

ing from 1682 that encircles the entire island and
was used for both civil and military purposes
until the middle of this century. When it is completed, walkers, cyclists and horse-riders will be
able to enjoy parts of the coastline only visible
at the moment from the air or the sea.

The custom of sailing round the island with
overnight stops on the way, always a tradition
among Menorcan families, many of whom posess
recreational craft for this purpose, has also become popular with the visiting tourists. At the
height of the season, the many boats to be seen
in the coastal waters form a heterogeneous procession in which all sizes, styles and degrees of
luxury have their place.

Those visitors who do not have the opportunity
to see the island by boat can console themselve
relaxing on any of the magnificent beaches whic
also offer the possibility of contemplating the
marine floor and its fauna. Diving enthusiasts
can choose between rocky and sandy sea beds;
the depths that are host to grouper and scorpion
fish, and the carpet of posidonia, reservoir of lif
and breeding ground to many crustaceans and
other species. This submarine meadow, of great
oxygen-generating potential, is another symbol
of conservationism and must be protected
against mankind, its greatest pillager.

Although many varieties of sea urchins, moluscs
and crustaceans are still to be found, along with
fish such as the wrasse, dentex, salema, saddle
bream and combers, both the monk seal and the
sea turtle have been irradicated from these waters by excessive and indiscriminate fishing
which has upset the delicate ecological balance
in detriment of these species.

la Mitjaneta

History and sociology

Since time immemorial, Menorca has suffered the logical transformations of a conquered land: many peoples and cultures have succeeded one another in occupation, imposing their customs and leaving their indelible mark. Their many and varied influences coexist here, forming the interesting mosaic that is Menorca today, enriched by centuries of change and adaption.

Peoples of the mainland of Spain and the eastern Mediterranean had settled here long before the Phoenicians, possibly as early as 4000 BC. Traces of their cultures are still apparent today in the many prehistoric monuments scattered over the island. In fact, Menorca can boast of having the greatest concentration of them in the world. After centuries of neglect, much of this unique archaelogical treasure has now been restored, and excavation work still in progress continually adds new discoveries. Recently, in a cave in the Ciutadella area, both human remains and others belonging to the *myotragus balearicus* (an extinct breed of goat) have been found along with bronze, ceramic and wooden objects, all in an excellent state of conservation.

The first recorded visitors were of a peaceable nature, first Phoenician and then Greek sailors seeking to expand their commercial activities across the Mediterranean. The Carthaginians, on the other hand, landed here with very different intentions. Lead by Magón, Hannibal's brother, they forcefully recruited the legendary *honderos*, slingshooters whose skill was to bring them fame in the Punic Wars.

The Greek name of Meloussa was changed to Minorica by the Romans when they conquered the island under Quintus Caecilius Metellus in 123 BC. They built roads and reinforced the settlements of Iammona (Ciutadella), Mago (Maó) and Sanisera (Sa Nitja), established by the

Carthaginians at a time when the Insulae Balearis was a newly created Roman province in its own right, previously having formed part of the province of Tarragona. Much has still to be discovered about the Roman occupation of the island as has become apparent following the new excavations being carried out in the port of Sanitja. Some of the findings are on show in the Ecomuseu de Cap de Cavalleria (see p.119). It appears that the natives of the island lived in harmony with the new occupiers until the 5th century AD and the arrival of the Vandals which gave rise to cruel persecution of the Christians.

For some time now, Christianity had become firmly established on the island. Bishop Severo's famous epistle of the year 417, describes travelling from Mago to Iammona with the aim of converting the city's Jewish colony. In 533, the Byzantine overthrew the Vandals, Christianity was restored and there follows a period about which comparatively little is known.

In the year 903, Menorca fell to the Moors. Under the new name of Minurka, the island was divided into four districts, the capital was established in Ciutadella (Medina Minurka) and the fort was built on Sta. Àgueda (Sen Agaiz). The majority of the populace was disseminated over the island and lived off the land which, thanks to the techniques of irrigation farming introduced by the Moors, became more fertile and productive and trading routes were established with Italian ports. Although few monuments dating from this time remain, the Moorish influence is ever-present today in many of the island's place names, for example, those starting with Bini which, in the language of the Moors meant "son or heir of"

Bronze statue of the Imhotep, a healing god. Found at the Torre d'en Gaumés site, it supposedly dates from the later Talayotic period.

Roman coin, with the value of a silver denarius, representing the goddess Roma. It dates from 146 BC and was found at the Sanisera excavation. Today it can be seen in the Ecomuseu de Cap de Cavalleria.

Small, bronze image of a bull, found at the Torralba d'en Salord taula. Probably a votive element, it dates from the 3rd or 4th century BC.

Punic amphora from Binicalaf, typical of the 2nd century BC when the eastern Mediterranean's commercial activity was based in Eivissa.

Pre-Talayotic funerary piece dated circa 1800-2000 BC. Found near Alaior, it now forms part of the Vives Escudero collection.

Reconstruction of a ceramic urn from the late Talayotic era. The remains were found at the Trepucó site.

The Catalan conquest

In the 13th century, the Balearics, along with the rest of the Iberian peninsula, were recaptured from the Moors for Christianity. Mallorca was taken by Jaume I of Aragón and in 1232 Menorca declared feudal allegiance to him which was maintained until 1287 when the island was conquered by a confederate army led by Alfons III. The Moors were taken as slaves or sent home in return for ransom. Of the latter, many never arrived but were thrown overboard shortly after setting sail. Alfons III shared the reconquered land as booty among his knights and this led to a certain deterioration of the island's social and economic structure.

After a brief period of progress and improvement, and until the end of the Middle Ages, the history of Menorca can be summarised as a time of epidemics, poverty, decadence and confrontation between the ruling classes and the peasantry. Following this, the 16th century can only be described in even worse terms, as, during the negligent reigns of Carlos I and Felipe II, many tragedies took place. In 1535 a fleet led by the cruel Turk Barbarossa admiral of Sultan Solimán II, sacked the city of Maó, razed it to the ground and imprisoned the populace. In 1558, the Turks attacked Ciutadella with similar consequences. More than three thousand people were taken as slaves to Constantinople, and the city's heritage of historical documents was destroyed.

The 17th century was as ill-fated as its predecessors. Epidemics of bubonic plague, the constant threat of pirate raids and the destruction of crops by swarms of locusts further undermined the peasantry while the nobility and the clergy grew stronger in the face of these adversities. The events of the 18th century and the change of sovereignty they brought were, therefore, beneficial. The century began with confrontations between followers of the Archduke of Austria, pretender to the Spanish throne, and those of Felipe de Borbón. The outbreak of the War of Succession in 1706 plunged the island into a state of civil war. France sent troops to support the Borbón cause, thus enabling Anglo-Dutch forces to disembark and take the island with hardly a shot fired. In 1712, the Treaty of Utrecht ceded the island of Menorca to the British Crown.

British and French domination

The British domination that lasted from 1708 to 1756 has been described by historians as the Golden Age of Menorca. If injusticies were committed by some members of the governing body, they were rapidly rectified and Richard Kane, the first Governor, is remembered with praise. He introduced fodder farming, imported fresh breeding stock, built the road across the island that still bears his name, abolished the Inquisition, and built schools. Under his rule, only the interests of Ciutadella can said to have been prejudiced. The British, Protestant domination was not well accepted here by the nobility and clergy and, as a result, the city lost its status as capital in favour of Maó which benefitted greatly from the consequent increase in commercial activity.

In 1756, the Duke of Richelieu, with a contingent of twenty thousand French troops, disembarked in Ciutadella where they were well received by the devoutly Catholic population. After a brief naval skirmish, the British withdrew with full military honours although Admiral Byng returned to England in disgrace where he was subsequently court-martialled and executed. For the next seven years, Menorca was ruled by the French. During this time, the Governor, Conde de Lannion, reinstated some of Ciutadella's lost status, founded the village of St. Lluís in honour of King Louis... and Richelieu discovered mayonnaise which was a great success at the court of Versailles. At the end of the Seven Years War in 1763, The Treaty of Paris returned Menorca to the British Crown.

During this second domination, the British were not as benevolent as they had been in the past, and the only notable work carried out by them was the demolition of the *arraval* of St. Felip and the transfer of its inhabitants to Georgetown, known today as Es Castell. A number of Menorcans, owing to the conditions of extreme poverty that now prevailed, emigrated to Florida in search of better fortune and others became privateers. After nineteen years of bad government and injustice, in 1782, a Franco-Spanish fleet, under Duque de Crillon, reconquered the island for Carlos III of Spain after a six month siege.

In 1798 the British returned for the last time, staying until 1802 when Menorca was finally returned to the

This Gothic inscription, commemorating the conquest of the island by Alfons III, once decorated the Pont de na Gentil bridge in Maó.

These oil paintings on canvas have been attributed, for the similarity in style and content, to the landscapist Joan Font i Vidal (1811-1855), although only the one in the centre, dated "10th October 1850", bears his signature.

Spanish Crown after seventy-two years of foreign occupation. Despite the good government of Conde de Cifuentes, Carlos III's representative on the island, the Spanish administration brought with it the seal of totalitarianism with a consequent loss of civil liberties, and, during the reigns of Carlos IV and Fernando VII, decadence and corruption prevailed throughout society. Once again, emigration was the only solution for many Menorcans who now ventured to Algiers and other north-African cities. Not until the middle of the 19th century did industrialization permit a relative economic recovery.

Recent history

This industrialization brought with it the beginnings of labour movements which, in turn, instigated many social changes. For example, a general strike was held in protest against the war in Morocco and the workers of the shoemaking industry formed an Anarquist federation. The collapse of the First Republic and the return of the Monarchy, supported by the landowning aristocracy, strengthened the position of the old ruling classes. The parliamentary elections of 1879 were won by the Conservatives in the Balearics, their member for Menorca being the Duque de Almenara Alta.

With the ascension to the throne of Alfonso XIII in 1902, the whole Spanish political system entered into a period of crisis and both Liberals and Conservatives failed in their attempts at innovation. In Menorca, only the Conservatives carried any weight within Monarchist circles, but the Republican party was strongly supported and in several legislations represented the island at Parliament. Proof of the Menorcans' truly democratic disposition at that time can be found in their lack of support for neither the candidatures presented by Joan March in Mallorca and Pere Matutes in Eivissa (which could be described as despotic or totalitarian by nature), nor the reactionary dictatorship of Primo de Rivera. At the local elections of 1931, whose results led to the proclamation of the Second Republic, the seat for Menorca was won by the *Front Únic* formed by Socialists and Republicans.

Following the Nationalist insurrection that gave rise to the outbreak of the Spanish Civil War, the military commander declared the island's allegiance to the Francoist rebellion. However, the very next day, 20th July 1936, a combined force of civilians and noncommissioned officers rose against the insurgent armed forces and, at the cost of great loss of

life, won Menorca back for the Republic. The island resisted until the end of the war in February 1939 and was, in fact, the last position in Spain to fall to the Nationalist troops. The bloody reprisals perpetrated in retaliation form one of the most traumatic chapters of Menorcan history.

The social and economic consequences of nearly forty years of dictatorship are too far-reaching and complex to be dealt with here in detail. The one-party system, strengthened by a powerful bureaucracy, generated political apathy among the popu-

⊙   *Anonymous painting, dated 1835, in which the activities of Maó harbour are illustrated in great detail. The warehouses in the foreground stand at the foot of the hill that connected the quayside with what is now the Miranda Square. Social classes such as merchants and clergy are represented, as are the different trades of the time: boatbuilders, peasants, fishermen, stevedores, gin distillers, etc.*

⊙   *Oil painting on canvas, dated and signed B. Pax 1859, showing the Industrial Mahonesa factory, opened in 1856 in Cala Figuera.*

ce and, until the 1950s, there was no apparent
gn of unrest at any social level. The latter end of
1e 1960s, a time of prosperity for the island, wit-
essed the first, albeit clandestine, indications of
desire for the revival of democracy. They were to
emain repressed until the 1970s and the flood of
vents that changed the course of Spanish history:
1e death of the dictator and restoration of the
1onarchy in King Juan Carlos I (November 1975),
1e reform process that led to the first democratic
lections since the Second Republic (June 1977),
nd the enactment by the King of the new Constitu-
on (December 1978).

1ore recently, in 1982, Parliament accepted the
statut d' Autonomía de les Illes Balears which
llows a degree of home rule for the islands under
1e Consells Insulars, or island councils.

Economy

he basis of the island's current economic profile
1ust be sought in the first shoe factories that were
et up in Ciutadella around the year 1850. The in-
ustrialization of the industry marked the start of
1 era in which Menorcan produce was successful-
 promoted abroad. Commerce with both the conti-
ent and the Spanish colonies brought notable
rogress and prosperity to the island and gave rise
 the creation of other subsidiary activities.

1 1856 the Industrial Mahonesa opened the island's
ioneer textile and cotton-spinning factory in the
ort of Maó (where the CAMPSA depot is now) and
1e following years were a time of prosperity during
hich many businesses and industries were set up.
he loss of the Cuban market in 1898 plunged the
hoemaking industry into a severe recession which
sted until the First World War. At the same time,
owever, by 1911 three thousand people were em-
loyed in the manufacture of silver purses, an activi-
y considered to be the precursor of the present-day
ostume-jewellery industry.

fter 1870, the extensive cultivation of cattle fodder
onverted dairy farming into the principal agricultural
ctivity with the consequent increase in meat and
1ilk production, the latter being made into cheese.

ourism, as an industry, arrived in Menorca be-
veen the end of the 1950s and the beginning of
1e 1960s, but its advance was far slower than in
1allorca or Eivissa due to the fact that, here, it was
onsidered an alternative source of income rather

Footwear and *Avarques*

A CENSUS CARRIED OUT IN 1782 (WHEN MENORCA
WAS ONCE AGAIN UNDER SPANISH RULE) INDICATED
THAT 281 ISLANDERS WERE SHOEMAKERS BY TRADE.
THEIR CUSTOMERS WERE MEMBERS OF THE ARISTOC-
RACY AND MILITARY OFFICERS, AND THE FIRST STEPS
WERE BEING TAKEN TO ESTABLISH AN EXPORT TRADE.
SINCE THOSE DAYS, THIS INDUSTRY HAS KNOWN TIMES
OF GREAT PROSPERITY BUT ALSO IMPORTANT SET-
BACKS AND RECESSIONS SUCH AS THE LOSS OF THE
CUBAN MARKET AT THE TURN OF THE CENTURY.
THANKS TO THE SKILL AND PROFESSIONALITY OF THE
CRAFTSMEN OF ALAIOR AND CIUTADELLA, THE PRES-
TIGE OF MENORCAN FOOTWEAR PREVAILS TODAY.
AS COMPETITION ITENSIFIED FROM OTHER SOURCES
WITH LOWER PRODUCTION COSTS, THE INDUSTRY HERE
WAS OBLIGED TO MOVE UP INTO THE MARKET OF FASH-
ION-DESIGN. NEVERTHELESS, ONE OF THE MOST SUC-
CESSFUL LINES ARE THE PEASANT SANDALS OR *AVAR-
QUES*, COMPRISED OF TWO PIECES OF COWHIDE AT-
TACHED TO A PNEUMATIC SOLE, WORN HERE SINCE TIME
IMMEMORIAL. THEY ARE NOW PRODUCED IN MORE SO-
PHISTICATED VERSIONS AND ARE SUCH AN INTRINSIC
SYMBOL OF MENORCA THAT MINIATURE CHINA COPIES
ARE SOLD AS SOUVENIRS.

than the mainstay of the economy. Even so, by
1973 it was important enough to be considered
as one of the three chief economic supports, the
others being arable and dairy farming, and the
costume-jewellery and shoemaking industries.

This balance has been upset by a series of events,
such as Spain's entry into the E.C. in 1986 which
has severely affected the dairy farming industry,
and the strong competition presented to the
costume-jewellery and footwear sectors by Asian
manufacturers whose labour and raw material
costs cannot be rivalled here. Isolation, such an
inherent part of Menorca's character, pays a high
price in terms of commercial viability, and it is yet
to be seen how the island's industries will deal
with the challenges to be faced in the near future.

Prehistoric monuments

Although an exhaustive discovery of the island's archaeological treasures may well be beyond the possibilities of the average visitor, the Southeastern Area car tour, see page 116, and the indications at the end of the Around Ciutadella tour, page 114, suffice as an introduction to this subject, one of Menorca's most fascinating themes.

The oldest remains (megalithic tombs, underground caves and *navetas*) have been dated by experts at around 2000 BC, but the most notable examples date from what is known as the *talaiotic* era, from around 1400 BC to the Roman invasion of the island in the last century BC. During this time, the structural conception, and even some of the materials used, changed considerably, to a certain extent as a result of increased contact with the outside world. Successive stages of this process are quite patent in some cases, the last recognizable influence being Punic, coinciding with the foundation of Mago, Iammona and Sanisera. These settlements were still inhabited by the native population during the Roman occupation.

The monuments that date from the talaiotic era are easily recognizable and are classified as: burial caves, burial chambers, *talaiots*, walled enclosures and *taules*.

Prehistoric settlement at Talatí de Dalt

Monuments from other historical periods to be found on the island are the early-Christian basilicas built during the 5th and 6th centuries during occupation by the Vandals and, supposedly, the Byzantines. The most famous is at **Son Bou**, where its proximity to the waterline has given rise to speculation about the possible existence of other nearby buildings. Indeed, some curious structures (visible from the air) do exist on the sea-bed just off-shore from the basilica, and their apparently regular shapes suggest the remains of a settlement. Archaeologists are, however, sceptic on this point. Inside the basilica, a baptismal font, carved from a single stone, is of particular interest. At **Es Fornàs**, near St. Climent, there is another basilica dated 6th century BC where we can see a superb mosaic of animal and vegetable motifs, and another on the **Illa del Rei** whose mosaics have been moved to the **Museu de Menorca**.
At **Cap d'es Port de Fornells** and on the **Illa d'en Colom**, two more are to be found, the latter currently undergoing excavation work.

Caves at Cales Coves

Burial caves

The most interesting of their kind are to be found at **Cales Coves**, on the south coast a few kilometres from Sant Climent, where nearly one hundred appear on the cliff face. There are more at **Caparrot de Forma** (near Es Canutells), at **Son Bou** (beneath a fortified wall on the cliff) and at **Cala Morell** on the north coast. All these burial sites date from the 9th and 8th centuries BC, but seem to have been in use well into the Roman era.

Burial *navetes*

Naveta des Tudons near Ciutadella

The name *naveta* (little boat) is derived from their appearance, resembling that of an inverted hull. The oldest, dating from pre-talaiotic times, are oval or circular in shape, but their construction evolved towards more elongated forms, for example, the **Naveta d'Es Tudons** of circa 1400 BC. A tiny doorway gives access to the interior which is comprised of an anteroom or entrance hall and one or two superimposed chambers. These constructions, of purely funerary use, are the oldest in Europe of their kind and can be found at **Biniac, Llumena, Rafal Rubí** and **Son Morell**.

Torelló talaiot

Talaiots

Talaiots are situated on rises in the ground or hillocks, from where other *talaiots* are usually visible at a distance. This fact has led to the supposition that they were used as defence towers or lookout points (*talaies* in Catalan) hence their name. However, remains have been found in small chambers inside these truncated cones which suggest that they were used as burial places. These great mounds of stone, up to ten metres tall, are to be found all over the island in varying stages of conservation.
The most notable stand at: **Trepucó, Torre Trencada, Talatí de Dalt, Torre Llafuda, Torre Llisà Nou, Torre d'en Gaumés** and **Binimaimut**.

Taules

These are the most exceptional of all the talaiotic monuments and are unique to Menorca, whereas constructions similar to *talaiots* are to be found elsewhere. They comprise of two huge blocks of limestone and owe their name *taules* (tables in Catalan) to their T-shaped form. Their most notable characteristic is their size: the *taula* at **Torralba d'en Salord**, which is imbedded two metres in the ground, weighs approximately 25 tons.

They are surrounded by a series of niches in the shape of a horse-shoe which were probably used for depositing offerings to the deity.
Opinions vary as to the purpose of the *taules*: sacrificial altar, central supporting pillar of a roof, symbol of a deity, or a fertility symbol in the form of the head and horns of a bull...
The most important are at: **Trepucó Torre Trencada, Talatí de Dalt, Torre Llafuda, Torre Llisà Vell, Torre d'en Gaumés** and **Binimaimut**.

Taula de Talati

Rural architecture

The rural arquitecture of Menorca, so different from that of Mallorca, Eivissa or other parts of the Mediterranean, forms an integral part of the landscape and, as such, has a significance that rises above and beyond merely practical considerations.

The whiteness of the farmhouses and hamlets scattered across the countryside is one of the island's most characteristic images. The task of whitewashing is an activity in which the islanders, usually the women, invest a great deal of time and energy, taking logical pride in the immaculate results they achieve. Their motives are not only aesthetic, however, as the frequent painting not only assures the cleanliness, but also the protection of the limestone walls that would otherwise be eaten away by sun, rain and wind. This stone, and *ullastre*, the wood from the wild olive tree, were the only raw building materials to be found on the island. Easily cut into ashlars, or building blocks, *marès* was readily available, either at the building site itself, or from any of the many quarries.

The basic configuration of Menorcan rural arquitecture was determined by the limited range of available raw materials and the prevailing climate. Houses were always built facing south, with a minimum of doors and windows on the north side to exclude the cold *tramuntana* wind. The sun heats the porches during the winter months and rainwater is collected by a curious system of gutters made from Moorish-style roof tiles that canalize it down from the roof to the cistern or water tank. All these elements make of the Menorcan farmhouse a clear example of man's adjustment to the means at his disposal.

Details of typical architecture

Another characteristic of the countryside are the endless dry- stone walls that, when seen from the air, appear as an enormous crisscross network. Their purpose is to divide up the *llocs* or farmsteads into individual *tanques* or fields for rotation farming. At the same time, their construction cleared the fields of stones and prevents the sparse topsoil from being blown away by the strong winds. Some of these stones were used to construct protective walls around tree trunks. True craftsmen, the few remaining *paredadors* still work in the same ancestral way building a double wall which is then filled in with rubble. To make them easier to climb, a few stones are left protruding up both side to form rudimentary steps known as *botadors*. The wooden gates, often made of twisted *acebuche*, another example of local craftsmanship, prevent cattle and sheep from straying and should always be left as they are found.

Marès was the only available building material in times gone by

Quarries

THE ASSOCIATION BETWEEN MENORCA AND STONE, WHETHER IN ITS NATURAL STATE OR MANIPULATED BY MAN, IS INEVITABLE. WHEN BUILDING STYLES MOVED AWAY FROM THE USE OF RUDIMENTARY, CRUDE STONE TOWARDS THE USE OF LIMESTONE ASHLARS, THESE WERE INVARIABLY OBTAINED FROM THE SITES THEMSELVES. LATER, THE INCREASING DEMAND GAVE RISE TO THE CONSTRUCTION OF QUARRIES WHERE THOUSANDS OF TONS OF RAW MATERIAL WAS HEWED, BY HAND, IN REGULAR SHAPED BLOCKS. TIMES HAVE CHANGED, AND THE INTRODUCTION OF NEW ELEMENTS HAS CAUSED THE QUARRIES TO FALL INTO DISUSE.

NO LONGER EXPLOITED, THEY SEEM DESTINED TO REMAIN AS SCARS UPON THE LANDSCAPE, BUT **LÍTHICA**, A RECENTLY FORMED ASSOCIATION, HAS PLANS TO SAVE THEM FROM SUCH AN IGNOMINIOUS FATE AND REFURBISH THEM FOR VARIOUS CULTURAL ACTIVITIES.

Fêtes and festes

Throughout the summer, each town celebrates in turn its own local *festes*, during which the islanders have always given rein to their ancestral love of merriment. Today they are enthusiastically joined by the many summer visitors and the first and most famous of these events is held in Ciutadella in honour of St. John the Baptist. These are the first *festes* of the season, and the cycle is closed by those of Maó on the 7th and 8th September. The *Festes de Sant Joan* begin on the Sunday prior to June 24th, when a man dressed in animal skins carries a sheep through the streets of the city, and reach their climax on the night of the 23rd and the 24th, St. John's day. At all times during the celebrations, the horse is the ever-present centre of attraction. The official acts are based on medievel traditions, and the strict observation of protocol is safeguarded by the *Junta de Caixers*, or committee, which represents the different historical social classes, peasantry, nobility and clergy all of which are symbolically rep-

resented in the processions. The *Festes de Sant Joan* are, without doubt, among the most colourful and exuberant to be held anywhere in Spain. No visitor should miss this remarkable medieval spectacle of jousting, tournaments and cavalcades, unique example of ancestral traditions and Mediterranean joie-de-vivre.

➲➲ *Jaleo in the Plaça des Born in Ciutadella. Popular folk group, adornments on a horse's tail, and detail of adornment Be de St. Joan.*

☻ *Engravings showing two of the symbols of Sant Joan.*

ES CAIXER FADRI

S'HOMO DES BE

From east to west

Maó

The façades of many buildings in Maó are again being painted the pale sienna colour that had been customary until, in an attempt to live up to the slogan "Menorca, the blue and white island", an over-zealous mayor ordered them all to be whitewashed. Much restoration and conservation has been carried out, not only by the municipal authorities, but also by private individuals who take pride in maintaining, for example, the English-style sash windows of their homes. In the early morning, before the first onslaught of traffic, it is easy to imagine the aspect the town presented at the height of its prosperity in the 18th century, and the liberal and cultured society that developed here.

Clustered high on the cliff, the old part of the city overlooks the harbour. The views from the stately houses on Carrer Isabel II are particularly splendid as befits their opulent interiors and the ample proportions of their frontages.
At one end of this street, the **cloister of St. Francesc**, the first convent built in Maó in 1719, is undergoing exhaustive renovation and will eventually house the archaelogical treasures of the **Museu de Menorca** where they will be exhibited in surroundings worthy of their historical value. At the opposite end of Isabel II in Pla de la Parròquia (or Pl. Sta. Maria) we find the church of the same name, the neo-classical **Town Hall**, the clock given to the city by Governor Kane, and the building known as **Principal de Guàrdia**. The Town Hall houses a collection of portraits of famous historical figures, notably that of Conde de Lannion by Giuseppe Chiesa and Conde de Cifuentes by Pascual Calbó.

View of the harbour

Market. Claustre del Carme

he **church of Sta. Maria** is home to one of the
ity's treasures: the magnificent organ of 3210
ipes, 51 stops and 4 keyboards built by the Ger-
an maestros Otter and Kirburz. The quality of its
egister delights those who attend the concerts giv-
n regularly by internationally renowned musicians
ho consider it a privilege to perform here. Behind
ta. Maria, built in the reign of Alfons III, a statue
f this king stands in the centre of the Pl. de la
onquesta, also site of the Can Mercadal palace
nd the public library. From one corner of the
quare it is a short walk to the viewpoint which
verlooks the **Costa de Ses Voltes**, a landscaped
tairway leading down to the port, one of the key
nages first perceived by visitors arriving by boat.
t its foot, the area of the port known as **Baixamar**,
hich in recent years has become a nucleus of bars
nd restaurants and centre of the city's nightlife,
articularly in the summer.

aces of the commercial activity that used to be
e main characteristic of the harbour can still be
und in the remaining old buildings, once the
orkshops of the *mestres d'alxa*, or artisan boat-
uilders. (In some, one can still see enormous
fters made from the salvaged masts of wooden

ships). Their skills are still renowned today and can
be appreciated in the custom-built *llaüts*. These
vessels are no longer used solely as fishing boats,
but have become the ideal recreational craft for the
many people who explore the island's coastline
during the summer months. Indeed, the whole aspect of the harbour has changed as a result of the
growing popularity of nautical sports, one more aspect of the influence of tourism. Nowadays, hardly
anyone remembers when merchant ships docked
here to unload grain for grinding in Menorcan mills,
en route to their final destination on the mainland
of Spain. Today, the craft found alongside the

Maó cheese

EVEN THOUGH IT IS PRODUCED ALL OVER THE ISLAND,
MENORCAN CHEESE IS REFERRED TO AS *MAÓ* AS ITS
COMMERCIALIZATION HAS ALWAYS BEEN BASED IN
THE CAPITAL. IT IS ALSO CALLED THUS UNDER THE DE-
NOMINATION OF ORIGIN, CONCEEDED IN 1985. SINCE
THE 1960'S, THE CHEESE PRODUCED ON THE ISLAND
CAN BE CALCULATED IN MILLIONS OF KILOS PER YEAR.
ITS QUALITY WAS ALREADY BEING PRAISED IN ME-
DIEVAL CHRONICLES THAT TELL OF THE PREDILECTION
OF THE CATALAN KINGS FOR THIS VARIETY

IT IS A SEMI-FAT CHEESE, MADE FROM FULL COW'S
MILK TO WHICH A MAXIMUM PERMITTED 5% OF
EWE'S MILK MAY BE ADDED. THE CHEESES ARE
SQUARE IN SHAPE WITH ROUNDED EDGES AND,
WHEN HANDMADE IN THE TRADITIONAL WAY, BEAR
CHARACTERISTIC MARKS CAUSED BY THE WHITE
LINEN CLOTH IN WHICH THE MILK, ONCE CURDLED, IS
WRAPPED. THE WHEY IS DRAINED OUT MANUALLY
AND THE BUNDLE LEFT UNDER WEIGHTS FOR TWEN-
TY-FOUR HOURS. THEN IT IS SUBMERGED IN SALT WA-
TER FOR TWO DAYS BEFORE THE DRYING PROCESS IS
STARTED. ACCORDING TO THE DEGREE OF MATURITY,
IT IS SOLD AS *TENDRE* (YOUNG), *SEMICURAT* (SEMI-
MATURE), *CURAT* (MATURE) OR *VELL* (VERY MATURE).

Maó from the harbour.

Club Marítim are modern, luxurious yachts, and more facilities for mooring and wintering are planned for the future.

But let's return to the starting point of our descent down to the waterfront - the **Costa de Ses Voltes**. This is where the fish market is to be found and, a little further on, the meat, fruit and vegetable market, situated in what was once the cloister and ground floor cells of the convent adjoined to the **Carme church**. The market itself is well worth visiting for the originality of its setting and it is also a short cut through to **Plaça Miranda**, another excellent viewpoint over the harbour. From here, via Plaça del Príncep, we return to the pedestrian zone of **S'Arravaleta** and **Carrer Nou**. This is the commercial centre of the town and the number and nature of passers-by are an indication, in summer, of the success of the tourist season, and in winter a mirror of Menorcan society.

The Cuesta Deià leads up to the **Teatre Principal**, inaugurated as an opera-house in 1829 and, as such, older than the Liceu of Barcelona, to which it had been compared in style until the Liceu was destroyed by fire in January 1994. The interior of the building is well-worth a visit, and this will again be possible when current refurbishment is completed.

Each spring, an opera week is held here to the satisfaction of Maó's notoriously music-loving inhabitants. The Montcada house on the corner of Carrer Bastion and Carrer Hannover has a striking modernist *uindou* (the name is a local evolution of the English window, an element often adopted here instead of typically Mediterranean balconies for climatic reasons. Further along, we reencounter the remains of the medieval city walls, the **Arc de Sant**

Modernist window

Roc which leads to S'Arraval, the dividing line between what was once the fortified city and the suburbs.

Another important central street is Dr. Orfila (or **Carrer de ses Moreres**), into which both Carrer Cifuentes and Cós de Gràcia converge from opposite sides. Following Es Cós, we arrive at the cemetery and **shrine of Our Lady of Grace**, patron saint of the city. The old orthodox temple of St. Nicolau stands on the corner of Carrer Ramon y Cajal which leads, in turn, to the **Es Freginal park**, once a place of communal market-gardening. The **scientific and literary Athenaeum**, home of an important collection of fossils and algae and site of many cultural activities, stands of Carrer Conde de Cifuentes and, behind it, **S'Esplanada**, the main square of the city.

Bordered by the barracks built during the first British domination, the construction in recent years of an underground car park has altered, yet again, the configuration of the old parade ground. Here people of all ages gather to pass the time of day and a street market is held twice a week. Its also the point of departure of the main roads that lead to other parts of the island and site of the bus terminus. Currently, it is rumoured that the remaining barracks are to be moved to another location. This would be a positive step in the Esplanada's evolution from military to civic centre.

Es Castell

The name of this town has been changed many times during the course of its history: Arraval de St.

Felip, Georgetown, in honour of King George III during the British occupation, Villacarlos after King Carlos III of Spain and, finally, **Es Castell** which has recently become the official name and refers to the Castle of St. Felip which stood here from 1554 until its demolition in 1781. Military history has played a vital role in the town throughout the centuries, and is still apparent in the barracks that surround S'Esplanada, the main square, alongside the colonial-style Town Hall. Inside the neo-classical church of Roser there is an interesting stone alterpiece that once belonged in the castle chapel.

Cales Fonts, down on the waterfront, was once the site of fishermens' boathouses but, over the years, has been transformed into lively centre of bars and restaurants. From here, sightseeing trips by boat can be taken around Maó harbour and over to **Lazareto**. This fortified precinct only became an island in 1900 when the Alfons XII canal was constructed, and it served as a quarantine centre in the 18th and 19th centuries. Today it is used as a congress centre and holiday accommodation for Ministry of Health employees. There is a small museum of medical instruments and other curiosities in one of the buildings.

Sant Lluís

St. Lluís was founded at the end of the 18th century during the French occupation. They layout of its streets was planned by Conde de Lannion, as was the building of some of the outlying hamlets. In those days, their function was purely rural, but of

Cales Fonts, Es Castell

Es Molí de Dalt, ethnologic museum, Sant Lluís

Panoramic view of Fornells harbour

late they have become residential areas. However, thanks to local legislation, their original outward appearance has been conserved.

In the town itself, the major landmarks are the governor's house and the church dedicated to the patron saint, St. Louis, King of France. Several old windmills still stand, and one, the **Molí de Dalt**, situated opposite the Plaça Nova by the bus stop, has been converted into an interesting ethnological museum.

The coastline around St. Lluís abounds in coves, beaches and urbanizations: **S'Algar**, **Alcalfar**, **Punta Prima**, B**inisafúller** and **Binibèquer** all bear witness to the growth of the tourist industry.

Alaior

In 1304, King Jaume II of Mallorca founded what we know today as **Alaior** on the site of a farmstead named *Ihalor*. It is sometimes called the island's third capital on account of its historical role as mediator between Maó and Ciutadella and the independence afforded it by a balanced economy based on farming, tourism and light industry. **Son Bou**, **San Jaime** and **Cala en Porter** are the main tourist centres of the area. The most notable buildings are **Casa Salord**, the **Town Hall** and the church of **Sta. Eulàlia** (rebuilt after damage by a tornado at the end of the 17th century). The cloister of the church of **St. Dídac**, now popularly known as *Pati de Sa Lluna*, has undergone a major transformation over

Aerial view of Alaior

the years. What were once the cells have been transformed into living accommodation by people of varied origins and life styles. Outside the town, the visitor may be surprised to see a number of houses of intriguing names and architectural styles that seem out of place in the Menorcan countryside. They were built by local people of past generations who ventured overseas during the economic recessions that afflicted the island and evoke memories of the exotic lands they visited.

Es Mercadal and Fornells

At the geographical heart of the island, at the foot of **Monte Toro, Es Mercadal** owes its name to the privilege bestowed by King Jaume II to Catalan colonials, authorizing them to hold a market here every Thursday of the year. This custom prevails today in a handicraft market also held on Tuesday and Saturday afternoons. This is a pictoresque little town whose old centre is crossed by a watercourse. The majority of the population is still employed on the many outlying farms. However, in neighbouring **Fornells** and the nearby urbanizations, the local economy depends almost entirely upon the tourist and service industries although development has been restricted to low-rise holiday homes and much of the atmosphere of the old

fishing village may still be enjoyed today. The island's only golf course is to be found near here at **Son Parc**.

The parish church of **St. Martí** in Es Mercadal is a renaissance building with some later additions dating from 1807. Also worth seeing is the cistern built under British patronage by Pere Carreras in 1735 that brought drinking water to the town for the first time and is named after Richard Kane, the British Governor of the time.

Home-made sweets and confectionery from **Ca's Sucrer** and *avarques*, typical Menorcan sandals from Biel **Servera's workshop** are two attractions for both visitors and locals alike. Several restaurants in

Es Mercadal from the road to Monte Toro

35

Rooftops of Ferreries

Es Mercadal specialise in traditional Menorcan dishes and of course **Fornells**, with its famous lobster specialities, is an indispensable port of call.

Ferreries

Ferreries exemplifies the transformation that has taken place on the island since the beginning of tourist-orientated development in the 1960's. The shoe, costume jewellery and furniture-making industries employ a sector of the population previously dedicated to agriculture, and dairy farming has taken over from arable farming as the major rural activity. Building, commerce and service industries complete the rest of the town's economic profile. Opinions are divided over the origins of the name Ferreries, some opting for the existence of a nearby monastery of friars, *fraria*, and others for the idea that it was founded by an iron-worker, *ferrer*. What is for certain is that the town was established by King Jaume II of Mallorca, in the 14th century, who built the church of **St. Bartomeu** which presides over the centre of the old town. However, the remodelled Pl. Espanya is the centre of activity today and on Saturdays hosts a handicraft market.

In the neighbouring area, places of interest include the **Algendar gorge**, **Cala Galdana** and **Mount Sta. Àgueda** (264m.) where the ruins of a Moorish fortification still stand.

Es Migjorn

Es Migjorn became a municipality in its own right in 1989, (previously it was dependant on Es Mercadal), but its origins must be sought two centuries ago during the second British occupation. Until then, the local farmers had to take their pro-

Church of Sant Cristòfol. Es Migjorn Gran

'a Plaça Nova and Ses Voltes

The Town Hall from the port

uce to Ferreries to be sold, but the construction
f the church of **St. Cristòfol** and surrounding
wellings offered them alternative trading oppor-
unities. Here, the peace and quiet of traditional,
ural Menorca is more apparent than elsewhere on
he island and, even in summer, when tourists
rowd the nearby beaches of **St. Adeodat** and
t. Tomàs, Es Migjorn Gran still retains much of its
ntrinsic charm.

Ciutadella

lthough **Ciutadella** can be likened to other cities
r towns of similar evolution, a series of character-
tics combine here to create a special atmos-
here, an intangible difference. Its inhabitants are
ware of this and maintain it with pride, as if in re-
liation for the loss of their city's status as island
apital. They offer visitors a generous welcome but
ever cease to be themselves, often emphasising
hese differences rather than seeking to atenuate
hem. In speech, as well, they use turns of phrase
nd expressions in Catalan that have fallen into
isuse elsewhere. For these reasons, visitors al-
eady familiar with the rest of the island may feel,

on arrival in **Ciutadella**, that they have entered
another world.

Of the old city walls, only two bastions have sur-
vived the course of history: **Es Born** on top of
which the **Town Hall** was constructed, and **Sa Font**
at the point where a stream once emerged into the
harbour. It is, however, easy to imagine the totality
of the original form of the walls as they have been
replaced by three consecutive avenues: Constitu-
ció, Jaume I, and Capità Negrete, known collective-
ly as **Sa Contramurada**. The **Camí de Maó**, name
given to the final stretch of the main road as it en-
ters Ciutadella, leads to the Pl. Alfons III where the
Porta de Maó gateway once gave access to the
city. It is a typically Mediterranean square, lively
with cafés and outdoor terraces, one of which oc-
cupies the recently restored **Es Compte windmill**.
Continuing along the **Camí de Maó**, we arrive at
Sa Plaça Nova and then Carrer José Mª. Quadrado,
or **Ses Voltes**, one of the most characteristic
streets, with its narrow pavement and vaulted ar-
cade. Although the ground floors of the buildings
that flank it are now occupied by all kinds of
shops, it has not lost it charm and medieval aspect. In Sa Plaça Vella, on top of a stone column,

stands one of the city's most emblematic symbols, the tiny *Be de Sant Joan* (Lamb of St. John), work of the local artist Maties Quetglas. Ses Voltes leads us to the **Sta. Maria cathedral**.

Built in Catalan Gothic style in the 14th century on the site of a Moslem mosque, **Sta. Maria** does not stand out from its surroundings in terms of height. It is however, an impressive, forceful building comprised of one sole nave that has been repaired and rebuilt so many times that elements of various architectural styles are to be found, such as the baroque **chapel of Ses Ànimes** and the neoclassical main façade. Historical events of all kinds have left their mark here, notably in 1558, the year of *sa desgràcia* (misfortune), when the cathedral was

Es Gin

<small>ALTHOUGH ITS ORIGIN CAN BE TRACED TO THE TIMES OF THE BRITISH DOMINATION OF THE ISLAND, THIS LOCAL BREW BEARS LITTLE RESEMBLANCE TO ENGLISH GIN, BEING MORE SIMILAR TO THE DUTCH VARIETY. ONLY ONE DISTILLERY, XORIGUER, REMAINS TODAY AND IN THEIR FACTORY IN THE PORT ONE CAN SEE THE ANTIQUE STILLS WHERE THE JUNIPER BERRIES CONTINUE TO BE PROCESSED IN ACCORDANCE WITH THE TRADITIONAL RECIPE THAT DATES FROM THE 18TH CENTURY. THE CLAY BOTTLES IN WHICH GIN WAS ORIGINALLY SOLD ARE COLLECTORS' PIECES NOWADAYS, BUT XORIGUER DOES COMMERCIALIZE PART OF ITS PRODUCE IN EARTHENWARE REPLICAS. GIN IS DRUNK STRAIGHT OR IN COMBINATION WITH *HERBES*, A LIQUEUR MADE LOCALLY FROM A MIXTURE OF WILD HERBS IN WHICH CAMOMILE IS THE MOST DOMINANT; WITH A SLICE OF LEMON AND A SPLASH OF SODA-WATER, IN WHICH CASE IT IS CALLED A *PALLOFA*; OR WATERED-DOWN WITH LEMON SQUASH AS THE FAMOUS AND OSTENSIBLY INNOCUOUS *POMADA*, LIFE AND SOUL OF MENORCAN FESTES.</small>

razed to the ground during ferocious Turkish reprisals. Recently, the **Portal de la Llum** has been restored and several gargoyles replaced. The **Palau Episcopal** adjoins the rear of the cathedral.

Before proceeding on to Es Born, or main square, it is well worth making a detour through the labyrinth of back streets that are steeped in the medieval history of the city. Facing the west entrance to the cathedral, the **Palau Olives** and a little further on, on Carrer St. Sebastià, the **Palau Squella**. On Carrer Sta. Clara , the **Palau Lluriach**, home of Menorca's oldest titled family, the Barons de Lluriach, and the **Convent of Sta. Clara** whose tales of martyrs, arson and abductions form an intrinsic part of Ciutadella's history.

Carrer Roser, on the other side of the **Pla de la Seu**, leads us to the **church of Our Lady of the Rosary** with its ornately decorated barroque doorway, site of the municipal art gallery. On Carrer Bisbe Vila, one of the **Saura palaces**, occupied today by a bank, and beside it the renaissance Augustinian **convent of Socors**. In summer, the traditional Music Festival and auditions for the **Capella Davídica** choir are held in the cloister. In Plaça de la Llibertat a picturesque open-air market is held daily alongside the newly-built Casa de Cultura. On Carrer Santíssim, two more interesting palaces: the **Palau de los Duques de Almenara Alta** and the **Palau Saura**, part of which has been converted into an antique shop. Carrer St. Francesc, Carrer Palau and Carrer St. Jeroni, all of which lead to Carrer Major de Born, form what was once *el Call* or Jewish quarter.

On arrival at the Pl. del Born, we come across the obelisk built in memory of the victims of the Turkish attack. The shadow it casts, like that of a sundial, points in turn to the many notable buildings that surround the square. To our left as we enter the square, the **Palaus de Salort** and **Vivó** and, further on, the **convent of St. Francesc**. To the right, the **Palau del Conde de Torre Saura**, probably the most splendid of all the mansions. Just beyond, the **Teatre des Born** and its neighbour, the **Cercle Artístic**. On the next block, to round off the ensemble, the **Town Hall**, built in the 19th century on the site of the Moorish governor's citadel. From the rear of this building there is a magnificent view over the port.

On the map we may observe that the interior of Sa Contramurada, the area we have dealt with up to now, opens onto a wide avenue which runs

View of the port with es Pla de St. Joan in the background

parallel to the bay. This avenue separates Es Born from the city's other open space, the **Plaça dels Pins**, is known as the **Camí de Sant Nicolau** and terminates at the castle of the same name. Here, in the forecourt, stands a bust of the Ciutadella-born **Farragut**, navy Admiral during the American Civil War. This is a perfect spot for watching the sun go down over the distant silhouette of Mallorca on the horizon. The aspect of this whole area may change if plans for increasing the capacity of the port are carried out.

Compared to Maó harbour, the **port of Ciutadella** almost resembles a Venetian canal, complete with bridge, and its diminutive proportions have a lot to do with its charm. It is barely a kilometre in length and has an average width of two hundred metres. Towering above, the Born bastion offers a stark background to the waterfront below with its terraces, passers-by, fishing boats and yachts that fill the little port with colourful activity. An unusual meterological phenomena takes place in the waters of the harbour from time to time, the *rissagues*. The water level drops drastically, to the point of disappearing completely, and then returns like a flash flood with sometimes catastrophic consequences for the moored boats, and even the quayside restaurants, as was the case in 1984. Scientific studies are being carried out to enable meteorologists to forecast the phenomena and thus minimize damages. From the Born area there are two ways down to the port, Portal del Mar St. just behind the Town Hall, or the steps of the Baixada Campllonch which lead towards the **Pla de St. Joan**, scene of an important part of the famous **St. Joan festivities**.

▷ Port de Maó
▷ Sa Mesquida
▷ Es Grau
▷ Far de Favàritx
▷ Na Macaret

The whole north-eastern coast is rugged, its configuration largely due to the violent action of the sea and the north wind. **Es Grau**, where the sea joins the saltwater lagoon of the **Albufera**, and **Port d'Addaia** which is formed by a natural inlet that extends more than 3 km. inland, are the only two places of shelter for boats along this stretch of coast.
For this reason, sailors are advised to stay on the south side of the island when the wind is from the north, and even the beaches can be hazardous on rough days, despite the attractions of **Sa Mesquida**, **Morella** and **Tortuga**.

The lagoon and marshlands of **S'Albufera des Grau** are an area of great interest to biologists and ornithologists. Many species of water fowl come here in their thousands during the summer to make their nests and raise their young and it is an important port of call on the migratory routes. The lagoon is separated from the open sea by banks of reeds, pines and sabine trees.

Cap de Favàritx, with its lighthouse overlooking a landscape of harsh black slate, is a tremendous contrast to the gently rolling hills of **S'Albufera**, particularly on stormy days when it takes on an almost Dantesque appearance.

Between this coastline and the town of Alaior, the countryside is comprised of woodlands of evergreen oak and pine trees which alternate with rock formations of varied and curious forms, such as the **Penyes d'Egipte** or the **Capell de Ferro**, and is an ideal area for walking on a hot day.

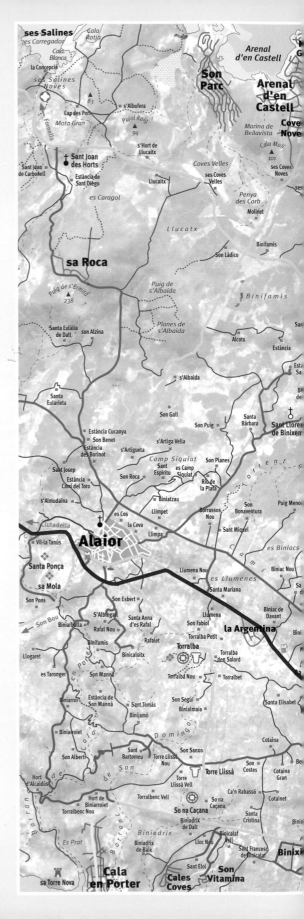

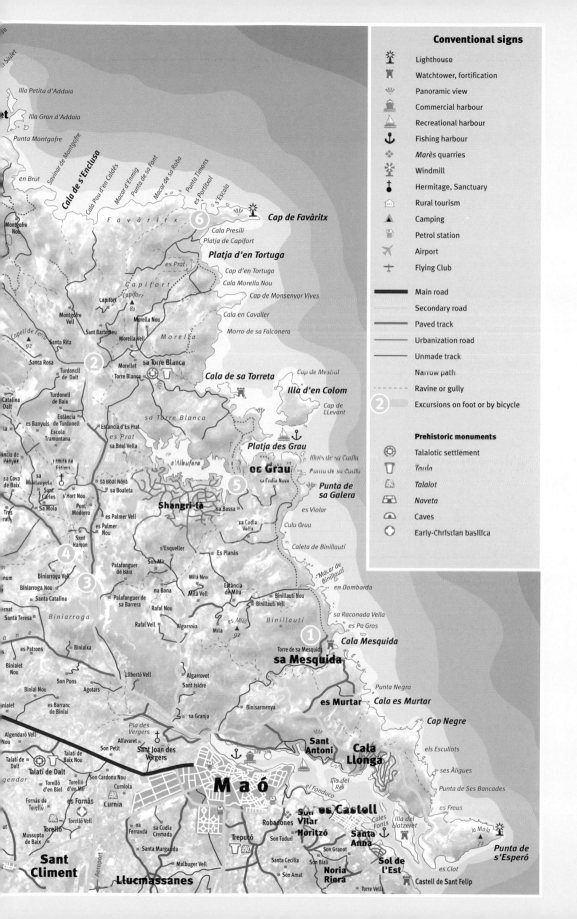

Conventional signs

☀	Lighthouse
♜	Watchtower, fortification
☀	Panoramic view
⛴	Commercial harbour
⛵	Recreational harbour
⚓	Fishing harbour
❖	*Marès* quarries
☼	Windmill
♁	Hermitage, Sanctuary
⌂	Rural tourism
▲	Camping
⛽	Petrol station
✈	Airport
✈	Flying Club

▬▬▬▬	Main road
─────	Secondary road
─────	Paved track
─────	Urbanization road
─────	Unmade track
─────	Narrow path
‑ ‑ ‑ ‑	Ravine or gully
②═══	Excursions on foot or by bicycle

Prehistoric monuments

◎	Talaiotic settlement
⊓	*Taula*
⌂	*Talaiot*
⊟	*Naveta*
⌒	Caves
◌	Early-Christian basilica

Illa Petita d'Addaia
Illa Gran d'Addaia
Punta Montgofre
en Brut
Cala de s'Enclusa
Savinar de Montgofre
Cala Pou d'en Caldés
Macar d'Enmig
Punta de sa Font
Macar de sa Roba
Punta Timons
es Portitxol
Escala
Montgofre Nou
Favàritx
Cap de Favàritx
Capell de Ferro 92
Lapifort
Capifort
Capiforr 81
Cala Presili
Platja de Capifort
Platja d'en Tortuga
Cap d'en Tortuga
Cala Morella Nou
Cap de Monsenyor Vives
Montgofre Vell
Morella Nou
Cala en Cavaller
Sant Bartomeu
Morella Vell
Morella
Morro de sa Falconera
Santa Rita
Catalina Dalt
Santa Rosa
Turdonell de Dalt
Morellet
Torre Blanca
sa Torre Blanca
Cala de sa Torreta
Cap de Meshul
Illa d'en Colom
Turdonell de Baix
es Banyuls
Estància de Turdonell
Escola Tramuntana
sa Torre Blanca
es Prat
Estància d'Es Prat
sa Boal Vella
Cap de LLevant
②
Ermita de sa Cova de Baix
sa Muntanyeta
Sant Carles
s'Hort Nou
Pont Modorro
sa Mola
es Palmer Vell
es Palmer Nou
sa Boal Nova
sa Boaleta
s'Albufera
Platja des Grau
es Grau
Illots de sa Cudia
Punta de sa Cudia
sa Cudia Nova
⑤
Shangri-là
sa Bassa
sa Cudia Vella
Punta de sa Galera
es Violar
④
Tres ...rats
Biniarroga Vell
③
Biniarroga Nou
Santa Catalina
s'Esqueller
Son Mir
Es Planàs
Palafanguer de Baix
Milà Nou
na Bona
Milà Vell
Estància de Milà
Culu Grau
Caleta de Binillautí
Santa Teresa
Biniarroga
Palafanguer de sa Barrera
Rafal Nou
Binillautí Nou
Binillautí Vell
Macar de Binillautí
en Bombarda
Rafal Vell
Algarrova
Mila
es Milà 92
Binillautí
sa Raconada Vella
es Pa Gros
es Patrons
Biniaixa
①
Torre de sa Mesquida
Cala Mesquida
Biniaiet Nou
Son Pons
Llibertó Vell
Algarovet
sa Mesquida
Biniai Nou
Agotars
Sant Isidre
Punta Negra
...iaiet
es Barranc de Biniai
sa Granja
Binisarmenya
es Murtar
Cala es Murtar
Cap Negre
Pla des Vergers
els Escullots
Algendaró Vell Nou
Alfavaret
Son Petit
Sant Joan des Vergers
Sant Antoni
Cala Llonga
ses Àligues
Talatí de Dalt
Talatí de Baix Nou
Son Cardona Nou
Curniola
Maó
Illa del Rei
el Fonduco
Punta de Ses Bancades
Torelló d'en Biel
Torelló d'en Mir
es Fornàs
Curnia
es Castell
Illa del Llatzeret
es Freus
Fornàs de Torelló
Torelló Vell
na Ferranda
sa Cudia Cremada
Robadones
Son Vilar
Horitzó
Cales Fonts
Santa Anna
la Mola 72
Punta de s'Esperó
Sant Climent
Mussupta de Baix
Torelló
Treputó
Son Tudurí
Son Granot
Son Biali
Sol de l'Est
es Clot
Llucmassanes
Santa Margarida
Malbuger Vell
Santa Cecília
Son Amat
Noria Riera
Castell de Sant Felip
Torre Vella
Aeroport

EXCURSIONS ON FOOT
OR BY BICYCLE

1

Sa Mesquida
Es Grau

As this walk follows a clearly defined path except for occasional, short stretches, it presents no difficulty but does require some stamina and, in summer, a hat or sunshade and drinking water. There are wonderful views of the open sea and small coves that offer the welcome opportunity of a refreshing and possibly solitary swim. To avoid having to walk all the way back, which would render this excursion impractical to all but the extremely energetic, consider the possibility of returning from **Es Grau** by bus, taxi or arrange to be met by car.
•TIME APPROX:
3-4h. (one-way)

2

Camí de
Montgofre Nou

This walk takes us, there and back, from the main road to the entrance to the **Montgofre Nou** estate, which is closed to the public, and back. On the way we can see the curious rock formations of **Capell de Ferro** (Iron Hat) to the west of the path. Also possible by car.
•TIME APPROX:
Less than 1h

3

Camí de sa Boval
Torre Blanca

The Camí de sa Boval crosses an extension of farmland which once formed part of the S'Albufera marshlands. The archeological site at Torre Blanca, complete with *naveta*, remains of a settlement and *taula* (the only one with a sea view), offers lovely panoramic views of the coast and the **Illa d'en Colom**. Totally practicable by car it is one of the excursions that allows us to discover the island's interior.
•TIME APPROX:
2h 30m (return)

4

Es Puntarró
Binixems

Starting from the same flat area described in the previous excursion, we follow the path towards higher ground and a protected zone of rich woodland (recently included in the protected areas), arriving eventually at the shrine of **St. Llorenç de Binixems**, one of the island's oldest, built at the time of the Catalan conquest in the 13th century and mentioned in the Treaty of Anagni.
•TIME APPROX:
2h 30m (return)

5

Es Grau
Sa Torreta

We cross the wooden bridge that spans the narrow canal leading us to Es Grau beach. On the far side of the beach we take the path that follows the coastline. Beyond a tiny cove with a house, we continue behind the **Punta de Fra Bernat** ignoring another path which branches to the left. As the path ascends, there are excellent views of the **Illa d'en Colom** and we will arrive eventually at the cove of **Sa Torreta** from where we will retrace our steps.
•TIME APPROX:
2h (return)

6

Favàritx
Cala Morella

After exploring the interesting scenery of the **Cap de Favàritx** headland surrounding the lighthouse, we return to **Tortuga**. An area of dunes and marshlands (usually dry in summer) lies just behind the beach. Our objective is to reach **Morella Nou**, crossing the headland that separates the two beaches. On this walk we will come across a great variety of terrains and natural environments.
•TIME APPROX:
1h 30m (return)

Port de Maó

ES CASTELL / CALES FONTS

Maó's natural harbour stretches inland for 5 kms. giving safe anchorage to vessels of all kinds- and has been highly considered by illustrious sailors over the centuries.
The panoramic views from the newly built avenues high on the cornice are magnificent, and a boat trip around the port is highly recommendable and offers an alternative persepctive.

Clustered around the bay, *Es Castell* is the first town in Spain to be awoken by the sun rise every morning. Counterpoint to this,the old fishing port of *Cales Fonts* is a busy nucleus of bars and restaurants that fill to capacity on summer nights, making this one of the island's livellest night spots.

The **Es Pa Gros** headland, 68 mts. high, overlooks **Cala Mesquida**. The French landed here to occupy the island in 1871. At the opposite extreme of the beach, we see the Sa Mesquida defence tower, built by the British at the end of the 18th century as protection against further surprise attacks.

Sa Mesquida

Es Pa Gros / Sa Raconada Vella

Behind **Es Pa Gros** appears another, quieter cove knows as **Sa Raconada Vella**. Fewer people come here as there is far less sand.

To the right, the nucleus of summer holiday homes belonging to Maoneses that has existed here for centuries.

The magnificent landscape of **Es Grau** with its ample beach and traditional houses to one side and the **Illa d'en Colom** to the other, has benefitted from the declaration of the **S'Albufera** as the island's first National Park. The unique nature of this sizeable ecological zone (1790 hectares are now protected) has, at last, been recognized and scientific and educational projects, instead of buildings and developments, are planned here for the future.

Es Grau

Parc Natural de s'Albufera

The declaration of **S'Albufera** as a National Park emphasizes the importance of this marshland zone that forms part of the migratory routes of many European and African birds. It is connected to the sea by the narrow Sa Gola canal.

Another place of interest in this area is the quiet and secluded **Cala de sa Torreta** which can only be reached on foot from Es Grau. It marks the end of the itinerary 5 on page 42.

Es Grau

Sa Torreta / Illa d'en Colom

The **Illa d'en Colom** can be visited on the motor boat that leaves from Es Grau.

The **Caló des Moro** is one of the two small but attractive beaches to be found on the islet.

Close to Favàritx, the lovely, un-spoilt cove of **Morella Nou** is surrounded by pinewoods and a typical old boathouse stands on the beach. It can be reached following the itinerary 6 on page 42.

Cala en Tortuga (Capifort) and **Cala Presili** are two adjacent coves very popular with those who choose to escape from the beaches of the more built-up parts of the island. There is a small area of marshland just inland from Tortuga.

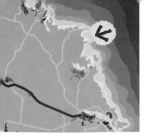

Far de Favàritx

Morella Nou / Cala d'en Tortuga

*The silhouette of the **Favàritx** light-house overlooks the black slate, almost lunar, landscape of the most desolate headland of the eastern coast. On stormy days, the sea breaking over the rocks is a breathtaking sight.*

The rugged outline of this part of the coast gives rise to hidden treasures such as the coves of **S'Enclusa** and **Montgofre**. In the background, the islets of Addaia and the fishing village of Na Macaret.

Another view of the solitary coves of **Montgofre**, largely protected from intrusion by their practical inaccessibility other than from the sea.

Na Macaret

At the mouth of the narrow and elongated **Port d'Addaia** and protected by the Illa de ses Mones islet, the pleasure harbour and, beyond, **Cala Molí** and the houses of **Na Macaret**.

The reefs that abound in the limpid waters around the **Gran** and **Petita Addaia** islets, render dangerous the entrance to the port which, in compensation, offers safe anchorage in its interior.

▷ Arenal d'en Castell
▷ Arenal de Son Saura
▷ Fornells
▷ Cap de Cavalleria
▷ Cala Pregonda

Es Mercadal is the geographic heart of this area, and **Fornells** its tourist centre. Its enormous bay, protected from the north wind and the sea by the Sa Mola promontory, is the ideal setting for all kinds of water sports. The nearby beaches, such as **Binimel·là**, are restful contrasts to the rest of the rugged coastline and **Pregonda**, because of its inaccessibility, remains hidden to all but the most determined visitors.

Owing to its very varied geological characteristics, it is impossible to generalize about the nature of this landscape: in **Cala Rotja**, in the bay of Fornells, there are copper-coloured formations (typical of the Triassic era also seen at the famous **Penya de s'Indi** or at **Cavalleria**) that are completely unrelated to the grey or black formations found close by. There is, however, one definitive common factor – the *tramuntana* wind that, in combination with the violent action of the waves it creates, erodes and changes the shape of all it touches.

This whole coastline has been declared a protected area under the Balearic Islands *Espais Naturals* legislation. Inland, **Santa Àgueda**, with its Moorish fortification, and **Monte Toro** are the two great vantage points of the island, and the countryside that lies between them, almost untouched by man, seems to have suffered no greater transformations than those imposed by the changing seasons.

EXCURSIONS ON FOOT
OR BY BICYCLE

7

Arenal de Son Saura Cala Pudent

A short attractive walk that starts at the extreme left of **Arenal de Son Saura** beach (looking seawards), and follows the rocky coastline to the tiny **Cala Pudent** and its transparent waters.
•TIME APPROX:
Less than 1 hr (return)

8

Camí d'en Kane

If we turn off the main road here, this stretch of the old **Camí d'en Kane** leads us through surprisingly luxuriant woodlands. An ideal excursion either on foot or by bike.
•TIME APPROX:
2h (return)

9

Santa Àgueda

An ancient cobblestone road leads us to the top of the mountain at 264 metres above sea level where the most notable traces of the Moorish domination of the island are to be found in the form of a ruined fort. It has been declared part of the National Historic and Artistic Heritage and restoration work is planned for the near future. Spectacular views.
•TIME APPROX:
1h 15m (return)

10

Ferreries Camí de Ruma

Heading north from Ferreries, the **Camí de Ruma** crosses the Hort de St. Patrici estate and, after a succession of uphill bends, we arrive at St. Francesc where we must leave the car and take the unmade path to the right which will afford us excellent and unusual views of both the north and south coasts on either side. Beyond St. Josep, the pathway becomes a rough track but presents no difficulty, and the rest of the circuit, which coincides partly with the **Camí de Tramuntana**, is easy to follow, becoming steeper beyond St. Antoni de Ruma. During this last stretch we can enjoy good views of **Sta. Àgueda** and **S'Enclusa**
•TIME APPROX:
3h 30m

11

Ferragut beach Binimel·là

Starting from either of these beaches, this pleasant, easy walk enables us to discover this stretch of the coastline and **Cala Mica**, a cove that lies between the two.
•TIME APPROX:
1h 30m (return)

12

Binimel·là Cala Pregonda

A short walk along the coastline from **Binimel·là** beach, this is the best way to discover the beautiful **Cala Pregonda**.
•TIME APPROX:
Less than 1h (return)

13

Cala Rotja

Twenty-two kilometres out of Maó, on the Fornells road, we come across a metal gateway on the right where we must leave the car and continue on foot, following the wide, unmade path until we reach a stone wall which must be climbed. From here we will take the left fork which leads through a pine wood to the curious geological formations of **Cala Rotja**. The characteristic, red clay flats which give the beach its name (*rotja* meaning red in Catalan) are a popular site for skincleansing mud baths or simply for enjoying the splendid view of the great bay of Fornells. The best way to return is by following the coastline via **Cala Blanca** and, on arrival at the abandoned saltworks and old house at La Concepción, take the path that leads back to our point of departure.
•TIME APPROX:
1H 30M

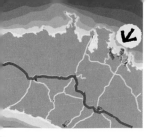

Arenal d'en Castell

MACAR DE SA LLOSA

Arenal d'en Castell, with its many hotels and tourist developments, is protected from the east wind by the stone mass of Punta Grossa. This is one of the island's most popular beaches.

The **Macar de sa Llosa** is another lovely spot lying within the same great bay as Arenal d'en Castell, from where it may be reached on foot. Access is easier, however, from Son Parc, an urbanization situated more to the north.

Arenal de Son Saura is frequently called Son Parc, partly with reference to the tourist complex that now surrounds it, and partly in order to distinguish it from the south coast Son Saura cove. And important area of dunes lie behind the beach and , in the vicinity, the island's only golf course is to be found.

The tiny *Cala Pudent* lies to the left of Son Saura. Its proximity to the sands of the Arenal and the beauty of the surroundings make it an attractive place to visit. (See itinerary 7, page 56).

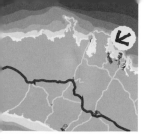

Arenal de Son Saura

Cala Pudent / La Mola de Fornells

The **Mola de Fornells** is a natural barrier between the north and northeastern coasts, and marks the northernmost point of the island. As such, the rocky headland stands as an impressive retaining wall against the violence of the sea and the fierce tramuntana.

The ample bay of Fornells and the surrounding area are protected as a nature reserve and this has prevented them from suffering the consequences of speculation and transformation.

The fishing village of **Fornells** has become an important tourist centre. The lobster calderetas served here in the restaurants have a lot to do with its popularity. The watchtower, built by the British after the demolition of the St. Antoni fort, can be seen in the background.

The installations of the old saltworks of **Ses Salines** can be seen at the end of the enormous bay of Fornells. Pinewoods almost reach the refreshing waters of **Cala Blanca** cove. (See excursion 13 page 56).

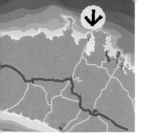

Fornells
SES SALINES / CALA TIRANT

The coastline opposite the quayside is dotted with tiny coves which emphasize the impression of a land-locked sea affording ideal conditions for sailing sports of all kinds.

At **Cala Tirant**, the name of a new urbanization, Playas de Fornells, confirms the fact that the townspeople consider this to be "their" beach. Beyond the sand, there is a marshland zone and tamarind trees.

The **Cavalleria** peninsula ends at this headland, where the lighthouse marks the northernmost point of the island. The **Porros** islet, seen here on the horizon, is often covered by the raging sea.

The beaches of **Cavalleria** and **Ferragut** with their red sands are ideal for bathing as long as the wind is not from the north. From here to the nearby beach of Binimel·la it is a short, pleasant walk as described in the itinerary 11 on page 56.

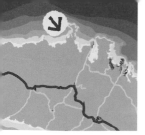

Cap de Cavalleria

Ferragut / sa Nitja / Binimel·là

Another view of the **Cavalleria** headland allows us to appreciate the different configuration of the two versants: high cliffs to the east and more gentle slopes down to the sea to the west. To the left, the old Roman port of **Sa Nitja**, where archaelogical excavations are being carried out.

Binimel·là beach is the largest and most easily accessible in an area that is well-known for the richness of its marine floor. The adjacent land, such as Es Pla Vermell, owes much of its fertility to the presence of fresh water springs.

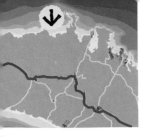

Cala Pregonda
PREGONDÓ

Inaccessibility by road has enabled **Pregonda** to remain unspoilt, conserving its idyllic combination of fine sands, transparent waters and surrounding pinewoods. The beauty of the setting is enhanced even more by its location in the centre of the rugged and inhospitable north coast. (See excursion 12 page 56).

The rocks that lie just offshore protect the cove from the open sea and would seem to have been placed there partly for this purpose and partly to add yet another attraction to this already privileged spot. The wider area of sand to the right is known as **Pregondó**.

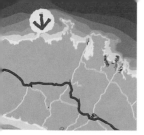

Cala Pregonda

Illes Bledes / Cala Barril
Cala Calderer

Cala Barril is protected by another rocky crag. The larger of the *Bledes* islets undoubtedly marks the extreme of the underwater prolongation of the headland.

Another lovely spot on this part of the coastline, the not easily accessible *Cala Calderer* in the foreground), forms part of one of the island's largest protected areas of special interest.

- ▷ **Cala Pilar**
- ▷ **Algaiarens**
- ▷ **Ciutadella**
- ▷ **Cap d'Artrutx**
- ▷ **Son Saura**
- ▷ **Macarella**

The western extreme of Menorca, which coincides with the municipal district of **Ciutadella**, is the driest and most barren part of the island and is bordered, to the north, by the green belt of **La Vall** and, to the south, by the gorges or ravines. It takes the shape of a great platform which slopes progressively down towards the south coast. Many prehistoric monuments are to be found in this area along with fine examples of wealthy landowners' mansions that remain today as evidence of past affluence.

The beaches on the south coast of this area have been saved from development as access to them is only possible by crossing private property. As a result, **Es Talaier**, **Turqueta** and **Macarella** are of an unspoilt, natural beauty unsurpassed almost anywhere in the Mediterranean. The beaches remain untouched thanks to the landowners' reluctance to permit entry via their estates. Access by car is controlled and limited at gates on the approach paths and, in recent times, even a charge (locally known as the "ecology tax") was made per vehicle. Here we have a classic example of a double-edged argument. If indiscriminate access to these beaches is allowed, they are in great danger of losing their unique, virgin status, but public opinion is divided and the controversy continues year after year. Apparently, the local authorities are about to take part in the issue, so, hopefully, some solution will be found in the near future.

Other beaches in the Ciutadella area such as **Cala en Blanes**, **Cala en Brut**, **Santandria**, **Cala en Forcat** and **Cales Piques**, are crowded in summer but offer all kinds of tourist attractions and services.

The city of Ciutadella with its marked Mediterranean character and aristocratic atmosphere is described in detail in its own section.

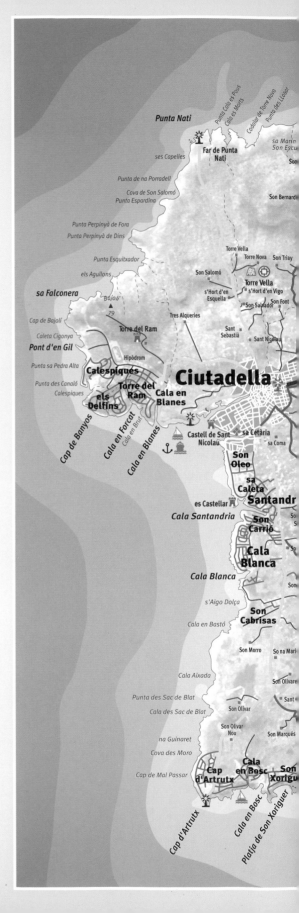

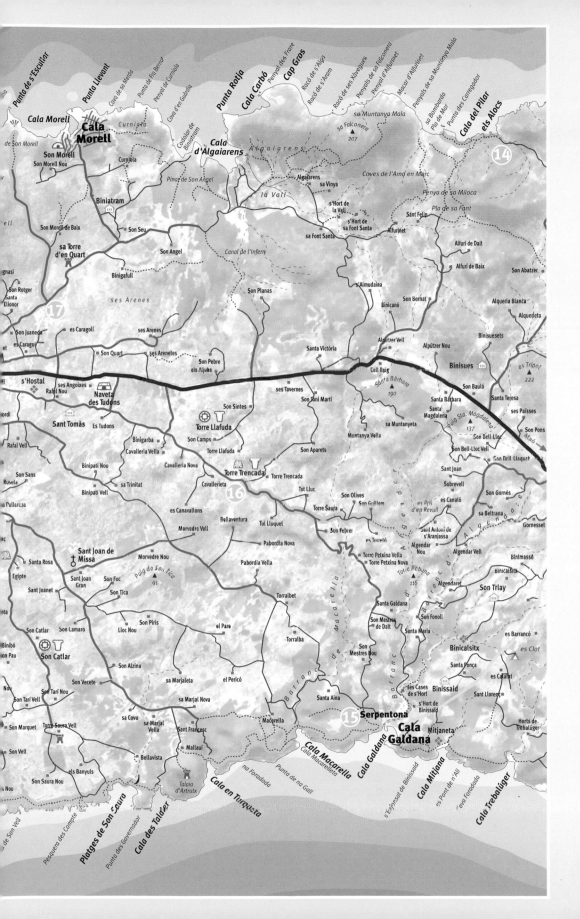

14

Els Alocs
Cala Pilar

Halfway up the cliffside, the path follows the coastline leading us to **Cala Pilar** beach, one of the most appreciated by solitary bathers who choose to escape from the crowds during the high season. There is even a freshwater spring, an added advantage at any time of year. Walking eastwards behind the Punta des Carregador, we find a curious work of nature: hundreds of rocks have been eroded by the sea to form pebbles of such disproportionate size that the beach they form has the appearance of a giant's playground.
•TIME APPROX:
2h (return)

15

Cala Galdana
Cala Macarella
Cala en Turqueta

The first stretch of the path is separated from the sea by pine woods. The beautiful coves of **Macarella** and **Macarelleta** are, in themselves, well worth the trip, but, after a refreshing swim there, it is advisable to carry on as far as **Cala en Turqueta**. If we wish to complete our discovery of the area, we can combine this walk with the one that follows, in which case we should allow another half an hour on top of the sum of the two individual timings.
•TIME APPROX:
2h 30m (return)

16

Torre Trencada
Algendar gorge

Leaving Ciutadella on the Camí Vell de Maó, we will make a first stop at **Torre Trencada** to visit the *talaiot* and *taula*. The site is well signposted and there is a car park. From here, we can walk to **Torre Llafuda** to see the smaller *taula* before returning to the car and driving to the fork that leads to the left of Son Guillem. We will leave the car where the tarmac road ends and continue, on foot, to the **Algendar gorge**. The old pathway, excavated out of the rock and still paved with cobble stones in places, leads us on an attractive walk to the gorge of the river bed, passing through luxuriant vegetation.
•TIME APPROX:
1h (return) on foot

17

Punta de s'Escullar

This short excursion brings us into contact with the northeast coast, which is rugged and solitary, except for specific points such as the nearby **Cala Morell**. Vehicles must be left where the asphalt finishes, and good views of the cliffs are to be had from the headland just beyond the road's end.
•TIME APPROX:
1h (return)

18

Son Xoriguer
Es Talaier

This walk can also be started from Cala en Bosc, crossing the built-up area that separates it from Son Xoriguer. The path is always close to the sea and several stone walls must be climbed with the aid of *botadors*, the rudimentary steps formed by protruding stones. Beyond the Son Aparets Nou estate and the entrance to Torre Saura Vell, we will encounter the ample, twin beaches of Son Saura. From here on, the track is not very clearly defined, but presents few obstacles. Passing the Punta des Governador on our right, we proceed to Es Talaier, another cove of fine, white sands, much smaller than Son Saura, but also surrounded by pine woods. The idea of combining this excursion with the previous one is worth considering.
•TIME APPROX:
3h 30m (return)

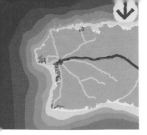

Cala Pilar

Cala Carbó

Although there is a good half an hour's walk to **Cala Pilar** (or perhaps for this very reason, as it discourages the majority of possible visitors) this beach is one of the most popular among those who wish to escape from the crowds. To the left of the beach, an interesting cove of giant pebbles, eroded by the sea over the centuries. (See excursion 14 page 70).

Cala Carbó is another characteristic enclave of the north coast, a small pebbled beach, hidden at the foot of the mountain. Its name – "carbó" meaning coal – comes from the charcoal stacks that were once found in the area. The ancient pathways that led to the beach have all but disappeared among the wild vegetation, and today the easiest route of access is from the sea.

The ensemble formed by the larger and smaller **Algaiarens** beaches and that of **Ses Fontanelles** is the high spot of one of the most interesting areas of the island which coincides with the **La Vall** estate. The Codolar de Biniatram appears in the background.

In **Algaiarens**, the beauty of the surrounding landscape of sand dunes and marshland combines with the clean sands and transparent waters to create an idyllic spot for bathing.

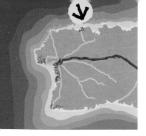

Algaiarens

Cala Morell / Punta Nati

The deep inlet of **Cala Morell** offers a welcome refuge to sailors on a stretch of increasingly rugged coastline. Among the houses of the new development, a few prehistoric caves remain as proof that the cove has been inhabited by man since time immemorial.

Punta Nati is a desolate region; the lighthouse stands on a cliff that drops abruptly to the sea and nothing but the sparsest of vegetation grows among the rocks. The only buildings are "ponts", curious stone constructions that were used as shelters for livestock.

Beyond
Cap de Bajolí,
the westernmost
point of the is-
land, the natural
archway of
Pont d'en Gil
appears like the
secret doorway to
a hidden cove.

To the north of
Ciutadella, tourist
developments
rise like fortifica-
tions around the
narrow inlet of
Cala en Forcat.

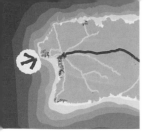

Cala en Forcat
Pont d'en Gil / Cala en Blanes

Cala en Brut is almost an estuary with hardly any sand, but sunbathers make use of the concrete platforms that litter the banks for this purpose.

Cala en Blanes is wider and deeper than the previous coves, but, even so, in summer it fills to capacity with both tourists and locals from the neighbouring Ciutadella.

The Gothic cathedral has always been the centre point of the old **Ciutadella,** but this perspective of the port will soon be a thing of the past. In the near future an ambitious project will be put into practice to enlarge the harbour far beyond its present limits in response to the ever-increasing demand for mooring space for both commercial and recreational vessels.

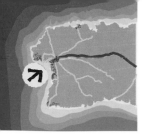

Santandria is a narrow and elongated inlet which has always been Ciutadella's traditional playground. It also played an important role in the 18th C. when it became the gateway to the city under the French domination.

Cala Blanca, further to the south, is a centre for both local and visiting holidaymakers. There are prehistoric caves around both the coves.

At *Cap d'Artrutx*, the south-western extreme of the island, the land slopes gently down to the channel between Menorca and Mallorca. The Cap d'Artrutx and Capdepera lighthouses mark the coastlines of the respective islands.

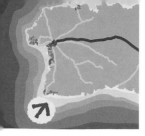

Cap d'Artrutx

SANTANDRIA / CALA BLANCA
CALA EN BOSC / SON XORIGUER

Cala en Bosc, the westernmost beach on the south coast, is surrounded today by holiday resorts of recent creation that include an artifical inland lake where a pleasure harbour has been built.

The natural bay formed by **Son Xoriguer** beach is flanked, on one side by the holiday resort of the same name and, on the other, by unspoilt terrain, seen in the foreground.

On Ciutadella's south coast, **Son Saura**, **Es Talaier**, **Turqueta** and **Macarella** comprise an area that has, fortunately, been protected from development and whose beaches remain unspoilt. Here, Son Saura, the largest of them.

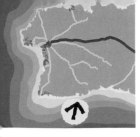

Son Saura

Es Talaier / Cala en Turqueta

Beyond Son Saura and the Punta des Governador, **Es Talaier** is a delightful spot. As in the case of the neighbouring beaches, the decomposition of the limestone soil has created the white sand that is so characteristic of this area.
(See excursion 18 page 70).

On contemplating **Cala en Turqueta** and **Macarella-Macarelleta** (shown in the following double page spread) it is easy to see why these beaches are considered among the island's finest. Access to them by road is fraught with difficulties but for boats they provide safe anchorage in idyllic settings.

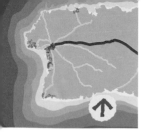

Macarella-Macarelleta

▷ Cala Galdana
▷ Trebalúger
▷ Son Bou
▷ Cala en Porter

Between the **Algendar gorge** that marks the boundary between the Ciutadella and Ferreries districts and the **Cala en Porter** gorge in Alaior, the countryside is characterized by the streams and torrents that have cleaved their way through the limestone land surface on their way to the sea.

The coastline, fairly elevated at **Cala Galdana**, drops slowly until it reaches **Binigaus**, starting point of an almost uninterrupted stretch of some of the island's most popular sandy beaches: **St. Adeodat**, **St. Tomàs**, **Atàlitx** and **Son Bou**, whose eastern extreme is marked by the cliffs at **Cap de ses Penyes**.

The limpid waters of the **Mitjana**, **Trebalúger**, **Fustam** and **Escorxada** coves are the great attraction of this area and **Cala Galdana**, despite the impact of the tourist development that has taken place there, is still the most symbolic of the Menorcan coastline. Groves of pine trees that grow down as far as the sandy beaches, emerald green waters, luxuriant vegetation and sweet-water springs combine to create an idyllic environment.

It is perhaps in this part of the island where the visitor encounters the widest and richest range of alternatives offered by nature: from long, open beaches packed with cosmopolitan tourists, easily reached from Ferreries, Es Migjorn or Alaior (see map and itineraries), to secluded coves only accessible by boat or on foot. There are hotels and appartments at **Cala Galdana**, **St. Tomàs** and **Son Bou** that offer all kinds of services and conveniences.

IV EXCURSIONS ON FOOT
OR BY BICYCLE

19

Ferreries
Algendar gorge

This is another way to visit the lovely **Algendar** gorge (see itinerary 16 on page 70). Shortly after the **Cala Galdana** junction, we must turn left and drive steeply up-hill along the road which, owing to its elevation, offers good views of **S'Enclusa** to the north. Turning then in a southerly direction towards the coast, it will lead us to **Es Canaló**, where we must leave the car and continue on foot down to the river-bed. Here, we will notice a radical change in the vegetation as we penetrate the micro-climate of the *barranc,* where palm and fruit-trees, lianas and ferns grow in almost tropical profusion. Crossing the river-bed, if we have arranged for return transport, we can join the previous itinerary, in reverse direction.
•TIME APPROX:
1h (return) for the walk

20

Sant Adeodat
Cala Escorxada
Cala Fustam

The first part of this walk takes us along the beaches of **Binigaus** and then, from behind the beach bar at the mouth of the gorge, we follow the path westwards into the pine wood to **Escorxada** and **Fustam**. See Itinerary 24 as an alternative.
•TIME APPROX:
2h 30m (return)

21

Cave of Na Polida
and Cave of des
Coloms

To reach these interesting caves we must leave the car park at **St. Adeodat** and walk to **Binigaus** beach where, near the middle, a path leads us to the left towards the gorge. After about three hundred metres, we leave the main river-bed to the left, climb a wall and follow the left bank of the stream for about half a kilometre. Here, we take the fork that takes us over to the other side to the **Na Polida** cave where, with the aid of a torch, we will see extraordinary marble-like stalactites which, unfortunately, show clear signs of vandalism. From here we return to the left bank and, about half a kilometre further up, crossing back to the right, we reach the **Es Coloms** cave, also known as *Sa Catedral* owing to its size - the oval-shaped entrance is 24 metres high. Archaeological finds seem to confirm the hypothesis that this was a prehistoric sanctuary.
•TIME APPROX:
2h 30m

22

Sant Tomàs
Son Bou basilica

From one extreme to the other of these two beaches (skirting around the outside of the hotel at the end of Sant Tomàs), this is quite a long walk, although not strenuous. From **Punta d'Atàlitx** there is a good view of **Son Bou** and, at the end, we may visit the remains of the **early-Christian basilica**.
•TIME APPROX:
2h 30m (return)

23

Son Mercer de Baix,
Trebalúger and
Sa Cova gorges

The main interest of this itinerary is, not only the archaeological site at **Son Mercer de Baix**, which includes the **Cova des Moro** and other *navetes*, but also the spectacular view of the confluence of the two majestic gorges. Access by car is possible until this point, but then we must leave the car if we wish to continue down to the cave known simply as **Sa Cova** or **Son Fideu** which is most impressive.
•TIME APPROX:
1h 30m (return) for the walk.

24

Cala Galdana
Cala Trebalúger

The path leaves **Cala Galdana** and leads through pine woods to first, **Cala Mitjana** and then **Trebalúger**. If one feels up to a longer walk, it is possible to continue on as far as **St. Adeodat**. See Itinerary 20.
•TIME APPROX:
3h (return)

25

Es Migjorn
Binigaus

This alternative route to **Binigaus** beach is, in itself, a pleasant walk, particularly the last stretch that takes us along the gorge. Access is possible by car as far as the Binigaus Nou farmhouse.
•TIME APPROX:
1h 30m (return)

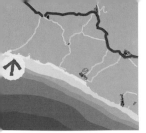

Cala Galdana

The surrounding landscape, rich in flora, fauna and pinewoods, and the perfect horse-shoe-shaped beach make *Cala Galdana* perhaps the most emblematic of the island's coves. In the first view, the gorges of **Algendar** and **Algendaret** can be seen as they channel their way down to the sea. In the second, the large hotel, built close to the cliff, stands as an example of the indiscriminate development of the early years of the tourist boom.

The following four photographs offer a an overall impression of the south coast beaches. Lying at the outlets of the successive gorges that cross the hinterland, they are invariably surrounded by pinewoods and the colour and transparency of the water, as seen here in **Cala Mitjana**, cannot be matched elsewhere.

The fertile soil of the **Sa Cova** barranc is exploited for vegetable and fruit farming. At the mouth of the gorge, **Trebalúger**, although a popular beach in summer, remains unspoilt thanks to its difficult access by car.

Trebalúger

Cala Mitjana / Cala Fustam
Cala Escorxada

*Another view of **Trebalúger** clearly shows how the beach acts as a separation between the sea and the approaching stream which rarely flows large enough to overcome this natural barrier. (See excursion 24 page 86).*

*Although **Fustam** and **Escorxada** are separated by the Punta de St. Antoni, the distance between them is so short that they are generally considered as a whole. The richness of the pinewoods and excellent state of conservation more than justifies their recent qualification as protected areas. (See excursion 20, page 86).*

In the central part of the south coast, the characteristic configuration of gorges and coves changes as the cliffs give way to a more gently sloping seaboard. Between the alluvial farmland and the sea, dunes are formed as seen here in **Binigaus**.

The beaches of **St. Adeodat** and **St. Tomàs** form a large resort area of hotels and appartments. This perspective, in which the opposite coastline can be seen on the horizon, serves to remind us of Menorca's size and configuration.

Son Bou

*Good panoramic views of Son Bou can be seen from the **Punta d'Atàlitx**. At this point the beach is at its narrowest but, as it is also more secluded, it is a popular spot with nudists.*

***Son Bou** is the island's longest beach (nearly 4 kms.) and also the most crowded. Its size, and the tourist attractions (including an aquatic games park) found near the hotels, make it an ideal beach for children. At the far end, an early **Christian basilica** can be visited.*

Son Bou

Beyond Cap de ses Penyes that limits Son Bou to the east, the coastline again tends towards tiny coves set among cliffs, such as **Sant Llorenç** that marks the outlet of the Torre Vella gorge.

Only the sparsest of crops grow in the shallow soil of the clifftop. Far below, the sea erodes the massive limestone block. To the left, the ruins of the **Torre Nova** watchtower built in the times of frequent pirate raids.

Cala en Porter
Cala Sant Llorenç / Sa Torre Nova

As it is one of the island's larger beaches, **Cala en Porter** was among the first to undergo tourist development. On the cliff face, a natural cave, **Cova d'en Xoroi,** has been converted into a discotheque and offers spectacular views of the surrounding coast.

Menorca can be unmistakably identified from the air by the geometrical shapes formed by the dry-stone walls that form one of the island's most characteristic features.

95

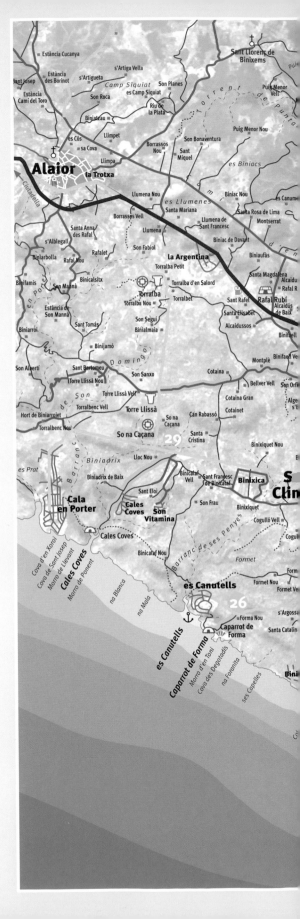

▷ Cales Coves
▷ Canutells
▷ Binibèquer
▷ Punta Prima
▷ Cala Alcalfar
▷ Cala Sant Esteve

This area is confined by, on one side, the **Cala en Porter gorge** that descends from Alaior to the sea and, on the other, by an imaginary line drawn from the innermost extreme of Maó harbour to Alaior. It is a varied landscape, although generally flat and sparsely vegetated except for the occasional area of woodland near the coast. During the winter months when rainfall tends to be high, the landscape is covered by a lush, green blanket, but the rest of the year, the twisted, dry branches of the wild olive are the most apparent element. In the gently sloping areas closer to the coast, the vegetation is more typically Mediterranean with pines and the occasional evergreen oak.

Cala en Porter, **Cales Coves**, **Es Canutells**, **Binidalí** and **Biniparratx** are examples of coves protected from the sea by high cliffs. From **Binisafúller** to **Punta Prima**, the coastline is less elevated but equally rocky. Punta Prima, the longest of these beaches, faces the **Illa de l'Aire**, the southernmost point of the island. From here to **Cala St. Esteve**, close to the mouth of Maó harbour, the coastline faces due east, and the permanent or temporary residents of **Alcalfar**, **Rafalet** and **S'Algar** are the first people in the Iberian peninsula to see the sun rise each morning.

Most of this coastline, with its many tourist developments and unspoilt hamlets, belongs to the district of **Sant Lluís**. Attempts are being made by the municipal authorities to rehabilitate the old *Camí de Cavalls*, or bridle path. Dating from 1682, it once circumvallated the whole island and one of its stretches leads from **Punta Prima** to **Alcalfar**.

26

Forma Nou
Caparrot de Forma

Once on the **Cala Canutells** road, we must take the left fork by the **Forma Nou** farmhouse. From here, a short walk will lead us along the cliff to the Morro d'en Toni headland, from where we will see the neighbouring troglodyte caves and an ample view of the south coast.
•TIME APPROX:
30m (return)

27

Punta Prima
Rafalet gorge

Follow the coastline from the extreme left of the beach, as we look seawards, as far as the old watchtower and **Caló Roig**. Enjoying lovely views of l'**Illa de l'Aire** along the way. From here we will see the protective rocky headland of Es Torn and the houses of **Alcalfar** clustered around the bay. To the right of the main St. Lluís road we reencounter the pathway that will take us across the **S'Algar** urbanization access road. We follow this unmade track, beyond the last houses, to the gorge, and descend through the welcome shade of the dense woodland between abrupt cliff faces to the diminutive cove for a refreshing swim.
•TIME APPROX:
3h (return)

28

Sant Climent
Camí de Cotaina
Torre Llisà

This excursion brings us into contact with the characteristic landscape of rural Menorca in an area where few transformations have taken place over the years.
At Algendar we must take the turn to the left and follow the gently sloping hill past the Son Orfila and Momple farmhouses to **Cotaina**. When we reach the Alaior-Cala en Porter road, we drive across and continue to the **Torre Llisà** farm where a signpost indicates an unusual *taula*. Here we should leave the car and enter on foot so as not to disturb the farm work in progress.

29

Cales Coves

Turn off the St.Climent-Cala en Porter road at the **Son Vitamina** urbanization, leave the car when the road becomes unmade and walk down towards the sea.
The cliffs that overlook the peaceful waters of the double cove are dotted with troglodyte burial caves, many of which are inhabited in summer and some all year round. The whole necropolis has been declared a National Historic and Artistic Monument and steps are being taken to prevent its degeneration.
•TIME APPROX:
1h (return)

30

Sant Lluís
Llucmassanes
and hamlets

We leave St. Lluís on the **Punta Prima** road and take the first turning to the right which will lead us to **Torret**. The narrow road meanders through this carefully conserved hamlet and emerges on the main **Binibèquer-Binissafúller** road where we turn left through **S'Ullastrar** towards the recently excavated *taula* at **Binisafuet**. Here we turn right and continue beyond Sa Parereta where we take another right turn to follow the old Volta d'es Milord (His Lordship's Walk), as far as the **Biniparrell** junction where we turn left towards **Llucmassanes**. As high dry-stone walls flank both sides of the road during much of this circuit, better visibility will be enjoyed by bicycle than by car. If we do not wish to return via St. Lluís, there are two accesses to the main Maó-airport road.

Cales Coves

The name of **Cales Coves** is derived from the many caves excavated in the cliff walls in prehistoric times. It is believed that they were burial places but, in recent times, they have been used as living accommodation. There is a project to convert the cove into an area which may be visiited as a site of special archeological interest. The shelter afforded by this double cove means that it is usually replete with pleasure craft. (See excursion 29, page 98)

People from St. Climent and Maó were, *at one time,* the only visitors to **Canutells** *whose small and protected beach has undergone great change in recent years.*

The landscape in **Caparrot de Forma***, once uninhabited and bare, has also changed of late. The high cliffs offer splendid panoramic views of the coast. (See excursion 26, page 98)*

From the sea, many caves are visible on the cliff faces where wild birds make their nests.

Canutells

CAPARROT DE FORMA / BINIDALÍ

*The headland to the west of **Binidalí** is another excellent viewpoint over this stretch of the coastline. Although the entrance to the cove is quite ample, the beach is diminutive but many natural platforms exist in the surrounding rocks for sunbathing or diving.*

At **Biniparratx**, the inlet describes a marked angle between the high cliff walls making it an ideal refuge for boats in bad weather. Here, too, prehistoric caves can be seen at its innermost extreme.

Beyond **Cap d'en Font**, the coastline of the St.Lluís area appears as an unbroken chain of developments and resorts. Just a few years ago, the cove at **Binissafúller** (in the foreground) comprised of no more than a few traditional weekend houses but is now surrounded by modern villas.

Binibèquer

BINIPARRATX / CAP D'EN FONT
BINISAFÚLLER / CALA TORRET

The "fishing village" at **Binibeca Vell** is one of the most visited tourist attractions. Its curious construction aims to reproduce the style and use of raw materials typical of traditional Mediterranean architecture.

Binibèquer, just beyond the aforementioned village, is a beach of fine sand protected from the wind by the Morro d'en Xua headland. The following inlet is **Cala Torret**, surrounded by the resort of the same name.

Binibèquer

Biniancolla is the last of the south-facing coves. The oldest of the houses stand, literally, in the water and their ground floors are used as boathouses.

Punta Prima was appropriately named Sandy Bay by the British during their domination of the island. Always a popular holiday spot among Menorcans, the resort has grown following the building of a large hotel.

Punta Prima
BINIANCOLLA / ILLA DE L'AIRE
ALCALFAR

The **Illa de l'Aire** which rises no more than 15 m. above sea-level at its highest point near the light-house, is home to a subspecies of endemic black lizards.

The little cove at **Alcalfar**, another favourite among Menorcans, was the site of the island's first tourist-orientated hotel. The defense tower stands as proof of its strategic importance in times gone by.

S'Algar *is a well-established resort situated on a rocky headland eroded by the sea. The absence of a beach is more than made up for by the many facilities available to the visitor. The tiny Cala Rafalet lies just beyond.*

*Although the cove of **Cala Rafalet** affords barely enough space to spread out a couple of beach towels, the beauty of the grove of holm oaks through which one passes on the way to the sea, and the views over the cliffs, more than warrant the walk.*

Cala Rafalet

s'Algar / Cala Sant Esteve
la Mola de Maó

*Cala **St. Esteve** is surrounded by the military fortifications that speak to us of Menorca's turbulent history. The recently renovated Fort Marlborough (to the right) can be visited as can the military museum that stands in what remains of the legendary Castell de St. Felip.*

*Returning to our starting point, the old fortress of **La Mola de Maó** overshadows the southernmost headland of the south coast. Its location has lost the strategic importance of times gone by, and, today, its monumental proportions, seen here in the view of the Punta de s'Esperó, appear to peaceably stand guard over Menorca and all her treasures.*

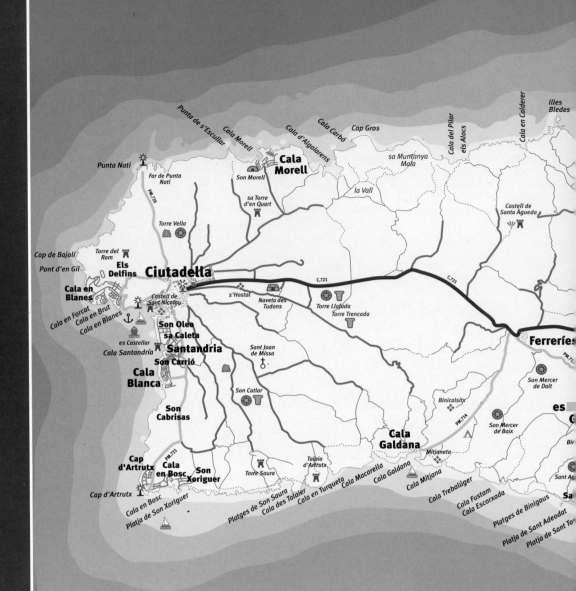

Punta de s'Escullar
Cala Morell
Cala d'Algaiarens
Cala Carbó
Cap Gros
Cala del Pilar
els Alocs
Cala en Calderer
Illes Bledes

Punta Nati
Far de Punta Nati
PM.720
Torre Vella
Son Morell

Cala Morell

sa Torre d'en Quart

sa Muntanya Mala

la Vall

Castell de Santa Àgueda

Cap de Bajolí
Torre del Ram
Pont d'en Gil
Els Delfins
Ciutadella
s'Hostal
Naveta des Tudons
C.721
Torre Llafuda
Torre Trencada
C.721

Cala en Blanes
Cala en Forcat
Cala en Brut
Cala en Blanes
Castell de Sant Nicolau
es Castellar
Cala Santandría
Son Oleo
sa Caleta
Santandria
Sant Joan de Missa
Son Carrió
Cala Blanca

Ferreríes

Son Mercer de Dalt

es

Son Cabrisas

Son Catlar

Binicalsitx
PM.714
Son Mercer de Baix

Bir

Cala Galdana

Mitjaneta

Sant Ag

Cap d'Artrutx
PM.721
Cala en Bosc
Son Xoriguer
Torre Saura
Talaia d'Artrutx

Cap d'Artrutx
Cala en Bosc
Platja de Son Xoriguer
Platges de Son Saura
Cala des Talaier
Cala en Turqueta
Cala Macarella
Cala Galdana
Cala Mitjana
Cala Trebalúger
Cala Fustam
Cala Escorxada
Platges de Binigaus
Platja de Sant Adeodat
Platja de Sant To

Sa

Conventional signs

⚲	Lighthouse
♜	Watchtower, fortification
♨	Panoramic view
⛴	Commercial harbour
⛵	Recreational harbour
⚓	Fishing harbour
❖	*Marès* quarries
✿	Windmill
☦	Hermitage, Sanctuary
🏛	Rural tourism
▲	Camping
⛽	Petrol station
✈	Airport
✈	Flying Club

Prehistoric monuments

◉	Talaiotic settlement
⊤	*Taula*
◭	*Talaiot*
⌂	*Naveta*
⌒	Caves
◇	Early-Christian basilica

▬▬	Main road
▬▬	Secondary road
▬▬	Paved track
──	Urbanization road
──	Unmade track
······	Narrow path
------	Ravine or gully

Car tours

Sa Torreta taula, from the air

1 FROM MAÓ TO SON PARC

- LA MOLA ▸ CALA MESQUIDA
- ES GRAU ▸ FAVÀRITX
- ADDAIA ▸ NA MACARET
- ARENAL D'EN CASTELL ▸ SON PARC

Starting from the innermost extreme of the port, **Sa Colàrsega**, the PM-710-1 road leads behind the power station and naval base, above the villas in Cala Rata and Cala St. Antoni and close by the colonial-style **Golden Farm** (allegedly a temporary residence of Lord Nelson, which can best be appreciated from the other side of the harbour). From here, or from the neighbouring **Cala Llonga** urbanization, we can enjoy splendid views of the city of Maó and Es Castell.

Further on, we arrive at **La Mola**, the fortress built during the reign of Isabel II to take the place of the demolished Castell de St. Felip which had stood on the opposite shore. Permission to visit La Mola, a restricted military zone, may be obtained from the Military Government in Maó.

From this point, the **Els Freus** isthmus, we can see the walled precinct of **El Llatzeret**, which became an island in 1900 as a result of the opening of the Alfons XII, or St. Jordi, Canal. We will have a better view of the Llatzeret when we retrace our steps towards the Cala Mesquida junction where we will turn right. It is on the low hills of this regions where Menorca's finest camomile can be picked.

Cala Mesquida is a nucleus of traditional holiday houses and jetties clustered around the little **Sa Raconada** bay with **Sa Mesquida** beach just beyond and an 18th century watchtower overlooking from above. From here, we return to Maó and start the second phase of our tour by taking the PM-710-2 road towards Es Grau.

This road diverts from the PM-710 Fornells road just beyond the **Pla des Vergers**, or Pla de Sant Joan, vegetable gardens, which we pass on our left, and travels northwards through uneven terrain right up to the beach and village of **Es Grau** from where we may choose to take a boat trip over to **Illa d'en Colom**. **S'Albufera**, a sea-water lagoon of notable interest to biologists and naturalists, is another point of notable interest. (See excursion 5 on page 42) To continue our tour, we must return to the junction with the PM-710 road and follow it 8 kms. to the **Hermitage of Fàtima**.

About 500 metres beyond, we turn right on the PM-715 road, as if following the direction indicated by a curiously shaped craggy rock known as **Sa Sella**, the Saddle, that stands alone in the middle of the plain. At the end of this road we come to **Cap de Favàritx** and the lighthouse of the same name. The last stretch is in rather poor condition, but the unusual, almost lunar landscape of black slate, eroded by the sea for millennia, more than makes up for the uncomfortable drive. The superb beaches of **Presili** and **Tortuga** lie just to the south of the headland and can be reached by a another rough, unmade road.

We return again to the PM-710 road and after about five km. take the turning to the right which leads us, first to **Port d'Addaia**, a long, narrow bay that penetrates more than three km. inland through a richly wooded area, **Na Macaret** where many people from Alaior have their holiday homes and boathouses and, finally, the beach and modern urbanization of **Arenal d'en Castell** with its hotels and tourist developments.

Son Parc is the next place to be visited. An important tourist centre here Menorca's only golf course is to be found along with various complexes of appartments and villas which surround the magnificent beach of **Son Saura**, or Arenal de s'Olla. To round off our tour, we will return to Maó by an alternative route, turning right at the Na Macaret-Addaia junction along the **Camí Vell d'Alaior** which leads us to the **Camí d'en Kane**. This drive offers the chance to appreciate the marked differences between the coast and the rural inland scenery of luxuriant woods of pines and evergreen oaks, farmsteads and old mansions.

2 FROM ALAIOR TO CAP DE CAVALLERIA

MONTE TORO ▸ BINIMEL·LÀ
PREGONDA ▸ CAVALLERIA
CALA TIRANT ▸ FORNELLS ▸ SA ROCA

Our starting point is the higher part of the town of Alaior where the recently paved **Camí d'en Kane** passes by the cemetery and then leads towards **Es Mercadal**. We pass through some woody areas and cross the **Pla d'Alaior** with its curious rock formations that stand out in the flat landscape, basically dedicated to cattle farming, with **Monte Toro** soon appearing ahead of us.

On arrival at Es Mercadal we will take another recently repaired road which winds its way up to the top of **Monte Toro**, Menorca's highest geographical point. From here we can enjoy a complete view of the surrounding island and visit the ermitage dedicated to Our Lady. (See page 8)

We return to Es Mercadal and, ignoring the signposts to Fornells, look for the sign that reads **Platges Costa Nord** (north coast beaches) which will lead us to the **Camí de Tramuntana**. This road takes us through an important agricultural area and, following the contours of the hills, offers wider, more panoramic views than is usual on the island. Generally, visibility from the roads is limited by the ever-present dry-stone walls. This is an interesting drive at any time of year, each season bringing with it a new colour scheme.

Follow the **Binimel·là** and **Pregonda** signposts which indicate roads or tracks to the right. The drive to Binimel·là is worthwhile in itself and the beach, in summer, is the perfect place for a refreshing swim or a drink at the beach bar. Worthily considered to be the jewel of the north coast, Pregonda can only be reached on foot. See excursion 12 of page 56 for more details.

Our next destination is **Cap de Cavalleria**, perhaps the island's most impressive scenario where the effect of the notorious *tramuntana*, or north wind, is most manifest. The lighthouse stands on a rocky headland where goats subsist on the few sparse shrubs that manage to survive in such inhospitable terrain. It is a sheer ninety metre drop to the sea below. From the cliff-top the views of the coast are most spectacular, particularly when the *tramuntana* and the sea combine to demonstrate the forces of nature at full blast. Care should be taken if venturing near the cliff edge on windy days.

On the way back from the lighthouse, on the right-hand side of the road, lies the little port of **Sa Nitja**, site of first, Phoenician, and then Roman settlements. The remains of an early Christian basilica are to be found near the watchtower on the Es Brau headland opposite.
We will now head towards Fornells, maybe stopping on the way to visit the rapidly developing tourist centre of **Cala Tirant** and the marshland zone which lies just inland.

Fornells is the safest port to be found on the rugged north coast and, as such, is invariably packed with boats, and the ample bay is ideal for windsurfing. Owing to the rapid growth of tourism, Fornells has been transformed from a sleepy fishing village to a busy, cosmopolitan town. Nevertheless, it retains much of its picturesque charm and offers pleasant strolls through the old streets or out along the quay where a watchtower dating from the British occupation still stands. No visit to Fornells is complete without trying the famous *caldereta de llagosta* at one of the many waterfront restaurants.

Leaving Fornells on the C-723 towards Es Mercadal. we then turn off on the PM-710 towards Maó until we reach the junction with the access road to the **Sa Roca** urbanization. This road will lead us back to Alaior, passing through woodlands and the **Hermitage of Sta. Ester** on the way.

Fornells

3 AROUND CIUTADELLA

- ▶ Punta Nati ▶ Cala Morell
- ▶ Algaiarens ▶ Cap d'Artrutx
- ▶ Cala en Bosc ▶ Son Xoriguer
- ▶ Cala en Turqueta
- ▶ Cala Macarella

From Ciutadella it is impossible to visit the three neighbouring coastal areas without repeatedly returning to the city as no circular road exists. Several separate excursions are therefore necessary.

The first starts at the Sa Font bastion from where we take the PM-720 to **Punta Nati**. The road is not in very good condition, but the trip is worth making as it takes us through some interesting countryside. After a few cultivated plots of land, the landscape becomes quite desolate and beyond the **Torre Vella** estate, where various *talaiots* are found, there is nothing but stone as far as the eye can see. The lighthouse, with a few surrounding bunkers, overlooks the rugged coastline, infamous for the many shipwrecks that have taken place here through the centuries. Here, Egyptian vultures, a bird of prey now extinct on the rest of the islands, can still be seen flying overhead and another curiosity of the area are *ponts*, strange stone constructions built as shelters for livestock. Just before the lighthouse there is a particularly notable, seven-tiered *pont* with a perfectly formed vault inside. Engraved in the stone, the builder's name and the date, 1857.

For our second tour, we leave Ciutadella's industrial estate on the road to **Cala Morell** and **Algaiarens**, the old **Camí de La Vall**. Along the first stretch of the road, what were once modest constructions for storing farming implements have been converted into chalets with vegetable gardens and orchards. Ahead, the fortified tower of **Torre d'en Quart**, after which we must take the road to the **Cala Morell** urbanization. From here, on the rock face of the gorge, we can see the caves of the prehistoric necropolis, some of which have elaborate entrances. The cove beneath is protected by impressive cliffs. Returning to the junction, we continue the way we were travelling to approach **La Vall d'Algaiarens**. This is a huge estate whose owners traditionally allowed families from Ciutadella to camp here in the woods close to the beautiful beach. Entry is now restricted by a timetable that finishes at 7 p.m., but it is still possible to park here and enjoy the lovely surroundings. The luxuriant pinewoods and the marshlands have recently been catalogued as of special interest to the environment.

For the third excursion we will leave Ciutadella from the Plaça dels Pins and head south along the PM-721. The scenery here, being a more built-up area, is very different from what we have previously seen of the environs of Ciutadella. Beyond the **Cala Santandria** urbanization we can stop at **Cala Blanca**, the best beach in the area, and then continue on to our destination at **Cap d'Artrutx**. To reach the lighthouse it is worthwhile turning off the main road to the right onto the road that borders the urbanization along the coastline which here, in contrast to what we have seen at Punta Nati, is low-lying and hardly rises above sea-level. On clear days, particularly at sunset, we will see the outline of

Sant Joan de Missa

Mallorca in the distance. Continuin[g] beyond the lighthouse, we cross th[e] urbanizations of **Cala en Bosc** and **Son Xoriguer** to the beach of the same name whose fine, white sand are characteristic of the south coast.

The last of the Ciutadella-based ex[-] cursions must be, in turn, subdivid[-] ed into three, and they all start fro[m] the **Camí Vell de St. Joan** near the Canal Celat.

(1) For the first, we branch off at So[n] Vivó towards the Son Saura beach to visit the archaeological site at **Son Catlar** with its *taula*, *talaiots* and walled precinct. Access to **Son Saura** beach is complicated as the road is barred by numerous gates which must be opened and closed behind us, making this trip worth-

Pont, near Punta Nati

while only if we intend to spend several hours or the entire day there.

(2) Retracing our steps to Son Vivó, we turn to the right towards the **St. Joan de Missa Hermitage** and take the Camí to Son Camaró in the direction of **Cala Turqueta**. Despite the fact that the road is unmade beyond the entrance to the Sa Marjal Nova estate, the beach is easily accessible, has a car park and is one of the island's loveliest.

(3) We must return again to the hermitage with its crenallated façade and then head towards **Macarella-Macarelleta**. Along this road, which is unmade beyond the Torralba farmhouse, we will come across very few buildings as it passes through an area of large farming estates and pastures. The coves of Macarella and Macarelleta, both closely surrounded by dense pinewoods, are two more prime examples of the island's natural beauty. As such they have become increasingly popular with both islanders and visitors alike and, in summer, have bar facilities. During the rest of the year they are almost deserted and truly idyllic.

Before closing this section, we would make one final recommendation. While travelling on the C-721 from Ciutadella to Maó, follow the signs to the **Naveta des Tudons** and the **Torre Llafuda** settlement which are further described in the Archaeology chapter.

4 FROM ES MERCADAL TO CALA GALDANA

▸ ES MERCADAL ▸ ES MIGJORN
▸ SANT TOMÀS ▸ SANT ADEODAT
▸ FERRERIES ▸ CALA GALDANA

The C-723 road that leaves Es Mercadal by the barracks leads us through a valley surrounded by high hills and tall pine trees and arrives at **Es Migjorn** alongside the beginning of the **Binigaus gorge** whose fertile slopes have been terraced for farming. This drive offers a different landscape from most of the island, being almost reminiscent of a mountainous area. Along the way we pass several old houses built on top of hillocks, probably for defensive purposes. The town of Es Migjorn is well worth a visit before continuing on to the beaches of **St. Tomàs**, **St. Adeodat** and their tourist developments. On the way, we will pass, on our left the prehistoric settlements of **Sta. Mònica** and, on our right, **St. Agustí** with a curious, hollow *talaiot* whose roof is supported by a central pillar.

On returning to Es Migjorn, and before continuing on towards Ferreries, we can visit the *talaiots* at **Binicodrell de Darrera** by taking the old Camí de Binigaus, near the cemetry. Back on the main road, it is a pleasant drive to Ferreries and a good view of the whole town can be seen just beyond the turning that leads to **Son Mercer** (see excursion 23 on page 86)

From Ferreries we take the C-721 in the Cala Galdana direction and then, just outside the town, turn left on the PM-714 which will lead us between the **Algendar** and **Trebalúger gorges**. We will pass on our left, first the turning which leads to **Cala Trebalúger** and then another which leads to **Cala Mitjana**. From the outskirts of **Cala Galdana**, the road drops quite steeply down to the beach which is surrounded by woodland and protected from the open sea by high cliffs. The mouth of the **Algendar gorge** serves as a canal for the mooring of small boats. Despite the presence of hotels and appartments complexes that have brought mass tourism to **Cala Galdana**, the natural beauty of the surroundings still place it among the most attractive of the south-coast beaches.

Sant Adeodat

5 SOUTH-EASTERN AREA

- ▸ TALATÍ ▸ RAFAL RUBÍ ▸ SON BOU
- ▸ TORRE D'EN GAUMÉS
- ▸ TORRALBA D'EN SALORD
- ▸ SO NA CAÇANA ▸ CALA EN PORTER
- ▸ SANT CLIMENT ▸ CANUTELLS
- ▸ BINIBÈQUER ▸ SANT LLUÍS
- ▸ PUNTA PRIMA ▸ ALCALFAR ▸ SANT ESTEVE

On this tour we will have the opportunity to visit several archaeological sites. We take the C-721 Maó to Alaior road and turn left just beyond the airport junction to **Talatí de Dalt** with its notable *taula* with lateral leaning pillar, a large, circular *talaiot*, and several burial caves. On our way back to the main road, on a turning to the right, we can see the two *navetes* of **Rafal Rubí**.

At the junction just outside Alaior, we turn left on the road to **Son Bou**, the island's longest beach. The demand for tourist accommodation has resulted in the drastic reduction of the marshland area, **Es Prat de Son Bou**, situated behind the beach, part of which once served as rice-fields. From **St. Jaume**, the overlooking hill, now a densely built-up area, there is a splendid view of such panoramic proportions that one can, almost, ignore the two monstruous, high-rise hotels that invade the horizon to our left. Apart from the usual tourist attractions, there is an aquatic games park near the hotels, an interesting early Christian basilica (see pages 20 and 86) and some excavated caves.

On our way back towards Alaior, we will make a detour to the right to **Torre d'en Gaumés**, one of the most complete of the prehistoric settlements. Apart from the large *talaiots*, there is much more to see, such as the enormous hypostyle chamber and the channels and water tanks that formed part of a drainage system. When this site was excavated, a 15 cm. bronze statue (circa 600 BC) of the Egyptian deity **Imhotep** was found, along with other elements dating from prehistory through both the Roman and Moor-ish occupations. From here it is a short walk to the megalithic tomb at **Ses Roques Llisses**.

From Alaior we will take the **Cala en Porter** road, stopping twice on the way at archaeological sites. At the first, **Torralba d'en Salord**, conservation work has recently been carried out by the *Fundació Illes Balears* whose well-documented, explicative pamphlets are available at the site. Passing **Torre Llisà Vell** on our right (see excursion 28 on page 98), just before the junction with the St. Climent road, we come to **So na Caçana** where we will see a *talaiot* crowned, curiously, by a geodetic measuring instrument. Findings here suggest that this was an important religious centre but, today, for some reason it is one of the less-visited sites.

Cala en Porter suffered the consequences of anarchic and excessive growth during the first years of the tourist boom and, although, an effort has been made to rectify some of the worst mistakes, it remains today as an example of man's insensitivity to his surroundings.
Half-way up the cliff to the left of the beach, the **Cova d'en Xoroi** is well worth a visit, particularly in the early evening to watch the sunset from the balconies, or at night for the romantic moonrises. During the summer it is transformed in the evening into a discotheque. The cave is home to one of Menorca's most popular folk legends: that of Xoroi, an earless Moor who lived here with a girl he abducted from one of the farms and their three children. The footprints left by him in the snow while out foraging for food, led soldiers to the hideaway, whereupon,

Detail of rural architecture

to avoid capture and enslavery, Xoroi and the eldest son leapt to their deaths in the sea below.

From **Cala en Porter**, we will continue via **St. Climent** to **Cala Canutells** situated at the mouth of a gorge and important tourist centre. The entire coastline of the **St. Lluís** area, to be visited next, is an almost continuous succession of urbanizations from **Binidalí** to **Punta Prima**. Set further back from the sea, and usually on rises in the ground, we will see a number of large old mansions overlooking the coast.

At **Cala Binidalí** there is an excellent viewpoint at the top of the cliff that overlooks the cove. Along with the neighbouring **Biniparratx**, it is one of the deepest in proportion to its width, and burial caves are seen in the rocks behind both beaches. In summer they are packed to capacity by boats taking advantage of the shelter afforded by these singular havens.

From here on, the coastline is less rugged and flatter beyond **Cap d'en Font**. Between the beaches of **Binisafúller** and **Binibèquer**, we come across the curious resort of **Binibeca Vell**, built to imitate the traditional architectural forms of the old fishing villages. The last beach in this area, **Punta Prima** in the extreme south-east corner of the island was popular among the islanders before the appearance of tourism and known at the time of the British occupation as Sandy Bay. Opposite, the **Illa de l'Aire**, famous for its lighthouse and indigenous black lizards, offers spectacular views in all weathers. There are bars and restaurants in the vicinity of all the aforementioned beaches. By turning right off the Punta Prima-St. Lluís road, we will arrive at **Cala Alcalfar** and **S'Algar**. The former was the island's pioneer tourist resort, whereas S'Algar, with its hotels, villas and appartments is of more recent development and offers many services such as tennis, horse-riding, deep-sea diving and parascending.

Before returning to Maó, our last stop will be **Cala St. Esteve**, where the restored Malborough fort may be visited, and **Es Castell**, perhaps rounding off the day with dinner at one of the popular waterfront restaurants in **Cales Fonts**.

Cala Alcalfar

The little harbour at Binibeca Vell

Information and suggestions

ART AND CULTURE

THE ATTRACTION THE ISLAND HAS ALWAYS HELD FOR ARTISTS IS MADE MANIFEST BY THE NUMBER OF THEM, BOTH OF LOCAL STOCK AND OUTSIDERS, WHO HAVE SOUGHT AND FOUND INSPIRATION IN THESE UNIQUE SURROUNDINGS OVER THE CENTURIES.

PAINTING

Painting has always been a particularly fruitful field with a marked emphasis on landscape painting in which the island's special quality of light has always played an important role. In the 18th century, the Italian **Giuseppe Chiesa** (1720-1789), who set up residence here following his marriage to a Menorcan woman, left an important pictorial record of the island at that time and introduced the Italian naturalist influence known as *veduta*. His Menorcan disciple

Pascual Calbó (1752-1817) was famous for both his scientific treatise and his artistic qualities. In the nineteenth century, the wide seascapes of Maó harbour under stormy skies, painted by **Font** (1811-1885), were recurrent examples of the romantic school of the time. **Hernández Monjo** (1862-1937) also left a legacy of seascapes, full of light and colour, in this case in the turn of the century modernist style.
Contemporary art is represented by two important landscape painters: **Joan Vives Llull** (1901-1982) in whose impressionist work nature is the most important element, and **Josep Torrent** (1904-1990), Ciutadella-born expressionist, whose original technique captures the essence and rhythm of the island. Also from Ciutadella, **Maties Quetglas** (1946), who has lived and worked in Madrid for some years, is known both nationally and internationally among the hyperrealist school.
Works by these, and other artists of more recent apparition, may be viewed at the following:

ART GALLERIES AND MUSEUMS

MAÓ:

Museu de Menorca. The old Convent of St. Francesc, Av. Dr. Guàrdia. Worth visiting for the building itself and its contents. Important exhibitions of the island's archaeological heritage, fine arts, ethnology and a library. Tel. 971 35 09 55.
Museu Hernández Sanz – Hernández Mora. In the Claustre del Carme. Maps and engravings dating from the seventeenth to nineteenth centuries, paintings and an important library. Tel. 971 35 05 97.
Sala de Cultura "Sa Nostra", situated in the old St. Antoni church, S'Arraval 32, holds temporary exhibitions all year round.

The **Scientific, Literary and Artistic Athenaeum.** Rovellada de Dalt 25. Works by *Vives Llull,* collections of drawings and paintings, Menorcan natural history exhibition. Cultural and sociological lectures are given all year round. Tel. 971 36 05 53.
Galeria Artara. Rosario 18.
Fortalesa de la Mola. Guided tours, information Tel. 971 36 21 00.

CIUTADELLA:

Sala Municipal in the Roser church on the street of the same name. Exhibitions.
Sala de Cultura "Sa Nostra" in the St. Josep church on C/Sta.Clara. Exhibitions.
Galeria Retxa. Seat of a collective group of artists with temporary exhibitions by others.
Museu Municipal Bastió de sa Font, Pla de sa Font, Tel. 971 38 02 97. Historical, archaeological and ethnological exhibits.
Museu Diocesà, adjoined to the Seminary. Pere Daura collection of contemporary painting, rare and antique exhibits of historical and religious value.
Casa-Museu Pintor Torrent, C/St Rafael.
Castell de Sant Nicolau. Tel. 971 38 10 50.
Pedreres de s´Hostal. Run by "Líthica", an association dedicated to the protection of stone quarries, this is an interesting ensemble of both the oldest and newest quarries just two km. from Ciutadella on the Camí Vell de Maó. Recommended itineraries are well signposted within the site. Tel. 971 48 15 78.

ALAIOR:

Centre de Cultura de Sant Diego. In the old St. Diego church.
Sala Municipal d'Art Contemporani, Major 11. Tel. 971 37 10 02.
Galeria Arths. Costa de l'Església 11.

S MERCADAL:

Ecomuseu de Cap de Cavalleria. Situated in the privileged surroundings of the Santa Teresa estate, this small museum offers the chance to discover the Roman history of Menorca, brought to light by the Sanisera excavations. Tel. 971 35 99 99. **Espai Hartung**, C/Vicari Fuxà. Summer exhibitions.

ES MIGJORN GRAN:

Johanna Byfield. C/St. Llorenç 12-14.

FERRERIES:

Museu de la Natura de Menorca. C/ Mallorca, 2. Tel. 971 37 45 05 / 971 35 07 62.

SANT LLUÍS:

s Molí de Dalt. The old windmill has been restored to full working order and contains an interesting exhibition of farming implements. Tel. 971 15 10 84.

ES CASTELL:

Pedrera d'en Robadones. "Centre del Patrimoni Marítim de Menorca". Here, in the largest of the subterranean quarries, more than forty traditional Menorcan vessels are on show. Camí d'en Verd, Tel. 639 601 354. **Museo Militar.** Plaça Esplanada. Tel. 971 36 21 00 / 971 36 59 47. **Castell de Sant Felip.** 971 36 21 00. **Museo Fort Malborough.** Cala Sant Esteve. Tel. 971 36 04 62.

MUSIC

The visitor may be surprised by the variety of musical activities that take place on the island and, indeed, by the very high standard of the performances. Menorcans are, by tradition, a music-loving people.

OPERA AND CLASSICAL MUSIC

Every year in the spring, the **Amics de l'Òpera** hold an Opera Week, the *Setmana de l'Opera*, traditionally in the incomparable setting of the Teatre Principal. Another very active group is **Joventuts Musicals**. From October to May they give concerts on alternate Mondays in the St. Josep church in Ciutadella and in Sta. María in Maó. During July and August they hold **Summer Music Festivals** which take place, in Maó in the Cloister of St. Francesc, and in Ciutadella in the Cloister of the Seminary. The nature of both these locations enhance the quality of the performances. During the last two weeks of July, in the *Aules de Cultura*, *Juventuts Musicals* organize a course in chamber music, violin, viola, cello and piano. In July and August a series of international concerts is organized by the Sta. María Organ Foundation and, in the summer, organ recitals are given each morning and one afternoon per week. In August, summer concerts are held in the church at Fornells and, in the chapel or cloister of the Convent of Socors in Ciutadella, both singing and organ auditions are held throughout the year by the **Capella Davídica.** (Here the voice of the world-famous, Ciutadella-born baritone *Joan Pons*, currently considered among the world's finest, was trained.) Among other activities, they organize the **International Organ Week** in the cathedral in February or March, and Easter, summer and Christmas concerts.

JAZZ

Although not such a long-standing tradition among the Menorcans, jazz does have a place in the island's musical scene. In great part this is due to the large number of British residents who, over the years, have created and maintained this interest. From Easter until November, jazz sessions are held in the **Casino at St. Climent** on Tuesdays, and in the winter on Thursdays.

ROCK - POP

There are many amateur groups on the island and they give frequent performances. One of them, **Ja t'ho diré** by name, has become successful on a national level.

FOLK

The *Jota Menorquina* (folk song and dance), *Havaneres* (which date from the time of massive emigration to Cuba) and traditional songs form the basis of Menorca's folk culture. Several folk groups exist and perform at all the local *festes*.

LIVE MUSIC

Jazz, rock and folk concerts are held throughout the year in Maó, Ciutadella and other points of the island with the participation of both local and visiting musicians. In recent years, weekly performances in the Cloister del Carme form part of the **Estiu a Maó** (Summer in Maó) programme. In August, outdoor concerts are held in Sa Plaça in Alaior. In Maó harbour, the bar **Akelarre**, on Moll de Ponent has live jazz and rock at weekends and open-air shows are given at **S'Hort Nou** several times a week in summer. In the **Sa Sínia** bar in Es Castell, live performances are given all year round. In Ciutadella the **Bar Asere** on the harbour, also has live music. An alternative attraction is the **Bar Salon** in Es Castell where imitations of cabaret-style entertainment are performed in most original surroundings.

THEATRE

The recently renovated **Teatre Principal** and the **Sala Augusta** in Maó and the **Teatre des Born** in Ciutadella, are the centres of the island's ever-increasing theatrical activity.

The theatre is a long-standing Menorcan tradition as is made clear by the existence and yearly performance of local works that have their origins in the 19th century. What is more, each town can boast of having its own theatre which, since the beginning of the last century to the present day, has been witness to Menorcan enthusiasm for amateur dramatics. Despite the island's small population, local groups abound and their performances are well attended by their fellow townspeople. The old-established **Orfeó Maonés** and the **Delfí Serra** and **St. Miquel** groups from Ciutadella have a long tradition. **La Clota-Groc** and **Mô Teatre** are more recently formed, the latter producing their own works. The *Aules de Teatre* (theatrical classes) have, in recent years, enabled actors to maintain a high level of interpretative skills.

LITERATURE

Menorca's contribution to Catalan and European culture has been quite considerable, although it remains comparatively unknown to the public in general. After the foundation in 1778 of the *Societat Maonesa de Cultura*, there was intense activity in this field within the enlightened trends of the times. Many members of this group studied in the south of France, such as **Joan Ramis i Ramis**, the leading exponent of Catalan neoclassic drama whose works include *"Lucrècia"* (1769), in defence of republican liberties, *"Arminda"* and *"Rosaura o el més constant amor"*. At this time, works by Molière, Goldoni, Metastasio etc., were translated on the island and linguistic treatises published, such as the *Principis de lectura*

menorquina, in which the author **Febrer i Cardona** clearly defined the unity of the vernacular language within Catalan territories. Scientific literature was particularly represented by the work of **Dr. Orfila i Rotger** (1787-1853) who studied chemistry and medicine in Paris and whose studies on toxicology enjoyed great prestige. He was physician to Louis XVIII of France and chair of chemistry at the University of Paris.

In the 20th century, the famous *Folklore menorquí de la pagesia* by **Francesc d'Albranca** is one of the best-known works and the *Revista de Menorca*, published since 1888 by the Scientific, Literary and Artistic Athaeneum, is highly considered in literary circles. The *Obra Cultural Balear* is the association dedicated to the production and diffusion of the *Enciclopèdia de Menorca*, a thematic encyclopaedia published in fascicles of which several volumes have been completed to date.

Contemporary fiction and poetry is also represented on the island by **Gumersind Riera**, **Ponç Pons** and **Pau Faner**, who, between them, have won both local and national literary awards. All the forementioned works can be found in the island's book-shops along with any new publications by native writers.

A curious place to immerse ourselves in the world of books is the **Café-Librería La Torre de Papel**, in Ciutadella, Camí de Maó, 46. A cosy, pleasant atmosphere invites us to combine the pleasure of reading with that of a hot drink. Here we will find both new and secondhand books in several languages.

RECOMMENDED READING

- Arxiduc Lluís Salvador d'Àustria. **La isla de Menorca**. Facsimile editions of volumes VI i VII of *"Die Balearen i wort und bild"*. "Sa Nostra" 1982.
- Armstrong, John. **Historia de la isl de Menorca**. Edit. Nura 1978.
- Ballester, Pere. **De re cibaria** *(cocina, pastelería y repostería menorquina)* Edit. Puig, 1986.
- Camps i Mercadal, F. (Francesc d'Albranca). **Folklore Menorquí**. 1987.
- Cao Barredo, M. **Flowers of Menorca**. G.O.B. 1996.
- Catxot, Santi, i Escandell, Raúl. **Birds of Menorca**. G.O.B. 1994.
- Faner, Pau. **Flor de sal**. Destino 1986.
- Florit, F. i Sauleau, L. **Pedreres de Marès**. Líthica. 1995.
- Garrido, Carlos. **Menorca mágica**. Olañeta, 1990.
- Lafuente, Lorenzo. **Menorca, costumbres i paisajes**. Edit. Nura, 1975.
- Martorell, Josep. **Guia d'arquitectura de Menorca**. La Gaia Ciència 1980.
- Mascaró Pasarius, Josep. **Geografi e Historia de Menorca**. (5 volums). Menorca. 1980/84.
- Mascaró Pasarius, Josep. **Las taulas**. Edit. Al-thor. 1983.
- Mata, Micaela. **Conquestes i reconquestes de Menorca**. Editorial 62. 1974.
- Mata, Micaela. **Menorca Británica**. I.M.E. 1994.
- Nicolás Mascaró, Joan C. de. **Guia des Camí de Cavalls de Menorca**. Triangle Postals. 1997.
- Nicolás Mascaró, Joan C. de. **Talaies i torres de defensa costanera**. I.M.E. 1994.
- Pallarès, Virgínia i Taltavull, Enric. **Guía Náutica Menorca**. Virgínia Pallarès. 1992.
- Pla, Josep. **Mallorca, Menorca e Ibiza**. Destino. 1950.
- Plantalamor Massanet, Lluís. **L'arquitectura prehistòrica i protohistòrica de Menorca**. Govern Balear. Treballs del Museu de Menorca, n. 13.
- Pons, Guillermo. **Historia de Menorca**. Menorca, 1977.
- Pons, Ponç. **Memorial de Tabarka**. Cruïlla, 1993.
- Riudavets i Tuduri, Pedro. **Historia de la Isla de Menorca** (1888) 2 volums. Al-Thor. 1983.

• Sabrafin, Gabriel. **Cuentos fabulosos y leyendas de las islas**. Olañeta, 1988.
• Sintes i de Olivar, **M. Pascual Calbó Calders, un pintor menorquín en la Europa Ilustrada**. "Sa Nostra". 1987.
• Vidal, Toni. **Menorca tot just ahir**. Triangle Postals, 2000.
• Vuillier, Gaston. **Les Illes Oblidades**. Edit. Moll, 1973.
• VV.AA. **Guia Arqueològica de Menorca**. C.I.M. 1984.
• VV.AA. **La ciutat des del carrer**. Ateneu de Maó. 1983.
• VV.AA. **La mar i Menorca**. *(La pintura a Menorca del segle XVIII a l'actualitat)*. Ajuntament de Ciutadella. 1993.
• VV.AA. Quaderns Xibau. **Col.lecció de Poesía Contemporània**. I.M.E. 1990/95.
• VV.AA. **Menorca, Reserva de la Biosfera**. "Sa Nostra". 1994.
• VV.AA. **Vives Llull**. "Sa Nostra" 1993.

HANDICRAFTS

Today, the traditional handicrafts of local origin still in production on the island comprise, in the main, of pottery and the making of *avarques*, typical peasant sandals. However, basketmaking, costume jewellery, leather work, textile and paper serigraphy are still carried out. Traditional Menorcan pottery is characterized by its use of local raw materials and the distinctive forms of the finished articles. Some of the most unusual are: pitchers, bottles, clay pipes with wooden mouthpieces, glazed bowls, demijohns, drinking and feeding troughs for farm animals.
At his workshop at 12 C/Curniola, in Ciutadella, **Artur Gener** makes pottery following an old family tradition, and in Maó harbour at 10 Moll de Ponent, the **Lora Buzón** brothers sell both traditional and contemporary designs. Customers can watch the whole process, from potter's wheel to end result, in the workshop on view to the public.
In the case of the *avarques* we have mentioned previously, although they are

found on sale all over the island, it is increasingly difficult to come into direct contact with the craftsmen who make them. **Can Servera** at 3 C/Metge Camps, Es Mercadal and **Can Doblas artesania** workshop at 1 C/Fred, Ferreries are exceptions. Other examples of local handicrafts can be found at the outdoor markets which take place daily in the summer and weekly the rest of the year: **Ses Voltes** and **S'Esplanada** (Maó), **Baixada Campllonch** (Ciutadella harbour), **Baixada Cales Fonts** (Es Castell) and the handicraft markets of Es Mercadal and Alaior. On Saturday mornings an interesting market is held in Ferreries where local farmers sell products such as honey, cheese, jam and preserves. Shoes and other leather goods of very high quality can be bought at the manufacturer's own outlets where, theoretically, the prices are lower than in the shopping centres. There are several of them on the outskirts of Ciutadella and on the main roads, and factory tours can be arranged by appointment. It is still possible to have shoes handmade to measure at a competitive price but this may not be practical for short-term visitors as it is quite a lengthy process as befits such a specialised handicraft.

ANTIQUES

The fact that antique dealers are to be found in most of the towns is hardly surprising on an island that has been enriched throughout its history by contributions from many different cultures. From the ancient civilizations, the remains of the Talayotic era that form part of Menorca's unique and protected archaeological heritage are the first examples, and are followed by Phoenician amphoras retrieved from the sea bed and Roman objects that have been discovered in the course of excavation and building work. Not to be forgotten are the fossils, nature's own "antiques", brought to light after millennia by the erosion of the elements. The British and French dominations left in their wake an

important legacy of characteristic everyday objects which, in the course of time, have become sought-after antiques. A prime example is the 18th century Chippendale and Sheraton furniture imported, in the main, during the last British occupation. (Although this was the briefest of the three, the influence exerted by the English was greater and more far-reaching than in the past.) The furniture found its way, over the years, through inheritance or sale, into homes of all social levels. Occasionally, authentic pieces can still be found for sale. Even locally-made rustic furniture came under the English influence and is more refined and sophisticated than its counterparts elsewhere. Many other decorative objects, paintings, trinkets and valuables of varied origins, dating principally from the 18th and 19th centuries, can be found in the antique shops that are tucked away all over the island, particularly in Maó and Ciutadella. In the past, Menorca had been a collector's paradise, but nowadays the prices have become more in step with the market in general and bargains are unlikely. A monthly, public auction is held in St. Lluís where a truly heterogeneous selection of items is put up for sale at quite reasonable prices. Even to the uninitiated, any of these establishments can offer a fascinating insight into the traditions and life-style of the island in years gone by.

FESTIVITIES

The horse is the undisputed symbol of the *festes* of Menorca and we have already mentioned those of Ciutadella and Maó. They are held in honour of the patron saint of the town and give rise to sporting and cultural activities as well as religious celebrations. The first note of the *tambor i es flabiol* (the drum and the pipe) is the anxiously awaited sound that signals the start of the **colcada** or procession. With the exception of Ciutadella, where centuries-old rituals surround and determine the course of the festivities which reach their climax with the **Jocs des Pla** tournament, the **colcada** and **jaleo** take place on the afternoon of the saint's day and the following morning. In recent years, the old tradition of the **corregudes des Cós** or horse racing in the street, has been revived in Maó and the townspeople take part enthusiastically.

Festivities in honour of the patron saints are not the only fêtes that are celebrated. As befits a Mediterranean culture, Menorcans maintain many Christian and pagan traditions of which we give details here:

CALENDAR OF FESTIVITIES

JANUARY

St. Anthony's Day (patron saint of Menorca) in commemoration of the conquest of the island by Alfons III.
16th Street parties in Maó, Es Castell, St. Lluís and Mercadal
17th Activities in all the towns. In Ciutadella a traditional market is held in Pl. de l'Hospital and on the 19th a gastronomic fête in Ciutadella.

FEBRUARY, MARCH, APRIL.

Carnival. Movable between February and March. Fancy dress balls and processions of floats in all the towns.

Particularly original are the Black and White Ball in Es Migjorn and the *Ball de ses Tauletes* at the Casino Nou in Ciutadella, both on the Monday.
Easter. Movable. Religious ceremonies and processions all over the island.
Of particular interest:
Good Friday. The Procession of the Holy Burial in Maó and the procession in Es Migjorn of very ancient origin.
Easter Saturday. The Sacred Concert at Ciutadella cathedral with religious ceremonies that conclude with the Foc Nou in the cathedral square.
Easter Sunday. Procession of the *Encontre* in Maó and Es Migjorn. In Ciutadella at noon, a bonfire set alight by shots from a blunderbuss. In St. Lluís, Es Castell, St. Climent, Alaior and Mercadal, choir singing in the streets.
Whitsun. Movable. Traditional outings and picnics in the country and beaches from Ciutadella and Ferreries.

MAY

1st Sunday In Ferreries, cakes and pastries are blessed and sold in benefit of the parish. This is an ancient tradition that has only recently been reinstated.
15th St. Isidore's Day. Patron saint of farmers. Religious and sporting events at the Hermitage of Fàtima.
24th or the following Sunday. Procession of Maria Auxiliadora in Ciutadella. Religious ceremony and procession through the old part of the city. At Sa Contramurada, a concert by the Municipal Band and a street dance.

JUNE

Dia des Be. On the Sunday prior to St. John's Day, a sheep, adorned with coloured ribbons is carried through the streets accompanied by a piper to announce the beginning of the festivities.
23rd-24th. Vespers at the church of St. Joan de Missa, followed by

medieval tournaments and processions, demonstrations of equestrian skills at the *Jocs des Pla*.
29th St. Peter's Day (or the following weekend). Festivities, games and dancing in Maó harbour and regattas featuring old sailing and rowing boats.

JULY

9th Commemoration of the Turkish assault on Ciutadella in 1558. The **Act of Constantinople** is read in public and the *Junta de Caixers* is chosen for the St. John festivities of the following year.
10th St. Christopher's Day festivities where vehicles are blessed.
15th-16th The image of the Virgen of Carmen is carried around the harbours of Maó, Ciutadella and Fornells by a procession of boats of all kinds that are decorated with lights and garlands of flowers.
24th-25th St. James's Day festivities in Es Castell.
3rd weekend St. Martin's Day festivities in Mercadal.
4th weekend St. Anthony's Day festivities in Fornells.
5th weekend (or first in August) St. Christopher's Day festivities in Es Migjorn.

AUGUST

1st weekend St. Gaietà's Day festivities in Llucmassanes.
1st weekend after the 10th, St. Lawrence's Day festivities in Alaior.
3rd weekend St. Clement's Day festivities in St. Climent.
23rd-25th St. Bartholomew's Day festivities in Ferreries.
Last weekend St. Louis's Day festivities in St. Lluís.

SEPTEMBER

7th-8th Our Lady of Grace festivities in Maó, another chance to see processions, horses and *jaleo*.
29th St. Michael's Day festivities in Es Migjorn with horses and *jaleo* every fifth year.

NOVEMBER

1st All Saints' Day. Traditional doughnuts with honey are sold all over the island.

ECEMBER

5th Nativity plays are performed in everal towns. Exhibitions of crèches nd Nativity dioramas in Maó and in iutadella at the Seminary and Sta. lara church.

1st The New Year is celebrated at idnight by the ringing of bells in wn squares and public dances.

OTHER FOLK TRADITIONS

ODOLADES

hese are popular poetic ompositions, usually of a satiric ature, whose metre differs in lenorca from other places. They tend make reference to local or ollective situations and affairs.

LOSATS

oetic compositions improvised by ifferent people in turn, accompanied y the guitar. Both these examples of aditional folk culture have been ept alive, in great part, thanks to roups from Ciutadella and Ferreries ho periodically give performances ll over the island.

SPORT

I RECENT YEARS MUCH HAS BEEN ONE TO IMPROVE THE QUALITY OF THE SLAND'S SPORTS FACILITIES AND, ODAY, NEARLY ALL THE TOWNS HAVE HEIR OWN SPORTS GROUNDS. MANY OTELS AND URBANIZATIONS ALSO AVE INSTALLATIONS.

CRICKET

he large number of British residents n the island has given rise to the ormation of a cricket club, the Menorca Cricket Club (or M.C.C.) to e found on the Biniparrell road, near t. Lluís. It is the only grass cricket itch in Spain.

GOLF

here is a nine-hole golf course at on ght hand side of the Fornells road. he high price the environment pays return for these facilities is subject

of considerable controversy and has prevented more courses from being developed.

HORSE SPORTS

We have already mentioned the important role the horse has always played in Menorcan society. The indigenous race of black horses is characterized by its medium stature and the long, straight profile of the head. Efforts are being made to encourage their breeding.

The **Maó hippodrome** lies on the road to St. Lluís and there is another in Ciutadella at **Torre del Ram**. Race meetings are held regularly and feature a variety of trotting races unique to the island. Betting is permitted.

The riding clubs belonging to the Federació Hípica Balear (Tel.971 37 82 20) are mainly concerned with classical Menorcan training, but also have horses for beginners to practise in the stables or to take out for rides.

Club Escola Menorquina. Ferreries to Cala Galdana road. From June to October, exhibitions every Wednesday and Sunday at 20h 30.
Tel. 971 15 50 59.
Club Hípic Alaior. Es Cos.
Tel. 971 37 82 43.
C H. Ferreries. On the road to Es Migjorn.
Tel. 971 37 42 03.
C. H. Ciutadella. Camí des Caragol.
Tel. 971 38 26 73.
C. H. Maó. Camí de Talatí.
Tel. 626 084 352.
C. H. Sa Creueta. (Es Migjorn) c/ Figuerenya, 18. Tel. 971 37 02 58.
C. H. Ses Ramones. (Es Mercadal) Maó-Ciutadella road.
Tel. 971 37 50 54.
Escola Eqüestre Menorquina. (Ciutadella) Camí des Caragol.
Tel. 971 38 34 25.
Grup Cavallers Cuadras Bintaufa. (Maó) c/ Cos de Gràcia, 56.
Tel. 971 35 23 47.

Other related options are the **Pony Club** (for children only), in the Sant Tomàs urbanisation, Es Migjorn Gran, Tel. 971 37 03 70, and the **Hort de Llucaitx Park** on the Maó to Fornells road (near the Son Parc turning).
Tel. 629 392 894.

TENNIS

Tennis is a popular game on the island and there are several schools and coaches who give private lessons and every town has its own cour.

The **Tennis Club S'Algar** is one of the most attractive as the courts are surrounded by a pinewood which affords welcome shade all year round. They also have artificial grass paddle tennis courts.

OTHER ALTERNATIVES:

At the **St. Lluís Flying Club**, light aircraft flights can be arranged and offer the chance to discover the island from the air. They also have a go-kart circuit.

The **GOB** (Grup Balear d'Ornitologia) offers another, alternative way to discover the island. They organize excursions for limited groups with country walks, trips to beaches and the archaeological routes which are of interest to both amateur ornithologists and nature lovers in general.

They can be contacted at 138 Camí des Castell, Maó, from 9h-15h, or by phoning 971 35 07 62.

Two sports are unique to Menorca, and one of them is exclusive to just St. Lluís. This is **La Bolla**, a kind of indoor bowling which probably originated during the French domination. It can be watched in the bar La Bolla, 56 Es Cós, St. Lluís. The second is **Joc Maonés**, more a kind of martial art of unknown origin than a game. The practice of this curious art was unique to only a few *aficionados* and their *maestros* who passed the tradition by word-of-mouth from generation to generation until quite recently when public interest has been revived and supported by local institutions. It is renowned for the singular elegance of the steps, tocs which increase in intensity prior to the combat itself, rodar. The participants are not in danger of injury as their optimum physical preparation is closely controlled by the teachers.

NAUTICAL SPORTS

As far as these activities are concerned, the possibilities seem endless. From sailing boats to pedaloes, passing through windsurf boards and motorboats, almost every kind of craft is available for hire. Until recently, despite the idyllic conditions for canoeing offered by Menorca's protected ports, this sport was not practiced on the island. Now, however, canoes are for hire from **Katakayak,** Fornells, on the promenade, from the **Diving Centre Cala Torret,** and at some other beaches. Excellent nautical sports facilities and services exist in Maó, Ciutadella and Fornells and, also, in many holiday centres. Visitors should bear in mind, however, that in the high season the demand for craft for hire is far greater than the supply. If you wish to focus your holiday in Menorca in this direction, arrangements should be made in advance and it would be wise to obtain one of the nautical guides that are available on the market. Whether you wish to hire your own craft or just take a short trip, the following information may be of assistance.

Maó harbour: Sailing and motorboat hire at **Menmar** and **Menorca Nàutic,** both on Moll de Llevant.

Years ago, the Maoneses who lived or holidayed on the opposite shore of the port would commute to and fro on the old *Barca d'en Reynes.* Nowadays, the increase in marine traffic, largely due to the ever-expanding tourist industry, has drastically altered the harbour's atmosphere but it still remains an enchanting setting, particularly in the early morning and evening. There are several boats that do pleasure trips around the harbour with running commentaries in several languages. They are to be found next door to the Trasmediterranea building.

Another, smaller taxi-boat is also available and also a glass-bottomed boat which offers views of the marine floor. The depth of Maó harbour, 20 to 30 metres in most places, does not permit the best of visibility.

Es Castell: Boat trips around the port also start from here at midday.

The **Llatzeret** island can only be visited in groups and by prior arrangement. Tel. 971 36 25 87.

Es Grau: A small cabin-cruiser runs a shuttle service to the Illa d'en Colom.

We have already mentioned Fornells harbour as a nautical sports paradise. There is also a taxi-boat and motor and rowing boat rental service at **Servi-Nàutic Menorca.** Sailing boats, catamarans and windsurf equipment can be found at **Windsurf Fornells,** and at **Club Nàutic ses Salines,** an important sailing schooll.

Ciutadella and Cala Galdana: Boat trips can be taken to the south coast beaches and some are glass-bottomed which, in this instance, is a very attractive alternative, given the variety and beauty of the marine floor in this area. In Ciutadella harbour there are facilities for boat rental such as **Sports Massanet** at Marina 66, Moll Comercial.

There are diving clubs in S'Algar, **S'Algar Diving** and in Binibequer, **Centro de Buceo Cala Torret.** In Fornells, **Menorca Diving Club** and in Port d'Addaia, **Ulmo Diving.** In Son Xoriguer and Son Bou, **Sub Menorca Centros de Buceo** and, in Ciutadella, **Ciutadella Diving.**

For further information contact: The **Federación de Actividades Subacuáticas.** Francesc de Borja Moll, 21. Ciutadella.

Federación de Vela. Av. Menorca, 96 4º A. Maó. Tel. 971 36 39 89

Two associations exist in Menorca with the aim of protecting the island's marine heritage: *Amics des Port de Maó* and *Amics de la Mar de Menorca.* Between them they aim to conserve the ports and the coastline, and safeguard the long-standing cultural and ethnological traditions.

ACCOMMODATION

Apart from the hotels, appartments and holiday accommodation in general, other possibilities, of a more environmentally-friendly nature are also available. There are a few small hotels that maintain the traditional style of rural architecture and, as a result, form a harmonious part of the surrounding countryside. Their very size and nature makes advance reservation an absolute necessity. A few examples are:

Hostal Biniali At S'Ullestrar, near St. Lluís.
Tel. 971 15 17 24,
Fax. 971 15 03 52.
A renovated mansion, laid back from the main road, with swimming pool and gardens. Nine well-appointed, elegantly furnished bedrooms and pleasant surroundings.

Hotel Almirante Near Es Castell on the main road from Maó.
Tel. 971 36 27 00. A remodelled 18th century house where Admiral Collingwood resided in Lord Nelson's time. Gardens, tennis court, swimming pool and, allegedly, a haunted room.

S'Engolidor 3 Major St. Es Migjorn. Tel. 971 37 01 93. An old farmhouse now integrated into the town. Boardinghouse with just four simple, but comfortable bedrooms, and a restaurant well-known for the quality of its traditional Menorcan cuisine.

Asociación Hotelera de Menorca, information and bookings: telephone 971 36 10 03. e-mail: ashome@infotelecom.es and website: www.infotelecom.es/ashome

RURAL TOURISM

ust recently, a new concept of holiday accommodation has been introduced on the island. Rural tourism offers visitors the opportunity of staying in country houses that have been adapted for this purpose and we list here a few of those that are already open.
Lloc de Binisaïd. Near Ferreries on the Cala Galdana road. Farmhouse in one of the most luxuriantly wooded areas of the island.
Tel. 971 15 50 63/971 35 23 03.

Son Triay Nou. On the Cala Galdana road, 2 km. out of Ferreries. Four bedrooms, swimming pool, tennis court, garden and pleasant rural surroundings.
Tel. 971 15 50 78/ 971 36 04 46.
Lloc de Biniatram. Near Ciutadella on the Cala Morell road. A stately home which offers the possibility of enjoying the life-style and gastronomy of rural Menorca. Four bedrooms, swimming pool and tennis court. Tel-971 38 31 13.
Lloc de Sant Tomàs. In Ciutadella on the Camí Vell de Maó, km.3. Three bedrooms. Guests have the chance to go on horseback rides and sample typical Menorcan cuisine.
Tel. 971 18 80 51.
Alcaufar Vell. Sant Lluís to Alcalfar road, km 7,3. Four double rooms in the rural surroundings of the eastern part of the island. Various facilities such as bicycle and horseriding, rambling... Tel. 971 15 18 74.
Matxaní Gran. Sant Climent to Binidalí road. Six bedrooms.
Tel. 971 15 33 00.
Talatí de Dalt. Camí de Talatí (Maó) Four bedrooms. Tel. 971 37 11 58.
For more information and bookings contact: **Asociación de Agroturismo Balear,** 971 72 75 08. e-mail: agroturismo@mallorcanet.com
Son Tretze, in St. Lluís, with eight bedrooms and a meeting hall offers the same style of accommodation within the town itself. Dinifadet, 20.
Tel. 971 15 33 00.
Another possibility lies in renting houses directly from their owners who use them only part of the time as holiday homes, either on the coast if the proprietors choose to stay in town, or vice versa.
Although no sleeping accommodation is provided, **Lloc de Binisues** on the road to Ciutadella, 31 km. from Maó on the turning to Els Alocs, is worth mentioning for its restaurant, traditional architecture and permanent exhibition of antiques and rural curiosities. Tel.971 37 37 28.

CAMPING

Camping on the island is very problematic as local people have never been well-disposed to the use of their land for this purpose. There are only two camping sites, both well-equipped, close to the beach and with swimming pools.
Càmping S'Atalaia. Four km. from Ferreries on the Cala Galdana road. Open in the summer, just 3 km. from the beach with all kinds of services and swimming pool. Communicated by bus with Ferreries and the rest of the island and also Cala Galdana.
Tel. 971 37 42 32/971 37 30 95.
Càmping Son Bou. Conveniently and centrally situated on the Sant Jaume road, 3,5 km. from Alaior and just 2,5 km. from the beach. Mini-golf, swimming pool, solarium, sports facilities in pleasant surroundings.
Tel/Fax. 971 37 26 05.
A number of country houses exist where youth organizations are allowed to use the sleeping, kitchen and bathroom facilities. In the event of there being vacancies, which is not probable in the high season, they are also available to private groups or families:
Es Pinaret. Near Ciutadella.
Tel. 971 38 10 50.
Torre de Son Ganxo and **Campament de Biniparratx.** Near St. Lluís.
Tel. 971 17 10 93/971 15 15 16.
St. Llorenç de Binixems. Near Alaior at the hermitage. Tel. 971 37 11 07.
Es Canaló. Near Ferreries at the beginning of the Algendar barranc
Tel. 971 37 40 72.
St. Joan de Missa. Near Ciutadella at the hermitage. Tel. 971 38 10 82/971 38 13 06.

GASTRONOMY

We have already mentioned gin and cheese, as the most emblematic of Menorca's products, but the island has much more to offer in the way of gastronomy. *"De Re Cibaria"* is a classic book of Menorcan cooking and is an excellent guide for those who wish to make an in depth discovery of the island's cuisine, whether in the form of every day dishes or other, sometimes archaic specialities.The simple tasting of local food suffices to identify its sources: the basic ingredients available, fruit of the land or the sea, and the influence of the different successive occupations (Arab, British and French) on their preparation. The origin of mayonnaise has been the source of international dispute between Menorcans and the French for centuries.

Oliaigo (literally oil and water), is a simple dish considered to be ideal for all seasons, eaten cold in summer and hot in winter. It is often served accompanied by figs. The basic ingredients are onion, garlic, green peppers and tomato cooked in a deep earthenware dish and served with fine slices of dry, white bread. **Caldereta de llagosta** (lobster stew), is the island's most famous dish but was regarded, before the arrival of tourism, as simple fare which the fishermen would prepare on board their boats. Today it is considered as food fit for a king. *Calderetes* are also made with other kinds of fish and shellfish.

Arròs de la terra (Rice of the earth) is a peasant dish made of ground maize, and baked aubergines. All the above-mentioned are traditional recipes whose simple ingredients tell us much of the limited natural resources of the island in years gone by, and man's ingenuity in transforming them into appetising dishes.

From the sea, apart from the wealth of fish caught in the surrounding waters, come **escopinyes**, sea dates, and **corns**. Different types of sausage are made on the island: **sobrassada**, **camot** and **carn i xua** and both

savoury and sweet pastries such as the **formatjades** and **coques** of Ciutadella, the famous **amargos**, **carquinyols** and **torró crema**t of Es Mercadal and **crespells**, **pastissets** and **ensaïmades** to be found everywhere.

Restaurants on the island are many and varied in quality, style and cuisine. Our intention is to give a few representative examples which, in no way, should be considered as anything more than a guideline.

TRADITIONAL COOKING

Good traditional food can be found at **Ca n'Aguedet**, 23 C/Lepant, Es Mercadal, and at **S'Engolidor**, Es Migjorn, which we have already mentioned in the previous section.

FISH AND SHELLFISH

There are many restaurants specialized in fish and seafood in general. At Cala Mesquida, **Cap Roig**, offers a wonderful view of the coastline. In Maó harbour, despite the ever-increasing number of restaurants, there are not many dedicated to fish. On Moll de Llevant, **Es Fosquet** being an exception. At Cales Fonts, **Trebol**, one of the busiest of the many quayside establishments and **Can Delio**. In Ciutadella, among others, **Tritón** and **Cafe Balear**, both in the harbour. In Fornells, **Es Cranc**, 29 C/Escoles, and **Es Pla**, **Cranc Pelut, Can Miquel Es Port**, on the sea front. Another style of restaurant typical of the island can be found in old farmhouses where the atmosphere tends to be informal and the surroundings traditional and simple.

Similar establishments also exist in the towns: **Andaira**, 61 C/ des Forn, Tel. 971 36 68 17, in the centre of Maó, is set in an elegant town house with tables in the garden. In Ciutadella, **Es Racó des Palau**, 3 C/Palau an old renovated bakery. In Mercadal, **Ca n'Olga**, Pont de Macarrana, tel. 971 37 54 59 and **Molí des Racó**, set in a restored windmill. In Es Migjorn Gran, **Bar Chic**, 7 C/ Major and, in Ferreries, **Liorna**, 9 C/ Dalt, serves good pizzas in a charming setting.

Of the farmhouse restaurants, many are situated in the Sant Lluís area: **La Caraba**, at S'Ullastrar 78 with both indoor dining rooms and a charming garden terrace, Tel. 971 15 06 82, and nearby, at Nº 46, **Villa Madrid** set in a colonial-style mansion, Tel. 971.15.04.64.

All around the island's coastline there are places to eat and drink just a few steps away from the sea (some very informal and others of a more serious nature). The style of food varies from the simplest to the most elaborate. Four km. from Sant Lluís, **Restaurante Son Ganxo** near a secluded cove, with swimming pool, terrace and indoor restaurant and **Es Caragol** between Biniancolla and Cala Torret.

TRANSPORT

BY PLANE

Iberia flies regularly between Menorca, Barcelona, Mallorca and Valencia all year. At Christmas, Easter and in the summer, services are increased owing to the high demand. Information: Tel. 971 36 90 15. Reservations: Tel. 971 36 56 73. Other companies offer regular flights to both Barcelona and Palma which connect to other destinations: **Air Europe**, information and bookings, Tel. 971 15 70 31 /902 240 042; and **Air Nostrum**, Tel. 902 400 500 **Norestair**. Air taxi and air ambulance. Tel. 608.530.606 or 971 35 13 07. The airport is on the PM-703 Maó–St Climent road. Tel. 971 15 70 00.

BY BOAT

Trasmediterránea covers the line Maó-Barcelona twice a week in winter and more frequently during holiday seasons. The trip takes about eight hours. Once a week they sail to Mallorca and then on to Valencia. Information: 971 36 60 50 Reservations: 971 36 29 50 **Iscomar** sails from Ciutadella-Alcúdia twice daily. This three-hour trip is an ideal way to visit Mallorca, taking one's own car. Tel. 971 48 42 16. **Cape Balear** also communicates Ciutadella and Cala Rajada (also in Mallorca) twice daily but only carries